The Trouble with Minna

The Trouble with Minna

A Case of Slavery and Emancipation in the Antebellum North

Hendrik Hartog

The University of North Carolina Press CHAPEL HILL

This book was published with the assistance of the Thornton H. Brooks Fund of the University of North Carolina Press.

© 2018 The University of North Carolina Press
All rights reserved
Set in Espinosa Nova by Westchester Publishing Services
Manufactured in the United States of America

The University of North Carolina Press has been a member of the Green Press Initiative since 2003.

Library of Congress Cataloging-in-Publication Data
Names: Hartog, Hendrik, 1948– author.
Title: The trouble with Minna : a case of slavery and emancipation in the antebellum North / Hendrik Hartog.
Description: Chapel Hill : University of North Carolina Press, [2018] | Includes bibliographical references and index.
Identifiers: LCCN 2017042874 | ISBN 9781469640884 (cloth : alk. paper) | ISBN 9781469640891 (ebook)
Subjects: LCSH: Slavery—Law and legislation—New Jersey—History. | Slaves—New Jersey—Social conditions—History. | Liability (Law)— New Jersey—History. | African Americans—Legal status, laws, etc.— New Jersey—History.
Classification: LCC E445.N54 H37 2018 | DDC 306.3/6209749—dc23
LC record available at https://lccn.loc.gov/2017042874

Jacket illustration: © AF-studio/iStock.

To Nancy,
for the wonders
of a shared New Jersey life

Contents

The Trouble with Minna

Introduction

In September 1822, Elizabeth Haines, a widow, rented a slave. The lease was for a term of just under four years and cost the widow sixty dollars. As a result of the lease, a woman named Minna or Minner, whose last name was never given, left the household of her owner, Henry Force, to live with Mrs. Haines in Elizabethtown, one township over and about eight miles away.[1]

At the time, the lease of a slave was a routine legal transaction. Like other rentals, it did not require an explanation. It is thus not surprising that Mrs. Haines never said anything about why she had rented Minna, nor did Mr. Force ever explain why he had let her go. Such limited-term transactions just happened.

What did the lease mean for Minna? For her, too, it was most likely not an unexpected event. The lease took place about a year after she had arrived in Mr. Force's household, and it was quite possibly not the first or even the second time that she had been treated as transacted and commodified property in motion. Each such transaction must have been a difficult, perhaps fearful, moment in its way. There would be no reason to assume that Minna was getting anything out of the transactions, other than the chance to work for different masters and mistresses. And the consequences could have been much worse than that. Still, these were the terms of her life, as an enslaved person living in New Jersey. Her movement from one household to another was her lot, as it was for others like her. The lease remained a routine legal transaction, even as it was shaped by the global slave trade, the Middle Passage, the capitalist market for commodities, and also, perhaps, the rise of an antislavery persuasion. Minna had been leased—transferred from the control of one white person to another.

But in 1836, more than thirteen years after the lease was made, long after the term had ended, Elizabeth Haines went to a county court to ask that Henry Force compensate her for the cost of Minna's care. That would not have been a routine act on Haines's part, and as far as I can tell, it was the only time Haines ever went to court to litigate a case. It was also a rare case of a lessee suing for compensation for the care of a lessor's slave. But according to Mrs. Haines's claims, Minna had been "worthless" as a worker;

she drank, and she had become blind in one eye. Mr. Force had refused to take her back, even though Minna remained Force's responsibility and her "care" was costly.

The county court ordered Force to pay damages to Haines. But in 1840, the New Jersey Supreme Court reversed the decision. Although Minna remained Force's legal and moral responsibility, the appellate court decided that Haines had no right to compensation for Minna's care. What Haines had done for Force, in caring for his slave and thus his property, was instead something the majority of the court defined as a "mere voluntary courtesy."

These events occurred in New Jersey in the throes of what is usually referred to as gradual emancipation. By 1804, New Jersey had legislatively committed itself to an end to the institution of slavery, and emancipatory practices had appeared even earlier in the state. However, this emancipation was gradual indeed. By the time *Force v. Haines* was decided, it had become a multigenerational process. As late as the Civil War, New Jersey still had a handful of "apprentices for life"—effectively slaves.[2]

Between the start of the nineteenth century and the 1820s, when Minna's story as we know it begins, the number of slaves in New Jersey had declined significantly. In 1800, there were 12,423 slaves in the state (5.9 percent of the population); in 1820, there were 7,557 (2.7 percent), even as the overall population of the state grew from 211,149 to 277,575. By 1830, the number had shrunk to 2,254 (.7 percent). By 1840, there were only 674 slaves (.18%) in New Jersey.[3] Why and how the decline occurred remain matters of speculation. Some slaves were being manumitted by masters, often as the conclusion of contracts made between masters and slaves or between masters and other white people. Some unknown and hidden number were being sold and moved to southern plantations, even though a series of statutes enacted by the New Jersey legislature made such sales illegal. The trade continued, allowing slave traders to move black people from New Jersey to the sugar plantations of Louisiana and elsewhere. Meanwhile, older slaves died, and most children born to the enslaved after the 1804 law (and not sold South) eventually became free. Other children and adults—with or without a "legal" manumission—walked or sailed away and disappeared into the free black communities of New York City and Philadelphia.[4]

But throughout New Jersey's long period of gradual emancipation, lasting through much of the first half of the nineteenth century, some white people continued to deal with black people as commercial objects. There were specific laws that applied to commercial transactions, and white people used them to justify their actions, even while the law was shifting. All of the judges and lawyers—even those with abolitionist sympathies, including some who would later become prominent members of the Republican Party and another whose antislavery credentials were celebrated by the abolitionist press—understood these laws as constituting a recognizable and enforceable (although necessarily complex) body (or bodies) of law.[5]

This was also true for the litigants in a case. They understood and worked within the implicit baseline legal rules that shaped ordinary transactions involving slaves. To take only one example, when Elizabeth Haines went to court in 1836, she asked for $2,000 compensation, figured at a rate of $1.50 per week over the decade from the end of the lease term in 1826 to the time she initiated suit. She did not, however, ask for compensation for the period between 1822 and 1826. From the moment Minna entered Mrs. Haines's household in 1822, she was supposed to have been—according to Mrs. Haines and other whites who testified on her behalf—"worthless." She was, they said, of no use in the household and a cost. But Mrs. Haines also knew that Minna's upkeep, no matter how costly, remained her sole responsibility throughout the roughly four-year lease term. She understood, as any competent property owner at the time understood, that as a lessee she was responsible for the care of the property she had leased. There would be no compensation from Force for her costs over those years.[6]

Once the lease was over, however, the situation changed. In 1826, at the end of the lease's term, Mrs. Haines tried to return Minna to Mr. Force— that is, to return his property to his care. He refused to take Minna back, and so Minna, although no longer Mrs. Haines's property, continued to live in Mrs. Haines's household for most of the next decade. And it was for costs incurred over that period that Mrs. Haines believed she ought to be paid.

When Mr. Force's attorney asked that Mrs. Haines be nonsuited, claiming that the case for compensation had not been made, the judges of the Middlesex County District Court refused. They ruled that Mrs. Haines was entitled to compensation and sent the case to the jury, which awarded her $300 in damages.[7]

It was that $300 award that the New Jersey Supreme Court reversed. A majority of the court characterized Mrs. Haines's actions as nothing but a "mere voluntary courtesy." No contract could be implied from her actions or those of Mr. Force. Without a contract—express or implied—Mr. Force's responsibility to provide care could not be used as grounds for having to pay Mrs. Haines for assuming that responsibility. What she did was, at best, understood as the actions of a good Samaritan.

Over the course of the next century, courts around the country often borrowed the language Justice Gabriel Ford used in writing what was treated as the majority's opinion in *Force v. Haines*, sometimes without attribution. The case became an occasional citation for the principle that Anglo-American law would not reward those who voluntarily took on care responsibilities. It shaped the boundaries of a nebulous and much-contested late nineteenth-century doctrinal category in legal thought: the realm of "quasi-contract." It exemplified the distinctiveness—the exceptionalism—of Anglo-American contractual theory, as often contrasted with Roman law and other European understandings. The activities of those understood in European law as "benevolent intervenors," including those who provided many forms of care work, were taken instead to be the acts of mere "volunteers" or "officious intermeddlers." Those who borrowed that language almost never identified it as coming out of a case about the care of a slave.[8]

According to Justice Ford and those later judges and lawyers and legal theorists, what volunteers did, the care they provided, they ought to have done for reasons other than the expectation of a reward. By definition, a volunteer did what he or she did without an explicit contract that bound the property owner (Force in this case) to pay the volunteer (Haines here) for the work that had been voluntarily provided. But further: it would sully the presumed virtue of good Samaritans if one reduced their actions to a calculus of compensation. Allowing compensation in such a case would have the effect of confusing truly good Samaritans with those who interfered with and intervened in the private lives and private business of those who were merely making decisions about their own lives and properties. It would also equate good Samaritans with those less good individuals who strategized to extract costs from property owners. In that regard, the contrast they drew was very like the one Oliver Wendell Holmes Jr. famously drew in *The Path of the Law* between a "bad man of the law," who does what he does out of an expectation of legal consequences, and a "good man," who acts without thought of legal reward or penalty.[9]

I first came upon *Force v. Haines* several years ago, while working on questions of intergenerational care: How to understand a legal and moral culture in which the hard work of caring for the dependent elderly could be construed as a voluntary "gift" that did not obligate the recipient to make any particular provision of pay or property to the gift giver? How to understand the notion of the caregiver as a volunteer? To answer those questions, I read the many nineteenth- and early twentieth-century New Jersey cases in which the image of the volunteer appeared. I kept seeing references to notions of "voluntary courtesies," and those references led me back to this obscure "slave" care case.[10]

This book began in an effort to make sense of that case. But doing so led me to confront and to conceptualize what gradual emancipation meant. To understand what happened to Minna, to Elizabeth Haines, and to Henry Force, I had to situate their case within a strange and unfamiliar legal culture—one defined by deep contradictions and one that differed from how American historians have ordinarily thought about the legal realms of freedom and slavery. Over a period of nearly two generations, black and white New Jerseyans fought, struggled, and negotiated within a jurisdiction—call it "New Jersey"—defined by both norms of freedom and norms of legalized and legitimate slavery, and committed both to the sanctity of property—including that of enslaved people—and to the moral and legal legitimacy of contract.

It was only after exploring that legal culture that *Force v. Haines* began to make a certain kind of historical sense. This book represents my effort to convey that sense, to situate and to explain what happened to Minna and Elizabeth Haines and Henry Force.

The result is not a history of how New Jersey evolved from a regime of chattel slavery to one of universal freedom. It is not a social history of African American life in antebellum New Jersey.[11] Nor is it a full exploration of the legal status of the voluntary or benevolent intervenor, a subject that academic legal theorists and comparatists worked through assiduously over the first two-thirds of the twentieth century. It represents, rather, an effort to reconstruct core features of everyday life within a legal regime just as mysterious as (but perhaps no more so than) our own. I am, in effect (although with provocative intent), normalizing a regime of gradual emancipation, a regime where slavery was usually but not always legal, where the apparently enslaved may or may not have been actual slaves. I treat slavery as a contingent and uncertain relationship nestled within a much broader terrain of unsettled relationships.[12]

That is to say that an understanding of *Force v. Haines* and its invocation of a "mere voluntary courtesy" required reconstructing how some African Americans struggled to establish their freedom and the freedom of their kin within a legal culture of very gradual emancipation. It required reading about white litigants fighting one another over the use and care and responsibility for people they often thought of as enslaved. It led me to explore the strategies and arguments of lawyers who moved seamlessly from representing a "wrongly" enslaved person in a habeas corpus case, to making arguments about technical features of the slave code, to representing white clients in search of compensation for lost human property. In the liminal legal space where all this occurred (New Jersey between 1790 and 1840), lawyers, litigants, judges, and others strategized and fought over the opportunities and costs that the laws identified with gradual emancipation seemed to offer them. And while they debated moral and legal dilemmas, they generally lived their lives without much thought about the coming of a future without slavery, in a present tense where slavery remained mostly legal and somewhat normal but also morally and perhaps legally problematic and offensive.

Making sense of that legal regime led me to try to move beyond our conventional understanding of the relationship of slavery to freedom. What might be called our "neo-abolitionist" commitment to the notion of an antonymic relationship between slavery and freedom—of a binary with an excluded middle—leaves us without resources to understand the in-between legal culture, neither "slave" nor "free," in which New Jerseyans lived in the years of gradual emancipation. The assumption of an inevitable and linear progression from slavery to freedom stands even more in the way of the understanding this book is after, even though that assumption was itself central to the worldviews of many of those who lived in that New Jersey.

Gradual emancipation or gradual abolition (the terms were used interchangeably) was a body of distinctive and evolving practices. It was certainly not a switch that flipped people from one status to another, from slavery to freedom. At least in New Jersey, gradual emancipation was defined by a legal culture in which white people and black people often continued to live habitual lives shaped by coerced labor, even as "freedom" became a norm. Slavery remained a lived experience in the midst of so-called emancipation. Meanwhile, it had become common for right-thinking white people to express antislavery sentiments and make known their moral qualms. Certainly, many white slaveholders began to shape their behavior and their dealings with their property through a lens defined by eventual emancipation, as well as by the declining prices that enslaved property fetched. Gradual emancipation incorporated habits and ways of being that drew both on moral and social discomfort with slavery and on expectations of continuity. (None of the moral complexities of such contradictory circumstances should be unfamiliar to sentient beings today. Just as the busser or the gardener or the nursing home care worker, who may or may not be a legal immigrant, helps constitute our experience in the world we live in, so it would be in the "free" [or freeish] society that was emerging along the Hudson. The cheap labor that many rely on today approximates the routine presence of enslaved or semi-enslaved black persons in any number of service positions.)

It may be that New Jersey's gradual emancipation was not exceptional, certainly not within the larger history of how emancipation came to be across the Atlantic world.[13] Until the 1860s, the end of slavery was understood as an incremental rather than instantaneous event. (Haiti, of course, provided a salient and much feared alternative story.)[14] Before the Civil War, the problem of emancipation was usually argued over as a problem of compensation—that is, who would be paid for the loss of enslaved property, and how would those entitled to compensation be paid (whether through commitments of continuing labor [apprenticeships] or in cash).[15]

In any case, I mean to explore how the people of early nineteenth-century New Jersey—women and men, white and black, legally trained and untrained—dealt with one another and managed both their legal relations and their care. I am interested in how they negotiated the terms of their lives and their relationships in a jurisdiction defined by uncertain boundaries between slavery and freedom. I am interested in law and the conditions of care and responsibility and freedom in a time and a place where "the conditions" of care and responsibility and freedom were contested. (In that sense, of course, it was a time not so different from our own.) And I am interested in exploring the parameters of a legal regime that comprised more than just the laws—the statute books and the case records—of the state of New Jersey. The New Jersey that is my subject extended vaguely outward, certainly to incorporate the laws of neighboring states—particularly those of New York. It also incorporated at least some of the legal horizons and expectations of the many immigrants to New Jersey over that period.[16]

I begin with an extended critical examination of what might be called my core primary sources: the opinions of the judges in the 1840 appellate case *Force v. Haines*. As I unpack the arguments made in those opinions, I move forward and backward and to the side in order to situate and contextualize those arguments. In particular, the first chapter includes reflections on the distinctiveness of the style of legal argument—the rhetorical forms and the recourse to precedents—that led to the conclusion that Mrs. Haines had offered only "a mere voluntary courtesy." It also provides an introductory reading of how those judges worked to connect and to distinguish poor relief and public responsibility for the needy (including the formerly enslaved). Throughout the first chapter, I work within the legal and factual assumptions and understandings that the judges in the case mobilized and brandished in their opinions. As we will see, those legal and factual assumptions and understandings obscured much about the actual situations in which Minna and the white litigants lived.[17]

In chapters 2 and 3, I move away from those legal and factual assumptions and understandings to the scene of the case: the legal world of gradual emancipation as it might have been experienced in its heyday, between the early nineteenth century and 1840. Here I use the tools of social and cultural history to trace a variety of stories about slaves and slaveholders and those who moved in and out of the "institution" during the era of gradual emancipation. My goal is to reconstruct some of the tacit norms and understandings that shaped what was known or knowable at the time—what it meant to be in that world—and to work to imagine what those who lived in that world saw around them. What I offer in those chapters will not be a social history of New Jersey slavery or of the lives of African Americans. I do not focus on what most slaves did within households or the conditions of labor or their intimate lives. Rather, I remain focused on the legal situations that gradual emancipation generated and the legal landscape within which enslaved people and slaveholders lived and negotiated with one another.

Finally, I return to the litigants—Henry Force and Elizabeth Haines—and to Minna, and I work in a speculative vein to try to reconstruct their understanding of their world and its contingencies and possibilities. It is only here, in the final chapter, that I offer my answers—speculative answers—to the mysteries at the heart of the case: why Elizabeth Haines went to court to try to make Henry Force pay for Minna's care, what she hoped to gain from her suit, why Henry Force did not or could not take Minna back, and who Minna was. While their story is not the grain of sand that can reveal the whole world (it is, after all, a peculiar grain found on a peculiar beach), I am confident that it offers an entry into some core mysteries of nineteenth-century American legal life—mysteries about how care should be paid for, about the relationships between public and private entities, about the relationships between moral and legal reasoning, and about a legal landscape that challenged simplistic notions of what it meant to live in freedom.

THIS IS, THROUGHOUT, a study of contractual behavior and of contract doctrine. To talk legalish, one might describe this as a book about questions regarding the law of "consideration" as it would have been understood in the legal culture of the early nineteenth century. Through the lens of care and enslavement, it explores how particular acts, expressions, and transactions did or did not produce legally enforceable duties and obligations, and how other acts, expressions, and transactions became the "consideration" for an enforceable contract. The reader's attention will be drawn to agreements and bargains, suggested and implied and challenged. The documents include not only the commercial documents conventionally identified with "contract law" (leases, sales, labor contracts) but also a range of writings that became something like contracts because they attempted to fix relationships in time. To take one recurrent example, consider the provisions in many wills that promised to free—or manumit—an enslaved person at the end of a fixed term. Or, to take another example that will be explored in chapter 3, the writing coercively imposed by a ferry owner on his free black employee to re-create a condition of slavery, at least for a limited term. Customs and implicit norms—what lawyers today often call reliance interests—are ever present in the narrative.[18]

Such writings were constitutive of a contractual world, even when mobilized to reproduce the material conditions we (and they) identify with chattel slavery. Usually they expressed a slaveholder's power. And yet they also extended a present relationship into a defined and bounded future, as contracts between free individuals are expected to do. They produced what poet and scholar of the ancient world Anne Carson calls a "now."[19] Each represented a limited but real effort to control the future, to thrust a present relationship—a "now"—into the future. Each carried the implication that the relationship in question—even one called slavery—would come to an end at the conclusion of the contracted-for term, a fixed and finite period of time. And once the contract was "executed," everyone, including the apparently enslaved, could walk away.

Such writings—deeds, wills, bills of sale, and scraps of paper—along with the legal arguments over their meanings, produce much of the documentary record that underlies this study. I have struggled to interpret conflicted meanings in the contractual language, and in legal arguments, and trial testimony in order to reconstruct the terms of the New Jersey slave regime and determine what gradual abolition meant in practice for the enslaved, for slaveholders, and for the communities that surrounded them. As is the goal of many historians, my goal is to reveal how lives were lived within those relationships in order to gain and share a fleeting insight into these people's present tense—their "now."

For many abolitionists, southern slaveholders, and historians alike, slavery has implicitly meant a denial of the fugitive and fleeting but delimited "now" of contract. Instead, the law of slavery was said to be founded on the belief that a property law writing—a deed, for example—could fix an identity in perpetuity. Indeed, our confident sense of the moral illegitimacy of chattel slavery (learned from abolitionists, among others) is enmeshed with its apparent denial of the boundaries that contractualism offered. That is much of what is captured by the familiar trope that slavery privileged property and denied personhood. And it was a standard understanding throughout the Deep South that contracting was inconsistent with the condition of being enslaved.[20]

By contrast, between the early nineteenth century and the 1840s, one finds negotiated and temporally bound slave relationships throughout New Jersey. These were relationships that incorporated a particularized and fleeting "now," a temporality that one ordinarily identifies with contractual freedom. As late as the 1840s, New Jersey continued to allow a few white men and women to know themselves as slaveholders. At the same time, 1840s New Jersey had a legal culture shaped by contractualism and ubiquitous contracting. That is the apparent paradox at the heart of this study.

As we have already seen, Minna's story (at least that part of her story that we know anything about) begins with a lease, an agreement; it ends, perhaps, with a court decision that the lease and the relationship it created produced no "implied" contract for care. In chapter 1 we will see how judges in 1840 struggled to account for what they sometimes called "implied" contracts for care and compensation. Much of that struggle occurred over the salience or relevance of particular analogies. Was the care of a slave like the care of other members of a household, such as the care of a wife or an infant child or an apprentice? Or was it more or less like the care, or lack thereof, that is part of what it means to own insensate (or apparently insensate) property? Was slave property a special kind of property? Or was slave property, in both its limitations and its possibilities, more like the property a household head possessed in the form of dependents who were under his or her control?

At the same time, all contracts occur within a particular historical site, in this case a "New Jersey" (the scare quotes used with intent) shaped by immense and easy mobility, indistinct jurisdictional boundaries, and a deep hostility to providing and paying for public welfare (including care for the poor and the dependent) through public taxation. The New Jersey within which gradual emancipation occurred incorporated much law from other jurisdictions, particularly from New York. The boundaries of the state were porous and may have been somewhat indeterminate for those who lived within it. Exit was relatively easy and a constant possibility. Loyalty may have been nearly nonexistent. New Jersey was, as Benjamin Franklin once quipped, a barrel tapped at both ends. In that, it may have been more typical of other jurisdictions (or legal landscapes) in early America than legal historians have typically acknowledged.[21]

That site, or jurisdiction, was shaped by a market revolution and a global slave trade. It was also shaped by a style of moral and legal reasoning, one often identified with legal liberalism. That style legitimated some forms of state action in pursuit of an emergent imagined public welfare, even as it privileged the freedoms of private actors. It harbored many contradictory tendencies, all of which found expression in a local regime of gradual emancipation. We will see all those contradictory tendencies mobilized in the judicial opinions in *Force v. Haines*, as examined in chapter 1. A range of judicial philosophies, or ideologies, about contracting and its moral significance contended as the judges tried to make sense of who was responsible for Minna's care.[22]

The two chapters that follow explore some of the many ways that contracting "infected" the field of slavery in New Jersey, even as state law retained a commitment to the legality of slavery itself. The point here is not simply the familiar one that bargaining is and was ubiquitous, found on a rice plantation in Georgia or in the Caribbean as well as in a household in New Jersey. Rather, the point is that in New Jersey, slavery coexisted with ubiquitous, recognized, and often enforced contracting. The law—judges and other public authorities—often took account. Sometimes—intermittently and haphazardly—the law allowed contracts to transform preexisting enslaved identities. But sometimes contracts extended slavery, or at least the coercive relationships that constituted what slavery was and how it was lived. And that is one part of a regime of gradual emancipation, as it was experienced in the present tense by participants of that regime.

All of this leads us back to the characters in our story, as we ask who they were and how they might have been changed by the relationships they formed and those they found themselves in.

This is the story of three individuals—Elizabeth Haines, Henry Force, and Minna—who lived in a relational regime of gradual emancipation. Who were they? Who might they have been? Who did they become?

CHAPTER ONE

A Mere Voluntary Courtesy

Ford

Gabriel Ford wrote the opinion for the court in *Force v. Haines*. It appears, though, that only one other justice, John Moore White, signed on to his opinion. A well known survey of New Jersey's judges characterized Ford as an "unreliable" judge. Still, he had once been a successful New Jersey lawyer, not solely because he came from one of the leading families in Morris County. Unlike his older brother, Timothy, who became a prominent South Carolina attorney, Gabriel Ford remained in Morris County, where he cared for the family house and estate, and practiced law until he became a judge on the state supreme court. By 1840, he was the longest serving and the oldest justice on the New Jersey Supreme Court.[1]

Gabriel Ford's legal life was enmeshed in slavery—not just because there would have been one or more slaves in his household in the early years, and not just because slaves had been a core labor force in his family's ironworks. In the cases he argued as an attorney and in the opinions he wrote, Gabriel Ford dealt with slavery as an unproblematic part of the New Jersey legal landscape. In one 1825 case, he testified that although he no longer "kept" slaves, he knew how to assess their value. Aside from his judicial opinions, I have not been able to find any expression of Gabriel Ford's personal opinions with regard to slavery; however, he seems to have never been a member of any manumission or antislavery society. His family, like that of many of the New Jersey elite, was intertwined with southern planter interests. In fact, his brother Timothy and his brother-in-law Henry were the two named partners in the leading Charleston law firm of Ford and DeSaussure, created to serve the needs of southern planters. The family's affairs revolved between Charleston and northern New Jersey.[2]

In *Force v. Haines*, Justice Ford's opinion began with a quick summary of the case. His version of the facts went as follows: Henry Force sold the custody and services of Minna to Elizabeth Haines for the period from September 1822 to June 1826. At the end of that term, Haines tried to return Minna. Force, however, refused to "receive" Minna or to be held "accountable" for her. Haines then kept the enslaved woman for two more years, when she "turned" Minna "out of doors." Minna was absent from the Haines household for the next six months but then returned. Mrs. Haines again "received" her and continued to "maintain" her—that is, to care for her—for about seven more years, when she initiated her action in court against Henry Force. This was an action in assumpsit, meaning she sued for compensation for Force's breach of a contractual obligation. One presumes that the breach was of Force's obligation to retake possession and care of Minna at the end of the lease term. At trial, Haines's evidence demonstrated that Minna "had a very bad temper, that she had lost the sight of one eye, by intemperance, and [that she] was partially and sometimes wholly blind of the other." Her "services" were "of little or no value," and her "maintenance," Ford acknowledged, cost Haines a dollar and a half a week. On the other hand, Ford added, there was no evidence at the trial that Force had ever asked Haines to maintain Minna or that he had ever promised to pay for the care Haines provided. Thus, there was no evidence that Force had taken on a contractual obligation.[3]

Force's attorney had asked for a nonsuit, essentially a dismissal, after all the testimony had been given on the theory that no action in assumpsit could be maintained based on such an array of facts. Taking the facts in the strongest light possible, they still did not justify the cause of action. A court should only allow such a case to go to the jury if it were satisfied that the care described in the case was furnished at the defendant's request or that he had promised to pay for it. But the evidence showed exactly the opposite: Force had refused to pay for Minna's care.

The judges of the lower court had rejected Force's attorney's request for a nonsuit. They sent the case to the jury. The jury found for the plaintiff, Elizabeth Haines, in the amount of $300. And then Henry Force appealed. The grounds for his appeal: That this was a case founded on the action of "indebitatus assumpsit." Assumpsit required the presence of a contract, either one made explicitly or one implied in law. Here, however, there was no evidence of a contract, either an express one or one "implied in law." Thus, there was no basis for the lower court decision in the plaintiff's favor. A reversal was called for.

Justice Ford agreed. For Ford, the case was entirely about what we would call contract law. It was not, as he understood it, distinctively or particularly about the law of slavery. Indeed, based on this opinion, one would not conclude that Ford believed in the existence of a law of slavery as a distinct doctrinal field. For him, the core question was whether it was possible to find an implied contract out of the facts (the judicially recognized facts) that had been constructed through the trial record. If so, Elizabeth Haines had a right to compensation. If not, she did not.[4]

Was there an implied contract that bound Force to compensate Haines for the care she had offered to his slave? Ford's answer to that question—what he regarded as the only relevant question—was contained in two very long paragraphs. The first articulated a general principle, "the great and leading" rule, that underlay his conclusions. The second reflected on an exception that sometimes limited the application of that principle but that he believed did not apply to this case.

And this general principle? An act done for the benefit of another is a "voluntary courtesy" for which no action can be sustained. Such acts occur constantly and do not imply the existence of an underlying contract. That is to say, such acts can be explained by many impulses, including that of simple human kindness and neighborliness, as well as the officiousness of busybodies. If such impulses automatically produced recoveries of compensation, it would lead to "the overthrow of personal rights . . . and civil freedom."

What acts did he have in mind? Ford expanded:

A man who has nothing else to do, goes to mowing in his neighbor's meadow; or when his team lies idle, to plowing in his neighbor's field; or a carpenter out of employment, goes to mending his neighbor's sleigh, without the slightest request to do so; taking away from that neighbor, the common right to mow and plow for himself, when he is unable or unwilling to hire and the right of doing without a sleigh, or of using it in the plight it was in, rather than incur the expense of repair; is it to be believed that they can maintain actions, and make that neighbor pay for such unrequested work, and with costs too, as Lord Mansfield said in a like case, "in spite of his teeth." No man's private business, in the mode or time of it, would be under his control, or free from the interference of strangers, perhaps idlers, drunkards, and perhaps enemies, under such pretences, drawing him from business into litigation.[5]

One might say that the rest of the opinion explained why the care of another's slave was just like mowing a neighbor's meadow or mending a neighbor's sleigh. Like those interventions into the affairs of another, this one involved providing a mere voluntary courtesy.

What's wrong with offering voluntary courtesies? One answer might well be "nothing." We want people to be charitable and giving, concerned for their neighbors and family and friends, willing to aid strangers and others who appear to need help. We want to reward charitable impulses, don't we? Just as the modern tax regime rewards taxpayers who make charitable contributions, we could imagine that compensating Mrs. Haines for her charity in taking care of poor and dependent Minna would encourage others to take on the burdens of care for those less fortunate. If those inclined to be helpful knew that their inclination was one that might be rewarded, might be understood as ripening into compensation, wouldn't that encourage helpfulness? Wouldn't offering compensation to those who in European law are often called "benevolent intervenors" encourage more benevolent intervention?[6]

Ford entirely rejected that understanding and, in doing so, articulated a perspective often regarded as intrinsic to and characteristic of Anglo-American common law. (Given that the notion of an officious intermeddler is not unrelated to the labels that southern proslavery advocates attached to northern abolitionists and others who "intervened" in their domestic institutions, one wonders if Ford was also silently reflecting or reproducing viewpoints presented to him by his South Carolina relatives about officiously intermeddling abolitionists.) For Ford, "benevolent intervenors" were nothing but busybodies who took from others their "common right to mow and plow" for themselves, to repair and maintain as they chose. Such people, people like Elizabeth Haines, robbed property owners of their capacity to use or misuse their property—to do as they pleased with what belonged to them. His great and leading rule expressed an underlying and conventional understanding of the right to property, at least in its early modern Anglo-American form.

What property law—more properly, the common law regime of property law—offered was the capacity to decide what we want to do with what is ours. Misuse—sometimes called "waste"—is in that context indistinguishable from use. Or rather, what is misuse and what is everyday use depends entirely on perspective. But property law decides the question of whose perspective wins: that of the owner. To return to the situation of Minna, the "worthless" slave owned by Henry Force: if Force did not want to care for Minna, wanted to "waste" her as a resource, that was his privilege. It was not Elizabeth Haines's business to interfere, however much Haines disapproved, even if by some external or objective standard Force was harming and ruining—misusing—what was his. As property, Minna was little different from the unmowed field or the unmended sleigh. She was nothing but a resource that Force had chosen not to fix or care for.

Ford left most of this implicit in his opinion. He did not, we might assume, need to do more than wave at this understanding, because his whole audience would have understood the point. That is, they would have known that the right to misuse or not care for was integral to what was understood as the right to possess or own. That right to misuse was the absent present, the implicit dark truth, underneath all the fuzzy verbiage about freedom and the untrammeled use of resources in property law. Just as land speculators knew throughout the nineteenth and twentieth centuries that they could hold land out of productive use, waiting for its price to rise, and just as in the infamous *State v. Mann* case, decided by North Carolina's chief justice Thomas Ruffin a decade before the appellate decision in *Force v. Haines*, in which a lessee, as a rightful possessor of property, was ruled to be free to harm—to shoot—his rented slave "without justification," so it was for Henry Force. It would be wrong—beyond what the law could do (at least as these judges imagined legal capacity)—to make Force take proper care of what was his. As such, the right to avoid or withhold care was integral to what we might mean by civil liberty—Henry Force's civil liberty, at least.[7]

Of course, the point is actually a good deal more complicated, as those in Ford's time understood. Public power—the state—compels owners to care for and manage, at least minimally, much that is ostensibly theirs. Not to misuse, not to waste—or only to waste in socially or publicly legitimated ways. We can't let our house become a meth factory or a shooting gallery. Depending on the locality, we may not even be able to decide to dry our clothes on a clothesline on our front lawn or to let our lawn stay unmowed. At the time that *Force v. Haines* was argued and decided, there existed a thick body of local and state rules that restricted and defined proper uses of property, limiting the freedoms of the property owner when his right ran up against community norms. Then, as now, it was taken for granted that to own was to subject oneself to a host of regulatory limitations on what could be done with what was ostensibly "ours." Judges, like legislators, understood themselves as administrators and managers of both a public environment and scarce and ultimately shared resources.[8] Uses had to be "restrained," in pursuit of the public welfare and a certain degree of civilization or Christian charity. In the 1840s and 1850s, cruelty-to-animal rules were being developed, which would eventually morph into cruelty-to-children rules. These were understood, among other things, as limitations on property—that is, a householder's property interest in beasts and children.[9] Gradual emancipation was itself one example of just such a public-regarding limitation on private property.

And so it was as well, with some awkwardness and embarrassment, with regard to the everyday use and misuse of slaves in a nineteenth-century New Jersey where the possession of human property was still mostly legal. Even in the South, many judges avoided the consequences articulated in *State v. Mann*, trying to claim some sense of slave owners' minimal responsibility for the care of their properties.[10] I suspect that Justice Ford would not have approved of the "logic" of Ruffin's opinion in *State v. Mann*, which seemed to give a slave owner the right to abuse his slave without risk of criminal indictment. Indeed, the two long paragraphs that compose the bulk of Ford's opinion suggest that he regarded slave property as more or less like other forms of domestic property (including children and wives and other members of a household). Therefore, it would be subject to somewhat parallel forms of regulation—which is exactly what Chief Justice Ruffin had denied in his 1829 opinion. For Ford, though, the use of slave property would be limited, if only minimally, by a state regulatory environment.

Henry Force, Minna's owner, was—as all the other judges who wrote opinions in *Force v. Haines* emphasized (although Ford did not)—responsible for Minna. That is, he was legally and morally responsible for her care. And the facts were well proven that he had not carried out or abided by those responsibilities. Thus, he had failed to do what he was legally and morally obligated to do as a slaveholder in nineteenth-century New Jersey. For starters, he had refused to take Minna back into his care at the end of the lease term with Elizabeth Haines. If he wanted to rid himself of direct responsibility or control of Minna, there were a number of legal ways by which he might have done so, although all of them might have left him financially responsible for her. Clearly he had not acted as he should have acted, yet the consequences of his failures were matters on which the judges disagreed.

Still, according to Ford and the other judges in the majority, Force's failures did not justify Elizabeth Haines's request for compensation from a court. Her actions were those of an officious intermeddler. As Justice William Dayton explained in his concurring opinion, Force's responsibility— his duty not to misuse—did not entitle Haines to a right to compensation for Minna's care, even if she was taking on what was actually Force's legal duty. Haines remained merely "a citizen," without official responsibilities to enforce care. At least within the common law world, the fact that an individual had responsibilities to care for and manage his properties did not mean that others could shoulder those responsibilities for him. And certainly if others did take on such care, they could not assume that they had gained a right to compensation for their acts.[11]

The judges' conclusion that it was not Mrs. Haines's business to intervene and to rectify Mr. Force's failures left unanswered who should make good Mr. Force's failures. Someone, after all, needed to care for dependents who were not being cared for by those who had responsibility for (and who potentially profited from) the control and power—the property—they exercised. Who should do the work of care when "household care" failed?

Ford ignored that question. Indeed, his opinion insisted that such questions of public policy were irrelevant to the case at hand because Mrs. Haines was not a public officer. She was either a good Samaritan or an officious intermeddler. In either event, she had no right to compensation.[12]

In the rest of Ford's first long paragraph (we are less than halfway through it), after having celebrated the civil liberty of the misusing property owner, he surveyed a sampling of assumpsit cases. This case was, he wanted his readers to understand, about a general problem, one epitomized by Elizabeth Haines's misunderstanding of her legal rights—that is, her misconception of what it meant to offer "voluntary courtesies." And that general problem had a general answer that could be found through the precedents established in Anglo-American case law. In elaborating on that general answer, Ford moved far away from any notion of slavery as producing distinctive legal problems.

Where did he get the phrase "voluntary courtesies"? He may have found it in a popular recent compilation of precedents, *Smith's Leading Cases*. In *Smith's Leading Cases*, each chapter begins with an older famous English case, followed by "notes" detailing both English and, by the time of the edition that Ford surely used, American citations and references.[13] The particular "leading case" that would have offered a point of origin for Ford's mobilization of the phrase was the seventeenth-century English case of *Lampleigh v. Braithwait*. The story of that case, like that in *Force v. Haines*, was one of folktale-like simplicity: Thomas Braithwait had killed one Patrick Mahume. Braithwait was convicted of the crime and asked an acquaintance, Anthony Lampleigh, to do what he could to obtain a pardon from the king. Lampleigh succeeded, and the convicted killer was pardoned. Braithwait then promised to pay Lampleigh one hundred pounds for the pardon. Braithwait reneged and did not do as he had promised. Lampleigh, the pardon obtainer, went to court. The court held that but for Braithwait's express promise, Lampleigh's good deed would have been understood as a "mere voluntary courtesy" for which no recovery was possible. It then went on to acknowledge the enforceability of the express promise to pay. As the rule in the case would be generalized in later years: an act (convincing the king to pardon a convicted murderer) that would be incomprehensible without the presence of a promise, followed by an express promise to pay for that act, could become an enforceable contract.[14]

Ford never mentioned *Lampleigh* in his opinion. Perhaps he avoided that detail to conceal that he was cherry picking from the notes in *Smith's Leading Cases*. In addition, since *Lampleigh* was a case in which the court in the end insisted on the obligation to pay for a benevolent intervention, it would not have been the best precedent to rely on. Instead, Ford began his survey of relevant precedents a century after *Lampleigh* with Francis Buller's 1767 English treatise on the law of *nisi prius*. (In his opinion, he suggested that he began in 1767, rather than with older precedents, just to keep things simple.)[15]

The principle Ford found in Buller's treatise was exactly the same as the holding in *Lampleigh* from a century earlier: If something is done for my benefit but without my request, and I am under no obligation to do it, then even if I promise to pay for that something, the promise is void—that is, unenforceable in a court of law. But if I am under a moral obligation to do that something and then promise to pay for that something subsequently to the doing of the act (as in *Lampleigh*), then the promise is good—meaning enforceable. That statement was then illustrated with an example: If a pauper were cured of a disease by an apothecary, and the local overseer of the poor—the town officer responsible for poor relief—subsequently promised to pay the apothecary for what he had done, then that promise would be an enforceable one because the overseer was under a moral obligation to provide for the care of the pauper. But, the passage continues, the general moral and legal obligation of the overseer to provide relief to the pauper would not create liability to pay the apothecary without evidence of an express promise on the part of the overseer to the apothecary. The overseer's admitted responsibility would not mean that he had to pay for the costs of medicine that had been provided "voluntarily" to the pauper—that is, at the request of the pauper or on the "voluntary" initiative of the apothecary.

So, to return to *Lampleigh*, if Lampleigh had obtained a pardon for Braithwait, and Braithwait had thanked him but not promised to pay him, then Lampleigh could not recover anything. And to look forward to *Force v. Haines*: Mrs. Haines would lose as well, because Mr. Force had never made an express promise to pay her. Indeed, he had forcefully refused to pay her.

Ford then gestured to a 1785 case decided by Lord Mansfield, the famous English chief justice, in which Mansfield refused to make one parish liable for a portion of the salary of a part-time sexton, as the parish had not expressly promised to pay that salary, and the whole of the salary had been paid by another parish. Next he turned to the slightly later case of *Jenkins v. Tucker*, which he took to be important for his argument because it offered a statement of the rule "beyond controversy." This was a case of a West Indian planter who had abandoned his sick wife in England. After he left, the wife contracted debts, became sicker, and finally died. Her father paid her debts and then sued his former son-in-law for compensation. The planter, Ford noted, was both legally and morally obligated to provide for his wife, perhaps especially after having abandoned her. But he had not asked his wife's father to pay those debts, and thus the father would not be compensated for having paid the debts she had incurred during her life.[16]

Ford's legal journey then left England and crossed the Atlantic. It first stopped in 1808 New Jersey, with the case of *Potter v. Potter*. Here, a widow had cared for her dead husband's aged slave. She sued her husband's children, his heirs, for the cost of providing that care. She won an award of $40, but the award was reversed on appeal. Counsel for the defendants on the appeal had argued that "it did not appear . . . that the maintenance of the wench [the enslaved woman] was at the request, or by the direction or authority of the defendants; that even if the defendants were liable to support the slave, which he denied, yet . . . it did not lay in the power of any person to furnish that support without their approbation or request, and then bring an action against them for it." And the court had agreed, although the court's holding was cryptic. Still, according to Ford, that holding had remained good law in New Jersey for the past thirty years and more, up to the time of *Force v. Haines*.[17]

One might imagine that *Potter v. Potter* was all that Ford needed—a New Jersey precedent based on facts that could be read as directly parallel to those in *Force v. Haines*: a widow who cared for a slave that was the responsibility of those who had inherited from her husband. What she had done was determined a mere voluntary courtesy, a kind act but not a compensable one.

But that was not enough for Ford. Why not? Perhaps because the only statement of that doctrinal conclusion came from the defendants' counsel; the judges in *Potter* had not explained why they ruled in the defendants' favor. It might also have been that, like many New Jersey lawyers and judges, Ford knew better than to rest his decision on early New Jersey precedents. And so Ford's unending paragraph of authorities continued.

He moved across the Hudson to New York, where legal authority more typically resided for legally sophisticated New Jerseyans. He took the 1813 New York case of *Dunbar v. Williams* as establishing the same principle as

Potter, but doing it better. This was a case about a doctor who had cured someone's slave of venereal disease. The facts appeared exactly as they had in the apothecary hypothetical that Ford had drawn from Buller's treatise. To allow slaves to obtain medical care and then charge the care to their masters would be dangerous to the rights of slave owners. That is, it would be dangerous to a slave owner's right to misuse (or waste) his property. The New York court had acknowledged that there existed situations of "emergency" or "necessity" in which there would be no time to secure a master's permission. In those situations, the doctor might be paid for his services, as a court could imply the existence of a contract. Venereal disease was not such a situation, however. What the doctor had done was provide a "mere voluntary courtesy" for the benefit of the master. That the master's property retained its value or even gained in value because of the doctor's care did not mean that the doctor had to be paid by the master.[18]

Ford added a second citation to a slightly later New York case involving a doctor suing the overseers of the poor for the care of an "ordinary" (non-slave) pauper. He concluded the paragraph with a reference to the 1822 New York case of *Bartholomew v. Jackson*, in which a man had removed a stack of wheat from his neighbor's property to save it when the stubble on the field was in flames. This kind and helpful act was, once again, labeled a mere voluntary courtesy. In the absence of a promise, "If a man humanely bestows his labor, and even risks his life, in voluntarily aiding to preserve his neighbor's house from destruction by fire, the law considers the service rendered as gratuitous, and it, therefore, forms no ground of action." (This contrast to the Roman law understanding that absentee property owners depended on the intervention of neighbors and should pay for their neighbors' benevolence must have been both implicit and obvious to Ford and his legally sophisticated audience.) And so the paragraph ended.[19]

One can imagine Ford taking a long breath before moving on to a second even longer paragraph, in which he reflected on the one exception he allowed to his rule: that compensation might be required if the care was provided as a matter of "urgent necessity."

Again, a survey of cases established the dimensions of the exception. His first stop returned to *Jenkins v. Tucker*, the 1788 English case about the West Indian planter who had abandoned his wife. Remember that the wife's father would not be compensated for the debts he had paid on her behalf—debts that paid for her "necessaries" in life. On the other hand, Ford noted that the English court did require the abandoning husband to repay his former father-in-law for the wife's funeral and burial costs. Unlike food and sustenance (or, one might add, a case of venereal disease), burial was a matter of immediate public necessity. "A dead body tending immediately to putrefaction, was incapable of waiting for either request or assent; the funeral became a matter of urgent necessity for common decency, not able to wait for either request or assent." To wait for permission while news of a wife's death traveled from England to the Caribbean and back was a recipe for disaster. And so, "as far as the debts are concerned, this case shews the general rule in its full strength, and as far as the funeral expenses are concerned, it shews the exception in its full strength."[20]

Lord Kenyon, the English chief justice, adopted the same rule in a 1795 case against a head of household who was sued by a doctor for the care of a "sick servant"—that is, not just an employee but someone for whom the head of household (or master) was directly responsible "in sickness and in health." (Like a slave, one might add.) The circumstances were such that the servant might have died before the master was found and able to respond. As a result, the master would be required to pay for the costs assumed by a stranger or a third party for the servant's necessary care. Ford assured his readers that Lord Kenyon did not mean that a physician might "hunt for patients in any family where he could learn there was a sick person." That would have turned the physician into an officious intermeddler, who had gone where he was not wanted, into the private sphere of a master or head of household. But he could provide medical care—he could heal—when called on in an "urgent case," even without the master's permission. As Ford interpreted the precedent:

> Sickness must prove fatal to every man living, sooner or later; and its mortality, till the last moment, being contingent, it always gives alarm to the sufferer and either awakens sympathy in the beholders, or exposes them for want of it, in that high court, revealed to us, of *dernier resort*, whose judgment will be, "I was *sick* and ye visited me not." A broken bone, a contused body, a burning fever, acute inflammation, or spasms, [but not, presumably, venereal disease] ask no permission of the common law, or any of its forms, to fall upon mortals. The law, knowing this to be so, makes human[e] provisions for such cases.[21]

Ford added that such cases commonly occurred in situations in which poor individuals—paupers—fell ill while away from their home or their settlement (parish), under circumstances for which it would be impossible to apply to masters or to the overseers of the poor responsible for their care.

Five years later, in 1800, Lord Eldon, the British chancellor, dealt with exactly that situation when a pauper away from his "settlement" was "flung" from a cart. Badly bruised, the pauper was carried to a nearby house, where he was nursed until he recovered. Those who had nursed him brought an action for compensation against the overseers of the poor responsible for the pauper—and won. "A person influenced by humanity may provide instant relief for an indigent, helpless creature overtaken by casualty and misfortune, without waiting for any request." Otherwise, "death may interpose."[22]

But absent such a situation "in extremis," care—that is to say, compensation—required the prior permission of the owner, master, or overseer who was being asked to pay, the one who was actually responsible for the dependent. That was, for Ford, the lesson of "the great [New York] case" of *Dunbar v. Williams*—the case of the slave cured of venereal disease—to which he next returned. The lesson of *Dunbar* was that the exception arises only out of "the concurrence of two facts": that there was a "legal and moral obligation" on the defendant, and that the act occurred "under circumstances not admitting of time for obtaining permission." Venereal disease, like Minna's need for care, was apparently not such a circumstance.

Ford concluded the paragraph regretfully. He admitted that a recent New York decision had rejected this statement of the rule and its exception, implicitly contradicting (or reversing) *Dunbar v. Williams*. This was a case involving elder care, *Forsyth v. Ganson*.[23] A son, John, had been promised a larger share of his father's inheritance on the condition that he care for his father and his father's wife, the son's stepmother, in their old age. After the father's death, John stopped supporting his stepmother. The stepmother's own son then stepped into the breach and took care of his mother for several years, eventually suing John for the costs of his mother's care. Justice Ford found it infuriating that the stepmother's son had succeeded in his suit for compensation for the care of his own mother. He allowed that John owed his stepmother support; he had made a valid promise to his father and should have been bound by that promise, at least as a moral obligation—just as Henry Force had some kind of duty to care for Minna. But her own son, who had actually provided support after the stepson's abandonment of his responsibilities, was, in Ford's telling, "an utter stranger" to the contract between the stepmother's husband and the husband's son—just as Elizabeth Haines was implicitly "an utter stranger" to Henry Force's duty to care for Minna. Both Elizabeth Haines and the son in *Forsyth* were providers of mere voluntary courtesies—or so the New York court should have held. Ford found it particularly absurd that the New York judge who wrote the opinion had analogized the situation in *Forsyth* to the responsibilities of a husband to provide for his wife's necessary costs. That analogy ironically put stepmother and stepson "on the footing of husband and wife." It depended on an "analogy, where none can exist without a supposition of incest." But he also noted that *Forsyth v. Ganson* stood "in full opposition and hostility" to the holding in *Dunbar v. Williams*, which he regarded as a leading and correctly decided case: "If one is law, the other cannot be so." And so New York law had been thrown into confusion.

But in a simpler New Jersey (here he invoked *Potter v. Potter*), as in the rest of the common law world, the "rule and the exception" stood undisturbed, according to a full review of the decisions. In a short final paragraph, Ford returned to Elizabeth Haines. Her care of the slave Minna gave her no rights to compensation. Doing otherwise would "legalize interference with the private business of others, in a manner subversive of law, and mischievous to society." Mrs. Haines should not have "harbored" Minna. If she felt "pity" for "an old servant," she should have notified the overseers of the poor, who would have found a way to compel the owner to "do his duty." Minna's care was not her responsibility.

Dayton

Justice William L. Dayton, who wrote a concurrence, was as young as Gabriel Ford was old. Like Ford, he came from an elite New Jersey family.[24] Dayton was appointed to the New Jersey Supreme Court in 1838, when he was just thirty-one, after attending the College of New Jersey (now Princeton) and practicing law for a few years. In 1841, not long after *Force v. Haines* was decided, he resigned from the court to become New Jersey's senator in Washington, D.C. Dayton spent the 1840s as a prominent Whig, but in the early 1850s, he became a founding member of the new Republican Party. In 1856, he ran (unsuccessfully) as John Fremont's running mate for the vice presidency. And in 1859, he was discussed as a possible presidential candidate. During the Civil War, he served as minister to France in the Lincoln administration. He died in France, suddenly and mysteriously, in 1864.[25]

Like Ford, Dayton understood *Force v. Haines* as a case in which apparently "benevolent acts" had resulted in a "voluntary support, for which no recovery" was possible. No one, he continued, could "assume another's burthens, without his assent, and then charge him with the cost."

Even as it agreed with Ford's holding, Dayton's concurring opinion offered both a querulous and a pointed critique of Ford's reasoning. It was querulous in its challenge to Ford's claim to offer a learned survey of cases (he directed the reader to *Lampleigh v. Braithwait* and to *Smith's Leading Cases*, revealing what Ford had apparently hidden), and it was pointed in its desire to locate the reasons for the holding in the concrete specifics of the law of slavery in New Jersey, as he portrayed those specifics, and in Mrs. Haines's moral status and situation.[26]

Dayton's political trajectory may have been toward the Republican Party, but he was no abolitionist, certainly not in 1840. His opinion took the law of slavery as nothing but a legal problem, part of the everyday landscape of New Jersey law. In Dayton's formulation, however, slavery lived within the law in a very different way from how Ford had conceptualized the institution. For Dayton, the law of slavery was a distinct doctrinal field, while for Ford, the law of slavery was close to a misnomer. For Ford, slaves were just property, part of a general legal field of properties or resources governed by a similar set of relationships. Transactions about them were covered by a commercial law that dealt with contractual problems and the boundaries between voluntary and involuntary transactions. Master–slave relations were a subset of a broadly defined law of persons, one that emphasized the continuities between various domestic relations (marriage, infancy, apprenticeship, slavery) that were present within households. As a result, Ford moved easily between cases that dealt with apprenticeship, marriage, and poor relief, and those about slavery. By contrast, Dayton, like many nineteenth-century American judges, regarded the law of slavery as a distinct legal subject, irreducible to ordinary problems of private property and private law. It was, in its nature, exceptional.[27]

Dayton began by acknowledging Henry Force's continuing legal and moral responsibility for the care of Minna. But, he continued, the reality of Force's responsibility did not give Haines any "peculiar" rights. She was just a private citizen like other citizens, without any capacity to make Force do his duty; without any capacity to compel him to compensate her when she did her duty. It should be up to a town's or locality's overseers of the poor to care for Minna, and it would then become their problem to seek reimbursement for their expenses from Force.

Implicitly, Dayton was chiding Mrs. Haines as a woman who did not understand the differences between private and public responsibilities, who apparently did not understand the rules of the male legal game. Dayton emphasized the need to distinguish legal from moral duties. For him,

Mrs. Haines's moral stature as a caring woman should not depend on a right to legal compensation; indeed, asking for compensation may have undercut her moral stature. To rule in her favor might be read as destabilizing the link between women and their supposedly natural tendencies for care.

In any case, Mrs. Haines should have understood that the overseers of the poor of a township had a legal responsibility for the care of slaves and ex-slaves put in their care. It was they who should have gone after a neglectful Force. Presumably, Dayton would have supported the right of those overseers of the poor to obtain compensation from Henry Force if they had taken over Minna's care. By contrast, Mrs. Haines had, at most, a weak moral obligation to provide for Minna's care, and her benevolent acts did not produce legal rights. She was, or should have remained, just a good Samaritan—particularly in this situation, in which there was no "emergency," no colorable claim of "necessity." Any other result would "constitute every man the keeper, at his option, of this class of the poor of his neighborhood."

What of Mr. Force's awareness that Mrs. Haines was taking on his responsibilities? What was the significance of Force's sharply expressed refusal to take Minna back when Haines tried to return her? Did his knowledge of Minna's need for care imply assent or an acknowledgment of responsibility? Perhaps it might have if Force had remained silent, but the fact that he had clearly told Haines that he would not provide for Minna was, for Dayton, significant. It countered Mrs. Haines's attorney's efforts to suggest that there was an implicit contract between Force and Haines for Minna's care, one that obligated Force to pay. Haines's attorney had tried to distinguish a hypothetical situation in which Force had said nothing about Minna's care, a situation that the attorney acknowledged might make Haines's actions into a mere voluntary courtesy. By contrast, what had actually occurred—Mrs. Haines trying to return Minna, and Mr. Force vigorously and explicitly rejecting any responsibility—gave the jury, according to Haines's attorney, the right to infer an implicit contract between the two. Dayton found that distinction specious, or "absurd." The potentially implicit had become explicit, and had been rejected. There was certainly no meeting of minds between Force and Haines, neither implicitly nor explicitly. And there was, as a result, no way for a jury to infer a contract from the facts of the case.

Dayton acknowledged that husbands and fathers and other heads of household were sometimes held responsible for the care of dependents, even in situations in which they had explicitly and loudly rejected responsibility, and even in the face of forceful efforts to avoid responsibility. And men with sufficient means could not legally abandon such responsibilities, leaving wives and children to burden the overseers of the poor. But the reasons husbands and fathers were held liable, "though rendered against . . . [their] express orders," were specific to the respectable identities of their wives and children: "It would be against public policy" to ask presumptively white wives or children "to apply for public relief on the ground of pauperism, preparatory to charging the husband or parent." Most wives and children would avoid the "degradation of holding themselves out to the world as public paupers." And so, if husbands and parents could not be sued for "necessaries" by the associates (friends and relatives) of their wives and children, "it would in most cases . . . exempt the husband or parent from all responsibility." And that exemption would violate our "public policy," our "proper respect for the relationship and reciprocal duties of husband and wife—parent and child."

But, he continued, "the same reasons" did "not extend to slaves." Unlike Ford, Justice Dayton was unwilling to see the situation in *Force v. Haines* as being at all analogous to those found in other domestic relations. Here he moved in ways that might remind the reader of North Carolina's Thomas Ruffin, who in *State v. Mann* worked to distinguish the law of slavery from the law of domestic relations. Other relations were defined by the public responsibilities placed on fathers and husbands. No such public responsibilities sat on the shoulders of slaveholders; or rather, what responsibilities slaveholders had for the management of what was theirs was defined entirely by "the general principles" that limited property rights and made private individuals who interfered with property into officious intermeddlers. Only explicit legislative enactments could have added to those general principles. Slaveholders were just property owners, for the most part free to use (and to abuse and waste) what was theirs. Husbands and wives and parents and children were special cases, exceptions to those general principles. Although a few cases had extended the exceptions to apprenticeships, Dayton thought that extension went too far. And it certainly did not lead to a further extension that would give Mrs. Haines a right to compensation for the slave Minna's care.

To put the point slightly differently: Husbands and fathers would be, or certainly ought to be, disgraced if they allowed those they were responsible for—their wives and children—to become public charges. And those they were responsible for would certainly experience poor relief as a disgrace as well. As a result, those who stepped in to care for those wives and children did so to maintain those dependents in a situation of decent respectability, providing the care that dishonorable husbands and fathers ought to have given. These people substituted for those husbands and fathers, and those husbands and fathers ought to pay as a form of compensation for the avoidance of disgrace.

But, Dayton continued, there was no disgrace in allowing slaves or exslaves to become public charges. What should be done with the Minnas of the world? They became the public responsibility of the overseers of the poor of the town in which the owner had a settlement. Those overseers might seek recompense from owners—men like Henry Force—who, according to New Jersey statutes, might be made to reimburse them for the costs of caring for slaves and former slaves. "If a slave be left destitute, let the public officer apply the remedy, and look over to the owner . . . [to] right the wrong." But, Dayton concluded, slave owners should not be burdened by the lawsuits of private individuals. Those, like Elizabeth Haines, who offered aid and care as private individuals should understand that what they did they did as a gratuitous act—that what they offered was never more than a "voluntary courtesy." They were, at best, merely good Samaritans.

In coming to this conclusion, Dayton had to ignore a great deal of hortatory language by the New Jersey legislature, language shaped by the legislature's worry that gradual emancipation would lead slave owners to dump their unprofitable slaves onto the overseers of the poor. The legislature had wanted to ensure that aged and dependent slaves did not become burdens on the various towns. Tax avoidance was the dominant concern; the legislature did not want township tax rolls swollen by expenditures for the care of dependent and needy ex-slaves that masters had abandoned. The result was a recurrent insistence that slaves in poor health (unavailable for ordinary labor) or over the age of forty (by 1840, Minna would have fit both criteria) could not be manumitted. Indeed, in the slave code of 1798 and elsewhere, and in the practices that developed in every county in the state, this was stated positively as a prerequisite for a valid manumission. A slave owner who wished to manumit a slave had to provide evidence that the slave in question "appeared to be sound in mind and not under any bodily incapacity of obtaining a support, and also [was] not under the age of twenty one years nor above the age of forty years."[28]

To justify his conclusion that the overseers of the poor ought to have been responsible for Minna's care, Dayton looked to an 1824 case, *Overseers of Poor of South Brunswick v. Overseers of Poor of East Windsor*. That case explored some of the unplanned-for consequences of the worry that gradual emancipation would produce new tax burdens. In 1802, a master had left the state without manumitting a slave, who remained in New Jersey and who by the 1820s had become a pauper in need of care (although apparently still formally enslaved). Who should pay for the slave's care? Chief Justice Ewing's opinion for the court had worked through the statutory language. After 1820, an ex-slave gained a settlement in the town where his or her master lived at the time of the manumission. An unmanumitted slave remained the responsibility of the master, and she or he had no settlement of her or his own. That is, no town had to pay for the slave's care, because that responsibility remained with the owner. Early on, the New Jersey legislature had provided for the possibility that a master might become insolvent and therefore unable to care for a slave. In that case, the slave did gain a settlement where she or he lived. Implicitly, the legislature assumed that insolvency was the equivalent of manumission (since a master no longer had the resources to be a master). But it had not provided for the situation of a master—competent in other ways (that is, not insolvent)—who had simply left the state, leaving the slave behind to become a pauper. So, what to do? The court in the *Overseers of Poor of South Brunswick* case ultimately decided that the town where the slave was located had to provide for him, even though it had no one to look to—neither a master nor the overseers of another town where the slave had a settlement—for reimbursement for the costs of the care provided. A needy and dependent person could not be left uncared for.[29]

Dayton worked to draw apposite language from Ewing's 1824 opinion for his own purposes. His goal was to prove that Mrs. Haines had no right to compensation because the overseers of the poor were there to assume the burden, and they would have a right to compel compensation from Mr. Force. But to reach that goal, he also had to ignore the holding in the case that said, in effect, that the overseers of the poor had no right to be compensated. They had no statutory capacity to compel an absent slaveholder to provide compensation; the town simply had to shoulder the costs of care of such an enslaved person. The case was not much of a precedent for the principle that the slave owner—Henry Force in this case—could be forced to reimburse the overseers of the poor for the costs they incurred in caring for his slave.

Even as Dayton tried to emphasize the public responsibilities of public officials, he could not look past the property rights of the slaveholder. If someone like Mrs. Haines could compel compensation from a slaveholder like Henry Force (as he imagined him), then slaves would be less enslaved and slaveholders would have a reduced "civil liberty." If Mrs. Haines were reimbursed for her costs, then perhaps a slave might go to a doctor against the wishes of his or her master. The owner's capacity to dispose of property as he or she saw fit would be compromised. Dayton did not believe an owner should have his or her property rights limited by the actions of private "individuals." If Henry Force failed to provide, "let the public officer who acts under the responsibility of official duties, right the wrong." Not Mrs. Haines.

Hornblower and Nevius

Two judges dissented in the case: Joseph Hornblower, the chief justice, and James Schureman Nevius. Hornblower was one of the few judges in the country—perhaps the only one in New Jersey—publicly identified as an abolitionist. A few years before *Force v. Haines*, he had defended New Jersey's relatively weak "personal liberty" law against the rights of southern slave catchers. That opinion had caught the attention of abolitionists, who republished and commented on it. A few years after *Force v. Haines*, after New Jersey had enacted a new state constitution, Hornblower would argue that the effect of the opening statement of rights in the new constitutional text— with its stirring declaration that "all men are by nature free and independent, and have certain natural and unalienable rights"—had brought a final end to the legality of chattel slavery in the state. Unfortunately, he wrote in dissent in that case as well. And the majority opinion there, drafted by Justice Nevius, opined that such constitutional rights language was merely aspirational. Only a positive act by the legislature could put an end to slavery in the state.[30]

But in *Force v. Haines*, Hornblower and Nevius stood together in dissent, although the reasons each gave for dissenting were distinguishable from the other.

Hornblower began by playing what modern lawyers might call the legal process card. The role of an appeal was not to second-guess the jury. An appeal was limited to consideration of questions of law, not fact. At most, the appellate court should evaluate whether the plaintiff was entitled to recover costs, given the sufficiency of the pleadings and the facts as brought out at trial. It was clear that the jury had rested its decision on sufficient evidence. There was certainly a legal basis for a holding in Mrs. Haines's favor; that should have been enough.[31]

Since a majority of the court disagreed, Hornblower felt obliged to continue. It was, he thought, inherent in the relationship of master and slave, based both on statute and on natural law, that a master must care for his or her slave, especially when that slave was disabled or ill. One might note the peculiarity of this statement coming from an abolitionist. Usually antislavery legalists argued that slavery rested only on "municipal" law, with no foundation in nature at all. That had been the conventional understanding for more than a generation, perhaps ever since Lord Mansfield's 1772 opinion in *Somerset v. Stewart*. Was Hornblower challenging that conventional wisdom? Indeed, should one wonder at his participation in this case? Was it possible to serve as a judge in New Jersey while being an abolitionist?[32]

Since Hornblower had spent his legal and judicial careers working in a jurisdiction where slavery was mostly legal, one has to assume that he had bracketed off those questions. Instead, Hornblower invoked a passionately felt commonsensical or Christian duty of care, one that humanized slavery but left it largely intact. Or, to put it differently, he implicitly argued that to choose to participate in the institution of slavery meant—inherently and inescapably—that one took on the responsibilities that came along with participation. Those responsibilities included a duty of care for enslaved women and men.

Henry Force's responsibility for Minna did not rest on a contract, a promise, or any choice he had made—other than the decision to become a slaveholder. According to Hornblower, the law made him do it: "Imperious duty imposes the obligation upon him, and righteous law *makes him willing* to perform it." And given that duty, Hornblower saw no reason why Mrs. Haines should not be compensated if she did what Force had refused to do but was obligated to do. Minna's situation was no different than that of an abandoned wife or child. Husband and father were required to pay for the costs of care, not because of a contract or an agreement but because of "imperious duty" and "righteous law." The law made them pay—and so it was in this case as well: "The law has not left it to the humanity, the avarice, or the caprice of the master, to say, whether he will or will not, support his helpless slave; nor yet, whether he will do it himself, or compel the public in the first instance to furnish such support and then look to him for remuneration."

One might imagine that Hornblower was responding to Ford's identification of Mrs. Haines as an officious intermeddler, and he suppressed any sense of her as merely a private actor, even as a benevolent intervenor. Instead, he worked to make her into the enforcer of state law. As he did so, he walked an uncomfortable line rhetorically: on the one hand, he would not have wanted to present her as akin to the abolitionist interfering with the slave regime's domestic institutions; on the other hand, he had to repress the extent to which she had been a willing and active participant in the rental of an enslaved woman.

Unlike the judges in the majority, who tended to see the problem of the case from the defendant's vantage point, that of Henry Force, Hornblower posed the problem from Mrs. Haines's perspective. What was she supposed to do? Ford and Dayton both regarded her as a woman who had stuck her nose where it did not belong. Hornblower offered a highly wrought alternative. Slaves were not "brutes." They had feelings that needed to be recognized (just as wives and children did). But Mrs. Haines had feelings, too. Hornblower imagined himself in her shoes: "What, if the owner of a blind and helpless negro woman, suffering at the moment, with hunger and nakedness, should thrust her into my doors, telling me, with brutal insult, at the same time, that if I relieved her sufferings, or administered to her necessities, he would never pay me[?]" Did that mean that Elizabeth Haines (or Chief Justice Hornblower, as he imagined himself in her situation) could be forced to choose between turning her "out of doors, blind, hungry and naked, . . . to perish like a brute" ("in violation of every feeling of my nature, and of every dictate of humanity") and giving her food, clothing, and shelter at her "own expense, however illy" she could afford it? Surely not. But that was the dilemma that the majority's holding forced on Mrs. Haines.

In his imagined dialogue with his colleagues, Hornblower acknowledged the answer they would have given to the dilemma he posed: Minna should be turned over to the overseers of the poor; there were real public agents responsible, and Mrs. Haines was not a public agent. But that answer suggested that the slave's owner, Henry Force, had the right to put Mrs. Haines to the "trouble" of mobilizing the overseers of the poor. Why give Force that power and Haines that burden, especially when it was clear that he was the wrongdoer in imposing enslaved Minna on Mrs. Haines? Why not allow Mrs. Haines to "relieve" Minna directly? Even if the overseers were bound to take over care under such circumstances (a proposition that Hornblower doubted), why wait when there was need? The machinery of "pauper relief" was a creaky one; it took time to put in motion. Not all overseers were scrupulous, and even those who were might live at a distance or be delayed for any number of reasons. In denying compensation to Mrs. Haines, the court had turned Minna the slave into "an anomaly in our law, . . . a human being with no more claims upon our humanity, or the protection of our laws, than a beast of burthen."

And what of the responsibility of the overseers of the poor? Hornblower's analysis here was complicated and needs some explication, shaped as it was by the chaotic state of poor relief in early nineteenth-century America.[33] It began with the parallels between Mrs. Haines's position and that of those ordinarily responsible for providing poor relief: a township's overseers of the poor. There was not, Hornblower confidently asserted, any statute giving the overseers a cause of action against a master who had positively refused to pay for the care of his slave. (Here he was probably drawing a fine distinction between the clearly stated and repeated statutory prohibition on slave owners *not* to use manumission to dump their no longer valuable or costly slaves on the overseers of the poor—a central feature of New Jersey's regime of gradual emancipation—and the absence of a statute giving a cause of action to overseers against masters like Henry Force, who "positively" refused to pay for the care of their slaves.) Without such a statute, on what would this kind of action be founded? What made a township's overseers any different than Mrs. Haines? Both should be able to recover because Force had neglected or refused to discharge a "legal and imperative duty." Anyone placed in such a situation by an owner should be equally able to maintain an action for compensation.

Next, Hornblower denied that the overseers of the poor had any distinct legal obligation in this situation. If they had intervened, they would have been "mere volunteers," just as Mrs. Haines was said to be. There was, of course, a thick body of statutes and practices that made poor relief officers responsible for the care of the so-called casual poor. But who were the casual poor? They were poor persons who became sick or had an accident while away from home. Thus, they were left to the charity of strangers. And in those circumstances, in cases of emergency, poor relief officials were, by statute, responsible for the costs of their care. But slaves were not, in their nature, to be understood as the casual poor. The casual poor were a problem that had to be dealt with by overseers of the poor because they were "masterless" men and women who moved about, ended up in other localities, and had to be cared for, and the costs of their care would not be reimbursed either by hometowns or by masters, husbands, or parents. But slaves were the opposite of the casual poor, the opposite of the unattended and free detritus of a mobile economy. Overseers of the poor had to take responsibility for the casual poor because no one else would. But in Minna's case, everyone knew who was responsible: Henry Force.

Meanwhile, Minna's situation was continuously one of emergency. "She was constantly, *in extremis*, and required constant care." If the overseers of the poor were not bound to interfere, who else was there? If Mrs. Haines had no right to stand in for the master, who could? Was purely private charity all that stood in the way of starvation? Was a coercive state entirely powerless in such circumstances? Surely not.

Hornblower then returned to the "exception" drawn for wives and children. Why distinguish the care of slaves from the care of other familial dependents? When "a man turns his wife, or his child out of doors, he sends his credit with them, for a support, equal at least, to his circumstances in life." Why not for the slave? "To suppose that the law, out of regard to the delicate feelings, or the family pride[,] of wives and children, will make provision for them, while it leaves the unhappy and degraded slave to the cold charities of the world, is to cast upon it [the law] a reproach which it does not deserve." Hornblower had to concede that there were no English cases to support his claim, but that was because slavery was unknown in England. (Here he relied on a common but probably incorrect understanding of what Mansfield's *Somerset* decision stood for.) The principles that he drew from the English cases had their "foundations in the rules of eternal justice," which compelled men to do as they ought and which implied "a promise on his part to do that which in justice and equity he is, by law, bound to do." Those principles were of direct relevance. And for articulation of those principles, he looked—as the other justices had—to *Jenkins v. Tucker*, the 1785 English case of the West Indian planter who abandoned his wife. From Hornblower's standpoint, the law of master and slave was "perfectly analogous" to that of husband and wife at common law. "Nothing . . . but a morbid insensibility to the claims of the slave for the sympathy and protection of the laws" could produce any difference.

And how did the other cases that Ford had mobilized stand up? Here Hornblower showed his skills as a lawyer, reinterpreting Ford's precedents to support his position. *Potter v. Potter* was simply a case about a woman who had provided care. In that case, no evidence had been offered of any "delinquency" on the part of the heirs to her husband's estate, unlike Henry Force. He believed that *Dunbar v. Williams*, the case about the doctor who cured the slave's venereal disease but would not be compensated by the slave owner, "so far from militating against this action, in my opinion, sustains it." The service the doctor provided was "voluntary"; it was not a case *in extremis*." The doctor was a mere volunteer, unlike Mrs. Haines. (He, like Ford, apparently regarded venereal disease as a non-emergency.) And *Bartholomew v. Jackson*, in which a neighbor put out the flames to keep the wheat from burning, "only shows, what is not disputed, that a mere gratuity, constitutes no ground of action."

Hornblower concluded with a quick riposte to Dayton's analysis of Force's vigorous denial of responsibility: Force knew that he was liable; otherwise, he would not have said to Mrs. Haines that "if she recovered any thing against him, he would put his property out of his hands." Force should not be able to excuse himself from paying, from doing what he was legally bound to do, "by simply refusing to do so."

IN HIS DISSENT, James Nevius was as pointed as Hornblower was effusive.[34] The only question he found worth discussing was what legal obligations the law imposed on masters. The 1798 law respecting slaves required masters to support their slaves unless they were insolvent. If a master was insolvent, then the slave became a pauper, eligible for support from the local overseers of the poor if the slave was unable to support him- or herself. But no slave whose master was solvent could be a pauper or have a settlement in the state. This meant that, putting aside any situation of emergency or "urgent necessity," the overseers of the poor had no more responsibility for the care of a slave than did any other person. In effect, Justice Nevius situated the overseers in exactly the same situation that Mrs. Haines found herself in because of the holding in *Force v. Haines*. Poor-relief officials would not be acting in any official capacity if they cared for a needy slave like Minna. Thus, if Mrs. Haines had dumped Minna on the overseers of the poor, as the judges in the majority ruled she ought to have done, an impossible situation might have resulted, in which no one was responsible. And so, Nevius continued, both the imagined overseer of the poor and Mrs. Haines should have available to them the same remedy for the care of a master's slave.

Nevius then reproduced the facts in the case in a way that justified the jury's decision to award damages to Mrs. Haines. "The girl" was a slave; she was "infirm and blind"; she could not support herself. Mrs. Haines had long supported her, and she had done so with the knowledge of the defendant, who was given "direct notice" of the care provided. Force had been asked repeatedly to "take charge" of Minna, but he had refused and indeed had declared that if suit were brought, "he would evade the payment by putting his property out of his hands." According to Nevius, Force's knowledge that Minna was in the Haines household, where she was being cared for, "amounted at least to a *consent*" to Mrs. Haines's support and an implicit promise to compensate her for that support. Force had an alternative, which was to take direct responsibility and care for his own property. When he did not do so, when he allowed Minna—his property—to reside with Mrs. Haines, he laid the basis for her suit for compensation. Mrs. Haines's "services" were therefore "not gratuitous and voluntary, but in a measure compulsory." It would be "a stain upon our laws" if a master could evade obligations under such circumstances.

Like Hornblower, Nevius flogged the major precedents that the judges in the majority had identified. *Potter v. Potter* could be distinguished because unlike this case, there was no request or promise to pay by the children who had inherited the slave. The two New York cases, *Dunbar* and *Bartholomew*, were situations involving "voluntary courtesies"; and in *Dunbar*, the master had no notice of the medical attention offered to his slave. *Jenkins v. Tucker*, in his rendering, "fully corroborate[d]" his understanding of the legal doctrine. There was, Nevius concluded, no distinction between the liability of a husband and a father for the support of a dependent and that of a master for a slave, except that the law inferred or presumed that husbands and fathers knew (had notice) of their dependents' care by others, while notice of support had to be proved in the case of a slave—as it was in this case.

What Lay Beneath (the Opinions)

The sharply posed disagreements among the judges who wrote opinions in *Force v. Haines* hide all the ways they agreed with one another. They shared a set of conclusions about the litigants, about the significance of ownership of a slave, about what it meant to be a private citizen, about the role of poor relief in the legal culture, and about Minna's status as a slave. They shared a sense of what evidence was relevant. (Not one of the judges bothered to mention that Minna had a son, Jesse—a child of eleven or twelve by the time of the trial, probably fourteen when the appeal was decided in 1840, a child who had been kept under the "care" of Elizabeth Haines. If Minna had returned or been returned to Henry Force, she would have been separated from Jesse.) And they shared a general sense that a mere volunteer, what in much of Europe would be known as a benevolent intervenor, could not claim a right to compensation. What they disagreed on was whether Mrs. Haines was in fact a mere volunteer, not the question of the legal consequences of being one.

Force v. Haines was framed as if it were a debate about a legal problem— the definition of a voluntary courtesy—in a place where the law of slavery was relatively clear. The state of the law was asserted forcefully and confidently. Henry Force should or should not have had to pay; Elizabeth Haines should or should not have known that she would not be compensated for her care; the overseers of the poor were or were not responsible for the care of needy Minna.

This was a case about slavery and about the care of a slave. That it occurred in a jurisdiction where slavery had long been legislatively declared to be on the way to abolition was entirely repressed. That the number of slaves had declined dramatically, to the point that the 1840 federal census records only one enslaved person in the city of Elizabethtown, could not be read out of the opinions, all of which assumed that this was a continuing subject worthy of their attention.

At least three of the judges who wrote opinions—Ford, Hornblower, and Nevius—were knowledgeable participants in many cases involving New Jersey slavery and abolition. They were all "repeat players." Each of them had advocated for and against slaveholders; each of them had judged cases in which the terms of gradual abolition had been debated. And yet the peculiarities—the specific features—of the regime seemed off the table. It is almost as if they had collectively decided to argue through this case by holding constant what was in fact definitively inconstant, changeable, vague, and imprecise. As we will see, on several crucial matters the judges knowingly misstated facts or drew inferences that they knew were not true.

The result was a discourse about an interesting philosophical or jurisprudential problem: the legal status of the "voluntary" actor. And yet one wonders what it took to construct that discourse.

CHAPTER TWO

Practicing Gradual Emancipation

Legal Lives

What do we know about our central characters—about Minna and the litigants, Henry Force and Elizabeth Haines? In particular, what do we know about them as participants in New Jersey's legal regime of slavery and emancipation?

Elizabeth Haines lived in Elizabethtown; Henry Force lived about eight miles away, along the Rahway River at the border between Woodbridge and Rahway. Elizabeth Haines had once lived in Rahway as well. It is at least possible that Elizabeth Williams (her maiden name) and Henry Force had known each other before her marriage to Benjamin Haines. Throughout the eighteenth century, Rahway had been a precinct of the extended Elizabethtown Township, until 1804 when Rahway Township was hived off. Woodbridge was an older rural community.[1]

In the early 1820s, Elizabethtown—the oldest English settlement in a colony that would become the state of New Jersey—was still a wealthy town. Throughout the eighteenth and early nineteenth centuries, it was the home of many of the prominent figures in New Jersey public life, the most distinguished Protestant ministers, a thick array of institutions—both charitable and educational—and one of the first state chartered banks. The College of New Jersey, eventually renamed Princeton University, was founded in Elizabethtown in 1746, although it only remained in Elizabethtown for a very short time.

Directly across from Staten Island, with a port that offered easy and quick access to New York City, Elizabethtown had long been a necessary stop for travelers to New York City from the south, who relied on its hotels, inns, and ferry services. During the 1810s and early 1820s, it was the site of the titanic battle over control of Hudson River steamship travel, which would end in 1824 with the U.S. Supreme Court's decision in *Gibbons v. Ogden*.

But by 1840, when *Force v. Haines* was finally decided, Elizabethtown (soon to be renamed Elizabeth) was beginning to decline in the face of the explosive growth of neighboring Newark. Its glory days were behind it.[2]

There had always been slaves in Elizabethtown, as even nineteenth-century booster-historians acknowledged. Advertisements for the purchase of slaves were a recurrent feature in the town's eighteenth-century papers. By the time Elizabeth Haines rented Minna in the early 1820s, the number of enslaved people held in the area had declined, though not as dramatically as elsewhere in the state. In 1820, there were still 659 enslaved people in Essex County, the county within which Elizabethtown was located. (There had been 1,301 slaves in 1790.) And according to 1830 census records, the households of a few of Elizabeth Haines's neighbors still included at least one enslaved person.[3]

By contrast, the 1830 census indicated that there were no slaves listed in the households of any of Henry Force's close neighbors.[4] As far as I can tell, Henry Force had never owned a slave until he purchased Minna approximately one year before he rented her to Elizabeth Haines.

For many years, Force, who had been born in 1780 or 1781 and had served in the War of 1812, had little land or personal property. He may have made a living as a lawyer—at least, late in life he called himself a lawyer—although nowhere in the published New Jersey court records is he referred to as an attorney. It is more likely that he bought and sold real estate. Around 1815 he began to run a sawmill on the Rahway River. His second wife died in 1820, leaving him with four small children. And in 1822, he was listed for the first time as owning thirty acres, two horses, two cattle, one dog, and one slave. Presumably, that slave was Minna. One might speculate that he purchased Minna because he needed help in his household while he ran his sawmill.

But whatever help Minna did or did not offer, she would not remain part of his household for long. Henry Force soon remarried and, shortly after, leased Minna to Elizabeth Haines. Had he exchanged a slave for a wife?[5]

In 1822, before she rented Minna, Elizabeth Haines had been a widow for more than thirteen years. She was almost fifty years old. Her daughter, Mary, who must have been born shortly before her husband's 1808 death, still lived with her.

In his will, Elizabeth's late husband, Benjamin Haines, had returned to his "dearly beloved wife" a house and lot in Rahway, which had been her sole property before their marriage. In addition, he gave her "a black Girl named Mary, and all the other moveable property now remaining that was her own." He continued: "Also the sorrel mare and the mare called the Burr mare, also my Riding Chair, also her Choice of two . . . cows, also provisions sufficient to support her and family for one year after my decease, provided that she . . . relinquishes her right of dower to the wood on my farm." He gave Elizabeth the use of all his property until Benjamin and Richard, his sons from a previous marriage, had each turned twenty-one. Mary Rebecca Haines, his infant daughter with Elizabeth (although her middle name recalled his first wife, Rebecca or Rebekah Townley), would get $1,200 when she reached the age of eighteen, if there were still sufficient funds at that time. And he directed his executors "to sell my Negroe man Named Ceazer only for the term of sex [six] years after my decease[.] At the expiration of the said six years, I give him his freedom."[6]

Fourteen years later, in 1822, Elizabeth Haines was still at least modestly well off, even after her stepsons had gained their inheritances. (That must have occurred in 1819 or 1820.) Over the years there were small changes in the assets in her household, at least as revealed to the Essex County tax collector. She had manumitted a slave, also named Benjamin, in 1817, but there is no evidence of what happened to the enslaved Mary that her husband had returned to her with her other personal property. Still, throughout the years between 1811 and 1822, there was always one unnamed slave listed among Elizabeth Haines's "tax ratables." As of 1821 and 1822, before Minna came, she owned a house on sixty-five acres plus a salt meadow, one horse, six cattle (reduced to one cow in 1822), and one slave.[7]

It is certainly possible, even likely, that Elizabeth Williams Haines and her husband were from Quaker families. Haines was a common name among the Society of Friends, as were both Townley and Williams. And yet no evidence survives of Haines's presence, or that of her husband, at any meeting. Benjamin Haines was buried in the Presbyterian graveyard in Elizabethtown, next to the gravestone of his first wife, Rebecca (or Rebekah) Townley Haines. And when Elizabeth's daughter, Mary Cross, testified at the trial in *Force v. Haines*, she did not object to taking an oath, as Quakers typically would have.[8]

And what of Minna, the subject—or object—of the litigation between Henry Force and Elizabeth Haines? She was in her late twenties when Elizabeth Haines rented and moved her from Woodbridge to Elizabethtown; she was well over forty by 1840, when the New Jersey Supreme Court decided that Haines would not be compensated for her care. As we will see, her age was of relevance in establishing both her eligibility for freedom and who would be responsible for her care. I am loath to give much credence to what white witnesses said about Minna when *Force v. Haines* was litigated. They all emphasized her drunkenness and "worthlessness," and that she cost her caretaker, Elizabeth Haines, much more than she returned in labor. Apparently Minna had lost sight in one eye during the lease years. In 1824 or

1825 she gave birth to a child, a boy named Jesse, to whom Haines apparently became quite attached. It may be that the birth of Jesse can explain much of what followed in the story that was *Force v. Haines*. Perhaps *Force v. Haines* was as much about the care of Jesse as it was about the costs that Force apparently imposed on Haines by not retaking possession of Minna. But as we have seen, Jesse was unmentioned by any of the judges in their opinions.[9]

NOW LET'S CONSIDER the early legal life of another important character in our story, Chief Justice Joseph Hornblower—one of the two judges who dissented in *Force v. Haines*. After his death in 1862, Hornblower's biographers and memorialists all emphasized and celebrated his antislavery credentials. One obituary characterized him as always "a practical anti-slavery man," who did his "best to extinguish the last remnants of the Slavery institution which lingered in some portions of his State." In 1836, he had challenged the enforceability—or at least the reach—into New Jersey of the federal Fugitive Slave Act. In 1844, as a member of the convention convened to draft a new state constitution, he argued strenuously for an absolute abolition of slavery, with no success. In 1845, in *State v. Post*, he argued that the constitutional statement of rights that opened the new state constitution made slavery an impossibility. Once again, though, he argued as a dissenter, without success. In 1857, as an old man, he wrote a young admirer that he despaired for his country because of the power that slaveholders wielded nationally. He had "lived to see my country in the hands of, and under the despotic rule of a few hundred thousands of lordly, slaveholding aristocrats, who are trampling out the very life blood of all American patriotism, and making the whole machinery of our government tributary to the perpetuation of the most anti-republican, soul-destroying, unchristian, inhuman and cruel institution, that ever cursed the human family."[10]

Earlier on, however, as a family member and a young lawyer, he had lived and practiced law within New Jersey's regime of slavery and very gradual emancipation. How comfortably he lived within that regime it is impossible to say. But we have to assume that he managed to reconcile his work life and his household and family life with his principles, even as he maintained his membership in manumission societies. He knew how to be a slaveholder, at least a New Jersey slaveholder, and he understood and worked within the terms of New Jersey law.

In 1823, he and his siblings manumitted a slave, Sarah, identified as having been their father's slave. Josiah Hornblower, Joseph's father, had died in

1809, fourteen years earlier. After his death, the inventory to his estate, for which Joseph served as executor, had included five enslaved people: two men each worth $200, one man worth $120, a "Negro Girl" worth $50, and a second "Girl" named Sal, who was worth only $20.

I suspect that Sal was the same woman that Joseph Hornblower and his brothers (and one brother-in-law) manumitted fourteen years later, as Sarah. But where had she lived between Josiah's death and her manumission? Presumably, the slaves Josiah Hornblower had possessed at his death had either been sold or, more likely, been distributed among his four children (with appropriate accounting and setoff). Thus, it is possible that she lived as a slave in Joseph Hornblower's household.[11]

In his will, Josiah Hornblower—a controversial engineer and inventor—had instructed his executors that he wished his slave Betty to be freed if she obtained the necessary security for legal manumission. Betty did not appear in the inventory to his estate, either because Josiah's instructions removed her from the inventory or because she was of no marketable value due to her age. She was probably over forty, which is why her manumission was premised on payment of security to protect the township's overseers of the poor from responsibility. If she could not find such security, she would, according to Josiah's will, be free to choose her own master and should be sold for a reasonable compensation." (It is of course significant that Josiah did not suggest or dictate that his executors should pay for her security. And we know nothing about how Josiah expected that Betty would find the resources to buy her freedom.) Since Betty's name does not appear with or without security in the Essex County manumission book, it is likely that she found a new master for herself. One is left to wonder whom she chose and how she made that decision, and also what if anything the estate received from the master she chose.[12]

In 1817 and 1818, Joseph Hornblower, who lived in Newark, manumitted his own slaves: a woman, Molly, and a man, Benjamin. Obviously those acts require us to conclude that up until that point, well into his adulthood, he had kept slaves in his own household. Census records for 1820 no longer exist for New Jersey, so it is impossible to know if he still had slaves after 1818. There were, however, no slaves listed on his 1830 census form, although there were three "free colored persons" living in his household: a male between the ages of ten and twenty-three, and two women—one between the ages of twenty-four and thirty-five, and the other between the ages of thirty-six and fifty-four. They might well have been his former slaves.[13]

Joseph Hornblower had been a successful lawyer for a quarter century by the time he became the chief justice of the New Jersey Supreme Court in 1832. Indeed, in his biographical survey of New Jersey judges, Lucius Elmer argued that Hornblower had been a better lawyer than a judge, that his temperament was better suited to advocacy. Like most successful lawyers at the time, his practice was a combination of trial advocacy and office counseling.[14]

In 1813, one of Hornblower's clients was Anne Ogilvie. Her father, Alexander MacWhorter, had been a famous minister in Elizabethtown and South Carolina.[15] MacWhorter had died in 1807, and Anne was his executor. Hornblower had been hired to help her settle her father's estate and work through other matters. Early on, that involved dealing with the death of Caty, Anne Ogilvie's "black woman." A letter from Ogilvie noted that Caty's death "agitated and affected" her "exceedingly." It was the loss of someone who had "acted a conspicuous part among my belov'd father's household," and it brought "tender remembrances into view." By 1813, Caty evidently lived on her own, "under the hill," apart from Ogilvie (although apparently not freed). With her death, rent was still owed and her "cloathing and chests" and her "bed, bedstead and rubbish" had to be removed and sold. Would Hornblower deal with all that, since Ogilvie was just "a fatherless, Brotherless, Childless Widow," who looked to "the sympathy and kindness" in his heart? Hornblower noted on the back of the letter that he had spent $20 on Ogilvie's behalf, including $2.25 for Caty's remaining rent and $6 for a coffin.

In December 1813, Samuel Beebe of New York City, a grandson of MacWhorter and a nephew of Anne Ogilvie, sent attorney Hornblower a note. A "black girl" who had once belonged to his grandfather had called on him because she had been told that Hornblower intended to have her sold as part of his management of the MacWhorter estate. Beebe wanted Hornblower to know that that was not possible. Anne Ogilvie had given "the black girl," called Leah or Elsie, to his sister Mary, who lived with their parents in New York City. According to Beebe, she had spent several years in the Beebe household, but recently Mary Beebe had told her that if "she thought she could procure a living she might leave her and be free." As a result, according to Beebe, Leah or Elsie could not be sold because she was no longer a slave. Beebe hoped that Hornblower would drop him a line on the subject.

If Hornblower did respond, the letter has been lost. And the next we hear of Leah or Elsie is more than eight years later, in January 1822. Hornblower received a letter from Theodorus Bailey, a New York attorney and politician, who enclosed an opinion letter from another New York attorney, the eminent Josiah Ogden Hoffman, with regard to the status of a "female Slave of the late Dr. MacWhorter."[16] The costs of her care—usually referred to as maintenance—were being litigated between the overseers of the poor of the township of Newark, New Jersey, and the MacWhorter estate. Evidently, Leah or Elsie had moved to Newark after Mary Beebe had released her from service, become a "pauper," and applied for poor relief. Under New Jersey law, as expressed in a 1798 "slave code," a slave owner might remain liable for the care of his or her now-dependent slave, even after having manumitted—freed—the slave. Such continued liability might apply if the manumission had occurred through private contract or deed or by testamentary gift, not according to the statutory forms set out in 1798.[17]

It looks like Hornblower, who by 1822 also represented the estate of Anne Ogilvie, who had died in the interim, had written to Bailey to ask him to solicit Hoffman's opinion about the legal status of a slave like Leah or Elsie under New York law. Hornblower must have been uncertain about the specifics of New York law and whether New York or New Jersey law applied to the situation; thus, he looked to Hoffman for an authoritative answer.

Hoffman's short, one-paragraph opinion letter was written in a telegraphic lawyers' code that would have been easily understood by a sophisticated colleague like Hornblower. On the other hand, it probably needs deciphering and expansion for those of us incompletely socialized into an archaic legal language.

His first point was that New York law forbade the importation of slaves. When Mary Beebe brought Leah or Elsie from New Jersey into New York (which is not, of course, what actually happened), Leah or Elsie "became ipso facto free," because that is what New York law prescribed as punishment for slave owners who violated New York law by moving slaves into the state: they lost their property. When Leah or Elsie lived in New York, then, even when she lived as a slave (that is, as if she were still a slave) in the Beebe household, she did so as a "free person," because she had been "imported" into the state when Mary's aunt, Anne Ogilvie, made a gift of her to Mary. (Such importations were certainly illegal under New York law. And as we will see, by 1822—although not in 1807, when MacWhorter died—such exportations were equally illegal under New Jersey law.)

Hoffman's second point was that the gift of Leah or Elsie from Anne Ogilvie to Mary Beebe was valid even though there was nothing in writing. An oral gift of "personal chattel" was valid—unlike real estate, whose validity depended on the presence of a written contract. Since the gift was a valid one, it constituted a complete transfer of the MacWhorter estate's (or Anne Ogilvie's) interest in Leah or Elsie.[18] Thus, even though Mary Beebe actually gained nothing from the gift from her aunt—because Leah or Elsie had become free as a result of the attempt to move her into New York as a slave—Anne Ogilvie and the MacWhorter estate retained no rights to Leah or Elsie. In other words, there was no reversion back to the Mac-Whorter estate when Mary Beebe lost or gave up her possessory interest, or title, in Leah or Elsie. That also meant that the aunt's estate, which Horn-blower was now managing, had no duties toward Leah or Elsie or to the overseers of the poor, and should not have to pay the Newark overseers for her care.

Hoffman's third point: Since the slave became free in New York "and so lived" as free (not just when Mary told her she was free but from the moment she came into the state, because Anne Ogilvie had no right to move her out of New Jersey or into New York), "it may well be questioned whether her subsequent return to New Jersey restored her to Slavery." A manumission "by force of law" should have the same effect as an actual and effectual formal act or deed of manumission. In either case, the result would be a full emancipation. Hoffman did not believe that jurisdictions had the power to reimpose slavery on those who had once become free.[19]

Hoffman's letter included the usual lawyerly qualifications. We might call them the language of lawyerly self-protection: "There may however be some provisions in the Statutes of New Jersey touching this species of Property" that would lead to a different result. But the conclusion Hoffman drew was that neither the MacWhorter estate nor Anne Oglivie's estate was liable for the care of Leah or Elsie. Hornblower's clients were emancipated from responsibility because Leah or Elsie was a free woman.

Hornblower must have sent Hoffman's letter on to the Newark overseers of the poor. Evidently, it did not convince them. In March, Hornblower received notification that the overseers were applying for a court order to require the "heirs and Executors of the Revd Alexander MacWhorter" to provide for the support and maintenance of "Elsie, a black girl, aged about thirty years, the slave & property of the said deceased at the time of his death, & now a pauper." Although they didn't give reasons, it is not diffi-cult to reconstruct how they would have interpreted the relevant law. What was the significance of the "force of law" that presumably made Leah or Elsie a free woman of color? The overseers would have questioned whether the illegal transfer of Leah or Elsie from New Jersey to New York, a transfer that destroyed her former owners' possessory rights over Leah or Elsie, also liberated those former owners from the duty to "save" the overseers of the poor from any costs incurred for the care of Leah or Elsie as a pauper. Several laws, in both New Jersey and New York, were drafted to avoid that result. The effect of an emancipation by force of law was not to liberate slaveholders from responsibility for poor or dependent slaves—even less so when the law that compelled emancipation was the law of a "foreign" jurisdiction, in this case, New York State. The burden should remain on former owners, and those owners should not be able to use transfers across state lines, whether done for strategic or gratuitous reasons, to escape liability. Further, one can imagine that the Newark overseers of the poor concluded that a manumission "by operation of law"—that is, a manumission founded on a slaveholder's violation of the law—should not have the same effect as a legally drafted and publicly recorded manumission, which might have protected those former owners from the risk of responsibility for poor relief.

In a cover letter that accompanied Hoffman's opinion letter, Theodorus Bailey gave his own ambivalent response to the situation. On the one hand, he was evidently less certain than Hoffman that the transfer of Leah or Elsie had worked an automatic manumission under New York law. Bailey also reported that his wife had talked with a Mrs. Jane Ludlow, another granddaughter of Dr. MacWhorter, who remembered that Mary had received the slave as a gift and then let her go free (which might, under both New Jersey and New York law, have left Mary responsible if Leah or Elsie became dependent on the overseers of the poor in Newark). But Mrs. Ludlow had disclosed one more "fact" in that conversation with Bailey's wife, one that Bailey believed, if substantiated, might change things. Apparently Dr. MacWhorter, who had spent several years as a minister in South Carolina, had also entertained "scruples" about slaveholding, and she remembered that Leah or Elsie had first come into her grandfather's household as a result of a twelve-year lease, not a purchase. The good reverend apparently believed that the rental of a slave implied a lesser or reduced commitment to the institution of slavery than the purchase of a slave. (This was not a belief that found much confirmation in the law in New Jersey—or anywhere else where slavery was practiced.) In any event, at the end of the lease term, Leah or Elsie should have "reverted" to the original owner, whoever that was, just as possession of and responsibility for Minna reverted to Henry Force at the end of her term of service with Elizabeth Haines. Even if Leah or Elsie were understood to be still enslaved, the original master—the master before MacWhorter—might now be the one who was liable for the costs of her care, if anyone were liable for the costs of her care.

But who was that owner? The letters tell us nothing.[20]

Whatever the truth or relevance of that new "fact," in June 1823, Hornblower asked another New York attorney to take depositions from two of MacWhorter's grandchildren: Jane Ludlow and Samuel J. Beebe, whom we have already met as the 1813 letter writer who challenged Hornblower's plan to sell Leah or Elsie. Mary Beebe, the granddaughter who had been the intended recipient of Anne Ogilvie's gift, had died, and so Hornblower looked for answers from her surviving siblings. These grandchildren reported that they knew Leah or Elsie when she lived in Dr. MacWhorter's household. They "understood" that "the said Servant Girl" had been given to Mary, who was sixteen or seventeen at the time. While Leah or Elsie was part of that New York household, she was "generally ordered & directed" by Mary's stepmother. After two or three years, the household moved to western New York. At that time, Leah or Elsie refused to move with them. The family "considered her free in Consequence of her having been brought from the State of New Jersey into the State of New York against the Laws of the State of New York," and "they never forced or attempted to compel her to go." They had understood her as free by operation of New York law.[21]

And so the matter ended, as far as the historical record shows, without any determination of what the New Jersey law said with regard to responsibility for Leah or Elsie. Leah or Elsie disappears from the record. As with so many women, especially women born into slavery, we have no way to trace her whereabouts, because we have no idea what her last name ever was or became.

The Law

What were the terms of the New Jersey legal regime within which Force and Haines's litigation played out? For starters, early nineteenth-century New Jersey slavery was understood by both defenders and critics as a "municipal" legal institution, to use a term familiar to William Blackstone and Lord Mansfield, as well as to those in New Jersey who were legally educated. "Municipal" meant that its regulatory terms conformed to no permanent or universal common law or natural law underpinning. It took its shape from the local and particular legal culture in which it found itself.

New Jersey's slavery was subject to continuing legislative tinkering through-out the years of gradual emancipation. And because New Jersey's slavery was different from the slavery found in other states, particularly in the neighboring jurisdiction of New York, what lawyers call the doctrinal field of "conflicts of law"—a field that offered ways to reconcile and distin-guish the different answers that jurisdictions gave to shared or similar legal problems—would become central to the question of what New Jersey slavery was as a legal regime. The mobility of both slaveholders and their slaves was ever present in the courts and in the legal consciousness of diverse actors. It was very easy to cross jurisdictional boundaries—to take a ferry to New York City, for example. What happened after depended on the differing laws and legal interpreters of at least two jurisdictions, and on how those laws interacted with one another.[22]

The governing law of gradual emancipation—the law found in New Jersey statute books and published cases, the law summarized in justice-of-the-peace manuals and guides—bore a close relationship to New York law. As we will see, the interpretation of what was and what was not "the law" flowed in complex ways around and across the Hudson River. Some of the time, apparently ruling legal interpretations in New Jersey emanated di-rectly from the courts and lawyers in the commercial metropolis to the northeast. Indeed, there are places in the New Jersey case records where it seems as if the lawyers or the litigants are, wittingly or unwittingly, substi-tuting or working through New York law in order to state New Jersey law (as Justice Ford did in his opinion in *Force v. Haines*). There does not, how-ever, appear to have been a similar flow of legal doctrine from New Jersey to New York, although the flow of people went in both directions. Indeed, one finds a certain disdain for New Jersey law expressed by New York lawyers and judges. New York legalists were affected by New Jersey law only because of the men and women, some of them enslaved, who moved to New York City from New Jersey and whose legal situations and identities shaped New York law.[23]

Historians have tended to identify abolition with the passage of a par-ticular statute or the handing down of a judicial decision—that is, with a moment in time. There is no escaping the political and rhetorical signifi-cance of such moments. Thus, New Jersey is conventionally understood to have entered into gradual emancipation late, in 1804, while New York began in 1799, and Pennsylvania in 1780.

At the same time, the legal foundations of gradual emancipation were both temporally and spatially broader than the terms of any particular statute. The nineteenth-century New Jersey regime of gradual emancipation was shaped by the continuing significance of earlier laws and decisions about relations between slaves and masters. Some of those laws and decisions dated back to the early eighteenth century. Even more, the changing moral and legal understandings of slave owners, as well as the mobile communities in which slave owners and their enslaved properties lived, affected the political decisions and compromises that produced legislation, legal strategies, and life plans.

Households and individuals that moved from one jurisdiction to another, particularly along the Hudson, carried and transformed enslaved and non-enslaved legal identities. In that sense, Leah's or Elsie's moves back and forth across the Hudson were exemplary. In 1792, to take a second small example, Robert Whiting of New York City sold Dinah, a young woman, to the miniature painter John Ramage. Dinah was soon sold or transferred to Mrs. Catherine Branford, who hailed from New Jersey, for thirty pounds, perhaps as something of a marriage settlement, since Catherine Branford was about to become Catherine Ramage, John's third wife. In 1801, John Blanchard of Meadow Ridge, New Jersey, agreed with Catherine Ramage that his enslaved "boy," Bob, and "her" Dinah could marry (John Blanchard wrote that he had "no Objections to the Alliance, but wont it be best they Marry for as long as they agree, and that we may think it best[?]"). Soon, Dinah gave birth to a child, also named Bob. The child Bob became part of Catherine Ramage's household, along with Dinah. All now lived in Orange Township in New Jersey (John Ramage died in 1802). More than a decade later, in 1813, Catherine Ramage "sold" young Bob to Ephraim Sayre, who promised to teach him to be a tanner. But then in 1815, Catherine Ramage took $125 from Robert Blanchard in exchange for Dinah and her three children, probably including young Bob. Who was the Robert Blanchard who had just purchased Catherine's property? He was, apparently, the older Bob, who had married Dinah fourteen years before, when he had "belonged" to John Blanchard. Now free, the older Bob was able to reconstruct a free family, merging together New Jersey and New York identities.[24]

Meanwhile, slaveholders remained confident that their rights over their human property would be recognized even when that property moved into or through free jurisdictions, away from New Jersey. Consider the 1812 letter Ann Gibbons Trumbull wrote to her father, Thomas Gibbons, a wealthy resident of Elizabethtown. She wanted the use of one of his slaves when she went with her husband, John M. Trumbull, to visit his Connecticut family. She assured her father that he didn't need to worry that his property would be lost to him when she took the enslaved person to a free state. Her husband's mother had written that there was "no trouble in taking a slave to Connt.—Keeping them & taking them away when ere you please— you can't sell them there, but you can command their service, so long as you chuse." The fertile category of the "sojourning slaveholder" protected Gibbons's property even when brought into a "free" state.[25]

The legislative foundation of the New Jersey regime within which Robert Blanchard achieved freedom and purchased his wife and children, and which also legitimated Thomas Gibbons's traveling property rights, lay in a 1798 statute, sometimes called a "slave code," drafted to summarize and reconcile a variety of contradictory eighteenth-century understandings and practices. Sections of that law incorporated both a regularized process of manumission and a body of slaveholders' rights and remedies. Much in the 1798 law restated (and sometimes clarified) what had been more or less vague up to that point in the state's jurisprudence. But the 1798 law also confused things in many ways, as we will see. The terms of that code would be amended over the next thirty years, and attempts would be made to integrate it with the very gradual emancipation that characterized nineteenth-century New Jersey. Still, into the 1830s it remained the essential starting point for settling legal questions about the rights and duties of slaveholders.[26]

Neither in 1798 nor thereafter did the legislature take much interest in specifying or detailing how masters lived with the enslaved peoples within their households. Little was ever said in the legislative record about discipline or the means of control. The code silently continued New Jersey's long-standing recognition of slave marriages, and it imposed a theoretical but largely unenforced duty on masters to teach enslaved children to read and write.[27] Another provision declared that any person who treated his or her slave "inhumanely" would be fined forty dollars, the fine to be used for the care of the poor in the township.[28] These provisions must have been small victories for Quaker and other antislavery advocates, who evidently lost most of the other battles over slavery in the New Jersey of the early republic. Such rules, however, were rarely if ever enforced. For the most part, the governance of the household was understood to belong to a minimally regulated private sphere.[29]

New Jersey's 1804 gradual abolition statute left in place nearly everything enacted in the 1798 code, even as it committed the state to a distant future without slavery. Using language that may have been largely copied from New York's 1799 gradual emancipation statute, New Jersey's 1804 statute had the following features: The children born to slaves thereafter would become free, though not until each child had reached a certain age: twenty-one for females and twenty-five for males. Until then, the children would serve their parents' masters as before, unless those masters turned them over to the local overseers of the poor by "abandoning" them. (Their parents, still enslaved, gained no control over them.) Abandonment had to occur within a year after the birth of a child. Once a master abandoned a child, the overseers would look after the child's education, at least until the child reached the statutory age of twenty-one or twenty-five, when he or she became "free." (As replacements for masters, the overseers were theoretically obligated to teach abandoned children to read.) The overseers could also, in theory, profit from the labor of the child. Whoever controlled these children during those years "owned" their labor, and that labor remained a tradable or leasable commodity, meaning the children could be sold for the duration of their "terms" of required service. But eventually, if they lived long enough and were not moved illegally or "kidnapped" to southern jurisdictions, the children of slaves would become "free."[30]

After 1804, the birth of every "free" child had to be recorded in a book maintained in each county, although the question of how to identify such children led to varied answers. Most slaveholders simply entered into the record "a child" or a "male child" born to "their" slave woman. But some slaveholders described the child as "a female slave." Others identified the child as a male or female "state pauper." In 1806, Mahlon Ford, Justice Gabriel Ford's uncle, wrote in the record book: "Please do register a Negro boy by the name of John, belonging to Morris Township & Born of a wench named Rose my property." Reflecting the complexities of a not-atypical situation, a white woman recorded the birth of three black children who were "the sons of Luce a black woman who becomes free on the 16th of April 1811." But she added, "The above mentioned" children "are Slave[s] to me . . . until freed by the law." In contrast, when Elizabeth Haines recorded the birth of Minna's child, Jesse, in 1824, she carefully described the birth as having occurred "during the term of service of my woman Minna." Minna was not characterized as a slave, although her child was registered in an Essex County record book dedicated to recording births to enslaved mothers.[31]

On the other hand, those enslaved people born before July 5, 1804, including the parents of children born after July 4, remained slaves for life. That is, New Jersey's slaves would remain enslaved unless and until a master manumitted them or moved them legally or illegally out of the state. Thus, the judges and lawyers involved in *Force v. Haines* took it for granted that Minna, who had certainly been born before July 5, 1804, remained enslaved even after she had given birth to a son who would eventually be free. As a slave, Minna would not possess any legal rights or control over her child. In the absence of manumission, either by formal deed or by some other mechanism (including, after 1818, being moved out of state), all who were slaves before July 5, 1804, would remain slaves until death.[32] As a result, a few elderly black people still survived as enslaved at the time of the Civil War, although by then state law called them "apprentices for life." While New York's legal practices clearly served as models for New Jersey's legal regime, in this regard New Jersey went its own way. In New York, by contrast, by 1817 the state had committed itself to an end to all slavery. And the last New York slave was freed, "by operation of law," in 1827.[33]

THREE INTERCONNECTED THEMES, or problems, shaped the New Jersey regime, each of which reflected the contradictory and almost incoherent goals that shaped the legislation. Together, these themes made questions about how to be a New Jersey slaveholder in an era of gradual emancipation close to unanswerable, at least for a legally scrupulous master.

The first theme centered on how an individual slave owner could go about abandoning slavery, how he or she could manumit those enslaved people (particularly those born before July 5, 1804) who would otherwise remain "slaves for life." Implicit in this theme was an unasked question: whether and how enslaved people could free themselves or their kin.

The second was the problem of what role or responsibility the state or other public agencies would take for the care of freed peoples and their children. This theme rested on the implicit reality, left obscure in almost every jurisdiction where enslaved people were a presence, that the master–slave relationship was actually a triangular relationship with public agencies and public authorities. Abandoning slavery immediately raised questions about who would be responsible for aged, dependent, or merely impoverished former slaves—that is, for women like Leah or Elsie, or for Minna and her son. (Unlike in the Deep South, however, there was never a serious public effort to remove the manumitted from New Jersey.) It also drew on fears that slave owners would use poor relief as a way to avoid their own responsibilities and that the public would have to shoulder the costs of care when slaves stopped being profitable, when dependents became aged or disabled, or when slave owners "abandoned" them. We saw the judges in *Force v. Haines* struggle with aspects of this second theme. (It is important to recognize that the question of the responsibility of a township's over-seers of the poor for the care of dependent formerly enslaved people con-stituted an extension and intensification of larger anxieties about poor relief and settlement law that were a pervasive feature of early American local government.)[34]

The third theme was the extent to which mobile slaveholders could re-tain control over slaves as they moved across jurisdictional boundaries. Could Thomas Gibbons's daughter take his slave with her where she wished? Could sojourners—a fluid legal category that included commercial travelers, slave traders, and those who might have made New Jersey their home for decades—bring slaves to and from New Jersey? To what extent could slaves still be conveyed into or out of the state during the years of gradual emancipation? This third problem, the largest of the three in terms of the production of case law and statutory activity, is the one that will capture much of our attention.

But behind all three legal problems was a different question, one that would not find open articulation in the statutory law or in the published cases but one that created many of the situations that produced the law: that is, How should masters and slaves (or quondam slaves or soon to be freed people) negotiate with each other over the terms of their relationships, and what should be the legal consequences of their negotiations?

And beneath that question and those three legal themes lay the uncom-fortable reality that what I am calling New Jersey's regime of gradual eman-cipation was only in part a legal regime. Or, rather, contemplating New Jersey's long period of gradual emancipation requires thinking hard about what one means by a legal regime. What we might label as "New Jersey slavery" grew out of discordant and unsystematized relations that emerged between the realm of slavery as such and other arenas of public life, in-cluding poor relief and labor control. It was also a regime defined by crim-inality and illegality. One will not be surprised to discover that not every master was legally scrupulous. Some masters relied on established habits of domination and subordination and violence and fear to sustain control over those who often were "really" no longer slaves. Legal rights were only one among several weapons in the arsenal of white power. It is also not surprising that many slaves felt no loyalty to the regime. For the enslaved, certainly, the ongoing regime of gradual emancipation was not a legal structure worthy of respect.

Like other legal regimes, New Jersey's gradual emancipation incorpo-rated a borderland of extralegal practices, including what must have been a flourishing discourse and lore among whites about how to move slaves into or out of the state under circumstances for which it was usually but not always illegal to do so. It also included a number of criminal subcultures. Some slaveholders knowingly worked to take themselves and their properties to the South or to sell their properties South when it was illegal to do so. One has to assume that the capacity of all parties to "exit" shaped and qualified whatever loyalty they might have felt to the law, to the legal form of the regime, and to the state of New Jersey. To put it differently: For many slaveholders, belief in the right to use what one had as one chose and to move where one chose—that is, to live as one pleased in a commercial slave-owning republic called "America"—trumped any sense of obligation to obey what they knew were contradictory, inconsistent, and sometimes unenforceable legal rules in a relatively unimportant legal jurisdiction called New Jersey.

A regime like that in New Jersey had predictable economic effects. Slave prices dropped with the passage of the gradual emancipation law, although inconsistently so. A slave owner committed to maximizing his or her economic position would certainly have experienced reasonable anxieties about the declining value of holdings. And slave traders from elsewhere, from a South in constant need of a replenished supply of slaves, saw this northern regime of gradual emancipation as an incentive structure for their trade— as a way to fill a growing demand. Just as drug prohibitions can be understood as producing a criminal drug trade, it might be argued that prohibitions on the movement of slaves out of New Jersey created and encouraged a trade in slaves.[35]

Some forms of legal and semilegal exit that shaped gradual emancipation in parts of Latin America—like practices of self-purchase and protection by religious orders—never came into open view in New Jersey (or have left few traces).[36] However, the regime was being structured and shaped by the still enslaved, who could and did escape to the vibrant free black communities of New York City and Philadelphia. Almost any issue of any northern New Jersey newspaper between 1800 and 1830 was replete with advertisements for the return of runaways. Those who stayed surely could and did negotiate the terms of their continuing or concluding enslavement, in the context of a regime that possessed inadequate enforcement mechanisms and an unwillingness to mobilize resources.[37]

The regime was not one that inspired loyalty. At best, it offered something similar to rules of a game. (And one might add that features of the regime came close to encouraging cheating.) Many slaveholders understood themselves as possessors of vested rights, entitled to do what they wished with what was theirs. Like property owners in many arenas of American legal life, they often regarded governmentally enacted restrictions on their property and the prospect of emancipation as problems to be solved or dealt with: How to maximize one's return on one's investment given the constraints that "gradual emancipation" imposed; how to use a changing legal environment to avoid having to change one's way of living.

UNTIL 1798, the practice of manumitting slaves had been understood as an exercise of private freedom by masters. To use a familiar metaphor, it was one stick in the bundle of sticks that constituted possession of property. Just as one might turn a horse out to pasture or let a pet bird fly free out of its cage, so might one release a slave. Or, as Justice Smith Thompson of the U.S. Supreme Court put it in an 1834 Tennessee case, "It would seem a little extraordinary to contend that the owner of property is not at liberty to renounce his right to it." There had been several regulatory acts passed by the New Jersey colonial assembly earlier in the eighteenth century intended to limit that freedom to the extent that manumissions produced costs for royal servants. But these were not initially understood as constraints on the exercise of the slaveholder's freedom to undo the relationship of master and slave and thereby abandon slavery. A slaveholder could not escape his responsibility to the crown, even as she or he remained free to abandon possessory control of her or his slave. Throughout the eighteenth century and the first half of the nineteenth century, manumission was legally conceptualized as a gift of freedom by a master or an abandonment by the master, rarely as something earned by a slave. Conceptually, manumission remained an exercise of a master's freedom and power.[38]

Manumissions seemed to have become more common in the immediate post-Revolutionary period. Over the course of the 1780s and early 1790s, the New Jersey courts rejected many challenges to manumissions. It may well have been that by then, much in the legal culture offered encouragement to those whites who contemplated abandoning slavery. Every county began to keep a "manumission book" for recording manumissions. In 1794, Quaker activists published a volume of "freedom" cases decided over the prior decade that collectively articulated a judicial presumption in favor of liberty.[39]

What was a manumission? It might seem obvious to us that a manumission meant an abandonment of power by a master, a dissolution of the master–slave relationship. Some of the manumissions that one finds in the county record books were like that: immediate and total acts of abandonment.

But much of the time, what one might think was an act of abandonment was rather a promise or a commitment or an undertaking to act or abandon in the future—or even an imposition of a duty on others, particularly on the executors of one's will. Benjamin Haines's will, discussed at the start of this chapter, may be read as typical (or certainly not atypical) of the legal documents produced by and for propertied white New Jerseyans in the late eighteenth and early nineteenth centuries. In them, enslaved peoples remained both transactable and donatable properties and, at the same time, were transformed into a more finite and spatially and temporally limited form. Wills and deeds by masters often placed term limits on the duration of enslavement, just as Benjamin Haines's will had, even as he also directed his executors to sell Ceazer in order to raise funds for the estate. Such slaves were sold to pay debts or to make money, but what creditors or purchasers received was then of limited duration and value. And courts would often—not always, but often—enforce such limitations when executors or purchasers (or later purchasers) resisted and complained. Contracts between masters and their slaves—for the terms of work, for how long enslavement would last, for the freedom of family members—while of uncertain enforceability, were also more or less routine features of the legal landscape.

One should add that even apparently generous impulses were often shaped by a continuity of power. Consider, for example, the certificate of Colonel Samuel Forman, found in the Monmouth County manumission book: "This is to certify that I . . . do set my Negro girl named Henrietta Free (who is now married to a free Negro man named Gabriel Crummul) at my death or before at my own will and pleasure. . . . Also her children to be esteemed free born—but under my direction during my life—and further I give unto her and her children two horses supposed to be worth as horses . . . Thirty five pounds, also two Cows, ten sheep and four hogs, such as may be in my possession at my death—also all my kitchen + furniture of every denomination, including negroes beds and bedding, . . . one wagon & gears, one plow, . . . and whatever provisions may be on hand for the years of my death. . . . Whatever misfortunes may pursue me, I am at this time possessed of a great sufficiency, therefore no incumbrances whatever can effect this present free act." Obviously, what he also retained, until his death, was his control over Henrietta and her children. Her capacity to enjoy freedom depended on whether she would outlive him.[40]

A crude and incomplete survey of deeds, wills, and advertisements across the 1780s, 1790s, and early 1800s suggests that by then it had become routine to include conditional term limits in transactions involving enslaved peoples. The boundary between manumissions and other transactions involving enslaved property was becoming blurry. Like Benjamin Haines's directive to his executors with regard to Ceazer, wills extended slavery for two, four, or six more years. Leases of slaves often ended with the manumission of the slave. Conveyances and wills included language requiring that a slave be freed at the end of a fixed term, defined by either a period of years or the arrival of a birthday in the life of the enslaved person.[41] A typical newspaper advertisement from 1809 noted that the strong, healthy, and able-bodied black man offered for sale, brought up to do farming, still had seven years and six months remaining before he would be manumitted. The ad does not reveal how that term limit had been produced or negotiated. The relatively complete papers of Richard Hartshorne of Monmouth County include five transactions for slaves. The first, from 1794, was a simple purchase of a slave. The others all involved term limits. In May 1804, Hartshorne bought a twelve-year-old girl named Jane from John S. Holmes; Jane would receive her freedom thirteen years after she came into the Hartshorne "family." Six months after buying Jane, he bought a thirteen-year-old "Negro Girl" named Gin, with similar terms. In 1812, he conveyed a "Negro Wench," aged twenty, to Garret H. Conover with "terms of her freedom." Next he tried to "bind out" a "black girl" named Ann to Robert and Mary Rhea, including "terms of freedom," but the Rheas apparently rejected the terms.[42] ("Binding out" was the English legal term for conveying apprentices to masters.)

How can we understand limited-term enslavement, or what others have called conditional manumissions? How can we understand these contracts and deeds? For the most part, slaveholders were not making emancipatory gestures. The documents delimited slavery and, at the same time, extended it over significant periods of a slave's life. Slave owning was certainly infected by contractualism. Yet slaveholding remained, and the legal significance of a promised-for freedom—that is, whether a term limit could be enforced on a term-limited master—remained contested and uncertain. Enslaved peoples might work for their freedom across many years, and still the enforceability of any promise on which they had relied remained uncertain.[43]

How would an enslaved person respond to such conditional promises? In 1800, Ceasar Brown, who lived in New Providence, Bahamas, wrote to Sophia Brown of Perth Amboy, New Jersey. Sophia Brown had apparently become his new mistress. His Bahamian master and mistress had died without fulfilling a past promise to make him free at their deaths. All of the slaves on the New Providence plantation were to be either sold or sent to Mrs. Brown of New Jersey. Why had he written her? His "only motive for intruding" was "to beg" that she consider his master's promise "which you know to be true." And she also must know "with what zeal & fidelity" he had served his former master and mistress. What did he want her to do? If possible, he hoped that she would make his "situation somewhat more independent." What that meant was not explained. He would, he allowed, "with pleasure" go and serve her "forever." But if she meant to have him sold with the other slaves, he begged her to lower the price assessed ($500). If she did so, he would try to purchase his own freedom "with the assistance of some friends." Whether she did so, and what happened to him, is not revealed in the records.[44]

It is easy to imagine a range of reasons why someone like Benjamin Haines did what he did in his will with regard to Ceazer. Term limits were sometimes ways to mark the favored position of some slaves as opposed to others, who were still to be treated as nothing but continuing property, as "slaves for life." Sometimes favored slaves, especially those with valuable and marketable skills, were favored because they had negotiated and paid for their privileges. The consequences of those privileges would play out over many years. A good deal of case law, in New Jersey and elsewhere, comes out of cases where a favored and freed—or soon to be freed—individual negotiated for or purchased the freedom of less favored kin.[45] On the other hand, the ability not to have to worry about the less valuable old age of a slave might have made the rental or purchase (or gift) of a shorter term for an older slave more attractive, with less downstream risk. Term limits also probably offered a way to control men like Ceazer and perhaps to make life easier for executors. Benjamin Haines might have hoped that Ceazer would calculate that it was worth his while to wait things out rather than run away. By reducing the incentives on slaves to flee, executors would not have to worry so much about assets of the estate disappearing in a place and time where disappearing was relatively easy for many slaves living in northern New Jersey.

Placing term limits into a will was also a cheap way for a slave owner to establish her or his beneficence. Or, more precisely, it put the costs of abandoning slavery onto heirs. Putting term limits into wills clearly told executors and purchasers that this was not property to be conveyed or sold into the plantation slavery of the South. Executors were implicitly directed not to participate in that extralegal practice. But in doing so, the master was in effect acknowledging that his estate would have a significantly reduced value. Such limits destroyed much of the value of crucial estate assets. Sale prices for an asset that would stay for only six years were going to be a small fraction of what a "slave for life" could fetch.

These conditional contracts and wills were in some ways directives to continue the enslavement of peoples—to continue to participate in the institution. Through their implementation, abandonment was put off. They were inadequate and incomplete provisions of freedom, mean-spirited gifts. And yet this is one instance where the half-full view seems to me more salient than the half-empty view.[46] A part of what was or would become the regime of gradual emancipation was a growing sense of the inescapability of contract and emancipation, a sense of the inevitable end to the regime. Implicitly or explicitly, these slaveholders were contractualizing their relationships with their slaves. Often they were doing so at moments when one would expect a good capitalist to want to maximize the value of his or her assets. Yet they chose (or were constrained to choose) not to do so. Their transactions, their use of their property, contemplated its demise, made dominion and control fleeting. And it should be added that in New Jersey, the delimiting of these terms of continuing servitude remained within a plausible contractual horizon, usually for less than a decade. (By contrast, in the early years of the Northwest Territory, slaveholders imposed indentures for terms of forty, sixty, or ninety-nine years. The goal there was to keep control of a servant for his or her whole life.)[47]

CONTRACTUALIZING AND EMANCIPATORY gestures by New Jersey slaveholders also led to controversy. Many whites worried about the growing presence of free black people, of masterless men and women no longer attached to households. Those racist anxieties translated or bled into questions of tax burdens and fairness and the contradictory structures of early modern poor relief.

To understand the controversy, and also to understand the arguments of the judges in *Force v. Haines*, it helps to take a short detour into the foundational norms and practices of poor relief in early modern legal culture.

In New Jersey, as in every outpost of English local government law, poor relief was a fundamental duty of local government. Every township had overseers of the poor, officers whose job it was to provide or arrange for the care of those who needed it and were entitled to it. Like other early modern offices, that of an overseer was understood as personal property, and the office also produced personal liability. Unlike other offices, there was little profit in "farming" the poor—that is, caring for paupers. With much liability and little gain, it was not an office that many wished for. Overseers usually placed those entitled to care in local households. (Larger towns would eventually build "poorhouses," but there were none in New Jersey in the early nineteenth century.) Often this was done by bid or by auction. Household heads who bid successfully to provide care were paid by the locality to the extent that an aged or disabled recipient could not be put to work or that she or he created costs for the household. (Obviously, an able-bodied "pauper" would have to work for and within that household.) Part of an overseer's job was to "charge" those with responsibility—like Joseph Hornblower's clients—for all costs expended on behalf of the pauper. Avoiding care for those not entitled to it and extracting costs of care from a recipient's family members (or others who were legally responsible for the recipient's care but were not providing it) were central tasks for an overseer of the poor. Only in the last instance would local taxes be looked to. Tax avoidance shaped the contours of poor relief.

To put it differently, the practices of local care drew on at least three distinct, sometimes contradictory, norms.

First of all, everyone in need was to be cared for in the local community to which she or he "belonged." The costs of that care were not understood as a form of charity. Rather, care was understood as a core and constitutive feature of a legitimate government.[48]

At the same time, the sites for actual care were the private households—headed by a parent or a husband or a master or a sibling—in which those with needs found themselves. Thus, the second norm was that household heads were ordinarily responsible for care, either by providing direct care for those in need of "relief" or by paying the overseers for the care that others provided for those in need. When household heads didn't do what they were required to do or when there was no household (often because the household or its head had moved away), only then did the township overseers have to act directly. In that situation, they would ordinarily place the dependent person in a new household. On the one hand, local public officers were a backstop for the family. They stepped in when there was no relevant, capable, or solvent household. On the other hand, the family was the workhorse of poor relief.[49]

And third: Poor relief was local relief, defined by the locale to which a recipient belonged. Everyone potentially eligible for poor relief possessed a settlement in a township. "Settlement" was a legal term with an immense and complex legal lineage. Settlement offered something close to a legal right. But what did settlement mean in an America where individuals and households were in constant motion? Those responsible for care often disappeared; families and individuals moved all the time. Marriages, apprenticeships, and other forms of migratory service qualified and complicated settlement. Townships struggled endlessly with one another in court to avoid or deny responsibility for the care of mobile paupers. Still, the legal culture demanded that every freeborn subject had a settlement (for tax purposes as well as for relief purposes). Slaves had no settlement; all others did.[50]

In the context of those divergent norms, what was the significance of a manumission? How, if at all, could a formerly enslaved woman or man come to possess a settlement? Would overseers of the poor have to provide care and placements—at taxpayers' costs—for needy and dependent freed people? Would former masters still be made to take responsibility? (All of these questions are implicit in *Force v. Haines*.) The relatively loose and encouraging manumission practices of the 1780s and 1790s, founded on incentives in favor of freedom, were often interpreted as little other than opportunities for strategic and calculating slaveholders to dump aged, dependent, and costly slaves on the overseers of the poor, thereby unburdening themselves and burdening township taxpayers. Was freedom an abrogation of a master's responsibilities, in effect a gift to the master? What would be the responsibilities of local overseers of the poor for those ex-slaves—for example, Leah or Elsie, or perhaps even Minna—who had become needy or who could not work?

In 1798, as a central part of its so-called slave code, the New Jersey legislature had responded to such questions by enacting a more formalized and mandatory manumission process. The new process made it illegal, at least in theory, to free a slave through a private act, either by contract or by will. Abandonment of possession was no longer understood as an act of private freedom. Instead, the code required a series of proto-bureaucratic practices that involved both overseers of the poor and county court judges. In formulaic language, those officials had to approve of the manumission and acknowledge that the slave was ready and able to fend for him- or herself. And masters were forbidden to abandon slaves under the age of twenty or over forty, or others likely to become dependent.[51]

The goal of the new process was obviously to protect townships from those who might dump unprofitable, aged, and needy slaves on public welfare resources. Those disabled in one way or another (as Minna apparently was) or those who were needy and could not work (like Leah or Elsie) were expected to be "kept" by masters, not "abandoned." For scrupulous masters who wished to free such slaves (that is, to stop participating in the institution of slavery), their only option was to secure (or protect) the town from future costs by the payment of bonds. And the required amount of the bonds, $500 in 1798, was very high.[52]

In 1806, the New Jersey Supreme Court used the occasion of a challenge to a "defective" manumission to confirm what an effective manumission required. In 1803, John Emmons and his wife drafted deeds that purported to free a black couple, Dick and Phebe. However, neither deed was executed in the presence of two witnesses, as required under the 1798 law. And in neither instance were any of the other formalities that the legislature required complied with. It is not clear what happened next, but by 1806, Dick and Phebe were living in the household of Isaac Emmons, John's son. And when Charles Ewing—a young lawyer who would years later become chief justice of the state supreme court—brought a bill of habeas corpus claiming their freedom, Isaac Emmons resisted.[53]

The three judges of the New Jersey Supreme Court each wrote an opinion in the case. Each began by noting the long history of manumission laws in New Jersey, spanning the eighteenth century. In 1713 and 1769, the colonial assemblies had imposed certain requisites on anyone who wished to make a valid manumission. In 1713, a master had to give £200 security to the queen and pay £20 yearly to the manumitted slave. In 1769, a master was to give his bond for £200 to indemnify the township against the costs of poor relief. The consequences of failure to comply with the rules as given was said, in 1713 and again in 1769, to be that the manumission "shall be utterly void, and of none effect."[54] Over the course of the eighteenth century, however, it had become settled understanding that the voidness of an informal—or inadequately formalized—manumission was solely with regard to the responsibility of the master for the slave's care and maintenance—his or her continuing duty to protect the public from the costs of poor relief. A master could not escape that duty except by way of a properly formalized manumission. On the other hand, and in spite of the apparently clear language of the 1713 and 1769 laws with regard to the relationship of master to servant, an informal deed was understood to be effective and valid. The slave was freed, even as the master remained bound because she or he had not complied with the statute.

What did the 1798 statute do to that received and settled understanding of the effects of informal manumissions? Clearly parts of the 1798 code were enacted as confirmatory of and continuous with past practices. Justice

Rossell, in his opinion, argued that the new manumission rules should also be understood through that lens: "Although our legislators have made use of different modes of expression in their formation, and have, according to the progress of humanity from time to time, made the terms of manumission more safe and easy for the master, and beneficial to the slave, . . . the same end appears always to be in view . . . : to prevent the public from being burdened in supporting *slaves*, whose masters from avarice, or some other motive, were desirous of throwing upon it."

As a result, in order to produce "uniformity" in New Jersey's decisions, "as well as in the aid of liberty and humanity, (which the law always favors)," he would have "exonerate[d]" Dick and Phebe from any further obligation of service to Isaac Emmons. They had become free, he believed, even as their former owner would remain liable for their support if either became needy.

But Rossell wrote in dissent. According to Chief Justice Kirkpatrick and Justice Pennington, the 1798 statute recast the law and directly changed how to produce an effectual manumission. The 1798 law obliterated past practices. The two judges recognized that in the first years of statehood, the new state courts had made several decisions that took as given "a distinction supposed to exist between emancipation, as it respects the owner, and emancipation as it respects the State," relying on a presumption "in favour of liberty." The courts had enforced manumissions that were not formally adequate. But, according to Kirkpatrick, the results had "become a subject of public complaint, at least in one part of the State." (Where? He does not say.) The 1798 law responded to those complaints. Pennington thought the separation of a master's public duty to pay for care and poor relief from the personal relationship of master to slave had made slavery incoherent, producing "doctrine wholly unintelligible to me." Slavery, he thought, was "an entire thing; . . . a man is either a slave or he is not." According to him, the 1798 law brought a new coherence to the law. The principle—reproduced in the State's brief and articulated by Rossell, writing in dissent—that "*liberty is to be favored*," although "humane and benign," was something close to a non sequitur. The reason to pass the statute was to change the law. The goal of favoring liberty could not be "set up as a bar to a positive provision in an act of the Legislature."

And Phebe and Dick remained enslaved, a result that the New Jersey Society for Promoting the Abolition of Slavery took worried note of as "materially and extensively" injuring "the cause of emancipation."[55]

The desire to save the larger public from costs also dominated legislative arguments about the freedom of children born to the enslaved, the presumed beneficiaries of the 1804 gradual emancipation law. The third paragraph of the 1804 law encouraged slaveholders to "abandon" those children to the local overseers of the poor. Initially, the state promised to maintain such abandoned children at statewide expense at a cost of up to three dollars a month, after each child reached the age of one. Presumably that reduced the local volatility of the issue, particularly in the northern and eastern parts of the state, where there were still many households dependent on slaves. A beneficent and generous state would compensate towns (and those to whom the towns gave the children) for the costs of caring for these abandoned children.

That bounty may have put too much of a burden on state finances. Non-slaveholders apparently protested that slaveholders were "abandoning" the children of their slaves in order to become beneficiaries of state payments. In March 1806, the state legislature admitted that the 1804 law had been a mistake, and the part of the law providing "bounties" was repealed. While children born after 1806 to enslaved women could still be abandoned by their masters to the local overseers of the poor, the state would not pay for the costs of the care that the overseers offered.[56]

In 1808, the legislature put in place a new and more complex system. Formally, township officers became responsible for the costs of care of abandoned children of slaves. There would be no state subsidy. But the new law also gave overseers a variety of tools to avoid any actual expense. The first paragraph ordered the overseers to "bind out" all abandoned children over the age of one, while stating a preference that those children should be "bound out" into the households where their still enslaved parents lived. If the abandoning masters of the parents were willing, but only if they were willing, such infants would remain with their parents (and their enslaved parents' masters). That was the content of the preference. And of course it carried the corollary that any owner of a slave was also free to refuse to take in her or his slave's abandoned child, leaving the child to be "sold" or "bound out" to others.

The second paragraph flipped the approach taken in the first paragraph. The overseers had the power to bind out a child for the duration of her or his period of semi-enslavement to someone other than the child's parents' master or mistress. If they decided to do so and the owner of the enslaved parents of the child did not "deliver" the "abandoned" child up to that "purchaser," then that owner (that is, the master or mistress of the still-enslaved parents) would be understood as having assumed all future costs of that child's care. The town would be held free of any further responsibility or cost. Thus, a master who felt morally or sentimentally obligated not to separate an infant from her or his enslaved parents offered towns the opportunity to escape from any liability, responsibility, or cost. All the town overseers had to do was threaten to remove the child (any child over the age of one). If the master refused to deliver the child, all future costs would be the master's responsibility.

The third paragraph of the 1808 law required the overseers of every town to publish a list of abandoned children found within their jurisdiction. This list was framed as if it were an advertisement for labor, intended to identify those children of slaves that "remain to be bound out, . . . in order that persons living in this state, . . . who may be willing to take such children, may know where to apply for the same." (As of 1808, none of those children were over the age of four.)[57] The result of this third paragraph was that for a brief moment, between 1808 and 1811, New Jersey's newspapers were filled with such advertisements. The advertisements drew on standard language that overseers had used throughout the Anglo-American world for more than two centuries to bind out the adolescent or soon-to-be adolescent poor into apprenticeships. But some of those advertisements came close to the form of slave sales. In 1810, the town of Saddle River advertised that there remained eighteen children abandoned according to the terms of the gradual emancipation statute: "Any person wishing to have one or more of them can by applying to the overseers . . . obtain them." In 1811, the overseers of the poor of the town of Harrington offered "to the inhabitants of the State of New-Jersey the following abandoned black children."

What would have led white New Jerseyans to bid for abandoned and costly infants and very young children? The answer lay in a qualification included in the 1806 law that ended the state bounty. No future state payments would be made for the care of children born to enslaved mothers after 1806. But the promise of a state bounty made in the 1804 gradual emancipation law was understood to have produced a vested property right. Payments to towns and to the assignees of those towns (like those who bid successfully for those abandoned children) would therefore continue until 1811. Those who purchased children between 1808 and 1811 did so because they expected to share in that vested and continuing state bounty, not because of the potential labor value of four- to six-year-old children. Once the bounty ended in 1811, so did interest in purchasing them. The newspaper advertisements disappeared.[58]

Meanwhile, for the still enslaved—all those born before July 5, 1804—a settlement for poor-relief purposes was a contradiction in terms. A slave had no settlement (belonged to no town) as long as she or he remained enslaved. No town was responsible for her or his care; no town had to provide support in case of dependency or need. A slave was part of an owner's household unless the owner chose to sell the slave, in which case the slave would be joined to a new owner's household, or unless the master decided to manumit the slave by formal processes that purported to save the town from any future costs. A slave was still a commodity, and a commodity, at least theoretically, is always in potential motion and belongs to no place. In other words, a commodity can have no settlement. Leah or Elsie could only make a claim on the support of Newark because she had become free. Minna, assuming she was still enslaved, had no claim at all on the support offered by the overseers of the poor of Elizabethtown, Rahway, or Woodbridge.

In 1798, at the same time that the New Jersey legislature declared the truism that an enslaved person would have no settlement, it also created an exception for the unmanumitted slave of an insolvent owner. In that situation, in which an impoverished slave could no longer be cared for—maintained—by her or his bankrupt master, the town where the slave was located would have to provide support and care for the unmanumitted slave. The insolvent's slave would be reconstructed as a pauper, indistinguishable from other free poor people who made demands on the overseers of the poor of a locality. Implicit in that legislative accommodation must have been a growing awareness that such enslaved people were no longer to be understood as movable commercial property that could be assigned to the insolvent's creditors. In that sense, gradual emancipation was slowly transforming the terms of the New Jersey slave relationship, making it something different than what chattel slavery was in the South.[59]

In 1824, the New Jersey Supreme Court added another exception to the 1798 legislation, involving an unmanumitted slave and an absent or abandoning owner. The 1824 case involved an owner who had moved away from the state more than twenty years earlier, leaving a slave to fend for himself. Years later, the slave had asked for support from a township's overseers of the poor. Would the township have to provide that support, even though it could not compel reimbursement from the enslaved person's solvent but absent out-of-state owner? According to the court, where a master of an unmanumitted slave lived beyond the capacity of state officers to compel him to support "his" slave, the township would have to provide the support the enslaved person needed. Humanity required it.

Effectively, the holding in this case suggested that an "abandoned" enslaved person was no longer to be considered enslaved. Without a master, there could be no slave. And that holding does say something about the distinctiveness of slavery in 1824 New Jersey. In southern jurisdictions, by contrast, the presumption was clear that abandoned enslaved peoples remained slaves, even without masters. More than a few mobile southern slaveholders used a decision to move away, perhaps to new lands in the West, as an opportunity to leave elderly, disabled, or otherwise valueless slaves behind, to abandon them. That situation would create a continuing problem for southern poor-relief officers.[60]

To return for a moment to *Force v. Haines*: part of what divided the judges of the New Jersey Supreme Court in 1840 was continuing doubt as to whether an overseer of the poor could be compelled to provide care for Minna, understood as an unmanumitted slave. Justice Dayton expressed confidence that a town's overseers of the poor would necessarily have to take on the tasks that Mrs. Haines had assumed. In doing so, he relied on this same 1824 case. It is not clear whether he understood that Minna would have been effectively manumitted, would have become a free pauper, if she had been turned over to the overseers of the poor. Justice Hornblower, in contrast, insisted in his dissent that no town's poor relief officers likely had any legal responsibility for Minna's care, given that she was still enslaved and that Mr. Force had inescapable responsibilities for her care.

On the other hand, by the 1820s, properly manumitted ex-slaves would have a settlement for poor-relief purposes, exactly as other citizens would. And the children of slaves gained a settlement once they had served their term of service—that is, once they had reached the statutory age. After 1820, they would have the same rights and capacities as white children who had been bound out in apprenticeships—at least with regard to poor relief. That is to say, once their term of service was completed, they could acquire a settlement in the town where they lived and worked. They could become paupers.[61]

To what extent, though, would other features of the long-standing laws of master and servant become applicable to the circumstances of the enslaved and their children? That question bedeviled the judges in *Force v. Haines*, who differed over the applicability—the precedential relevance—of apprenticeship cases to Minna's situation. That uncertainty was already manifesting earlier in the century. In 1806, Nimrod Washington sued James Tallman before a justice of the peace for the loss of his slave Phebe. Washington relied on the provision in the 1798 apprenticeship statute that forbade "the counseling, persuading, enticing, aiding and assisting" of a clerk, apprentice, or servant "to absent herself from . . . service." We don't know anything about the circumstances of the supposed "enticement" that had occurred, whether Tallman was Phebe's lover, a potential employer, or the owner of Phebe's husband or lover.[62] In any event, a justice of the peace awarded Washington the thirty-dollar penalty given by the statute for what he had lost when Phebe left his service. When Tallman appealed, offering as one reason for reversal that Phebe was a slave, not a servant or an apprentice, the New Jersey Supreme Court affirmed the award. At that moment, neither Justice Kirkpatrick nor Justice Rossell saw a problem in the mobilization of the apprenticeship statute in support of a slave master's rights; Justice Pennington disagreed, but he was evidently outvoted.

Three years later, though, in a case on similar facts, a unified supreme court came to the opposite conclusion, as it reversed the decision of a justice of the peace who had awarded compensation for a slave's "enticement." The justice of the peace had, according to the appellate court, misapplied the apprenticeship law when he ruled that while "all servants were not slaves, he considered all slaves as servants." The apprenticeship law could not, the supreme court justices believed, "be construed as extending to slaves." Slaves were not servants, and thus were not enticeable. Besides, the 1798 slave code had "made provision on the same subject by creating a penalty for employing, harboring, or concealing a slave."[63]

In the short run, this 1810 case settled the question that slaves were not enticeable apprentices, although questions regarding the enticement of slaves or the apparently enslaved would continue to shape the regime, as we will see in chapter 3. What is striking is the assumption, already shared by several lawyers and judges in the state, that enslaved peoples could be seduced away from those they were obliged to serve. In this, they were actors in relationships. Masters had remedies for loss, just as husbands and parents had remedies for the loss of value of the services that dependents provided. They had rights against those competitors—other masters—who would convince slaves to leave their service. Those remedies, however, were very different from the remedies that traditionally compensated for the taking of property. For those lawyers and judges, the wrongs done to those masters were not the same—not as compensable—as the loss of property would have been. The arguable possibility of an action for enticement of one's slave signaled the presence of a more contractual understanding of the relationships enslaved people had with their masters.

One might add that Elizabeth Haines's acts of "voluntary courtesy," in caring for Minna, had parallels to the enticement situation. In keeping Minna, or allowing her to remain in her household after the end of the lease term, Mrs. Haines was not unlike someone who had enticed a servant. She had kept Minna from going (or staying or being) where she belonged (though where was that if not with Henry Force?). What that meant in terms of Minna's status as an enslaved woman was not brought out by any of the judges, however.[64]

SEVERAL SECTIONS OF THE 1798 code and much law making in the two decades thereafter were devoted to the formulation of rules and penalties for moving slaves into and out of the state. These laws increasingly followed New York law. They also qualified and limited the notion that a New Jersey slave was a mobile commodity, available for trade and use. The implicit goal of the statutory language was to stop the movement of slaves into or out of New Jersey. By sharply limiting the potential market for slaves—that is, restricting slave sales to the area—prices for slaves would decline. Slavery would become unprofitable and disappear.[65]

The ironic result of the decline in the value of slaves as assets, however, was that in the years after 1808, New Jersey slaves became a particularly attractive opportunity for slave traders and plantation owners from Louisiana and the new slave territories in the Southwest. New Jersey slaves sold at what was understood as a steep discount, certainly as compared to slaves in the upper South. The only problem for those seeking to profit was getting those slaves out of the state, which required manipulating or violating state law.

The statutory language used in 1798 to "forbid" the movement of slaves into and out of the state exemplified the contradictions and compromises that shaped the New Jersey regime. Section 12 of that law declared that from then on it would be unlawful for anyone to move a "negro or other slave" into or out of New Jersey, "either for sale or for servitude." Any violation led to a $140 fine. A clear directive, one might think. But the rest of the paragraph undid the effectiveness of that section: "That nothing in this act contained shall be construed to prevent any person, who shall remove into this state to take a settled residence here, from bringing all his or her slaves without incurring any of the penalties aforesaid, or to prevent any foreigners or others, having only a temporary residence in this state, for the purpose of transacting any particular business, or on their travels, from bringing and employing such slaves as servants during the time of his or her stay here, provided such slave shall not be sold or disposed of in this state." Slaves could not be brought into the state for sale. But whites who wished to move to or pass through New Jersey could keep their slaves as they went about their business. Even the question of sale would be qualified and limited to effective irrelevance. How long one had to be in the state before one regained the right to alienate one's property was not stated. And in 1801, the law was amended to allow the sale out of state of any slave convicted of a crime.[66]

It is possible to read those provisions as containing competing political agendas: Quakers and other antislavery voices, on the one hand, getting the opening sentence, and slaveholders, on the other hand, getting the rest. In truth, it is hard to read the legislation as providing any kind of coherent guide to action.

In other sections of the statute, limitations on slaveholders' capacity to convey were developed further, again drawing on New York precedents. Sheriffs were instructed to seize any vessels outfitted for the slave trade, indeed any vessels outfitted for the transport of slaves to any place outside New Jersey. Any slave who had lived for a year in New Jersey could not be removed from the state without her or his consent. Consent would be established by means of a "private examination" before a justice of the peace (later, before two justices of a county court of common pleas). In theory, a slave would be asked by the justice about her or his willingness to be moved. The examination should occur out of sight or out of earshot of an owner or other authority figure. Masters who wished to move enslaved children had to secure the consent of the children's enslaved parents before they could be removed. (As this was 1798, before the passage of gradual emancipation, the children were understood to be enslaved.) Such rules about private examinations for slaves mimicked the rules that required private examinations for wives before a husband could use her property under his control or change the family's domicile. According to the 1798 code, any person (that is, any free person) who removed a slave without first obtaining that slave's consent (or the consent of his or her enslaved parents) would be fined fifty dollars, which would be given for the support of the poor of the township within which the slave lived. One has to wonder how the legislature planned to execute such fines on whites who had left the state with nonconsenting slaves. And one should note that this fine, like the fines on abusing masters and those who did not teach slaves to read, gave a bounty to townships without benefiting the affected slaves (who were in any case ineligible for support from the town). Indeed, in most cases, the slaves would by then have been living far from those townships (as would their usually unreachable masters). But even that theoretical fine was effectively countered by the statutory language, which finished with the proviso "that nothing in this act shall be construed or understood to make any person or persons liable to the above penalty, who may or shall remove to and reside in any other of the United States, and take his, her, or their slave or slaves with him, her, or them." In other words, the law was, for the moment and for the most part, an ineffectual signifier. The rule against moving slaves out of state was balanced by language that permitted exactly that.[67]

In New York, by contrast, slaves who were moved into the state for purposes of sale would be emancipated. Or, to put it more accurately, slaveholders who moved their slaves into the state after 1788 ran the risk of discovering that they had lost their property "by operation of law"—exactly as Mary Beebe and her siblings discovered after Leah or Elsie was given to Mary by her aunt. (There remained in New York, as elsewhere, an exception for "sojourners.") Before the 1810s, when the end of the international slave trade produced an intense demand for New Jersey slaves who could be transported south using coastal and inland routes, there was already a significant judicial history of cases dealing with the machinations and efforts of slaveholders to move New Jersey slaves into and out of New York City for purposes of sale. In those cases, the New York courts interpreted the legislation—both New York's and New Jersey's—through the lens of a presumption in favor of freedom.

The first such case, *Fish v. Fisher* (1800), found a divided New York court struggling with the question of what constituted a sale that would result in an enslaved person's freedom. Fish, the slave of Van Voorst, a resident of Bergen County, New Jersey, had run away to New York. Van Voorst followed him, evidently found him, and recaptured him. Van Voorst then rented Fish to Fisher in New York City for $225 for a twenty-year term (Fish was about twenty-five years old at the time). Was that lease effectively a sale, forbidden under New York law, even though it took the form of something less than a sale?

The majority on the New York court agreed that this lease produced the "mischief" the New York statute was meant to prevent. According to Justice Radcliff, New York law should be interpreted "liberally" in favor of "personal liberty." Although Fish had moved to New York City (one might say, voluntarily) to escape from his New Jersey owner, that owner, Van Voorst, had made Fish's movement across the river into his own act by chasing him, finding him, and then negotiating with another white for his lease in New York City. "If we should adopt a different construction, it would be easy for masters having the absolute control of their slaves, to evade the prohibition, by suffering, or tempting them to [e]scape into this state, and thus, by a new mode, introduce a fraudulent traffic, contrary to the intent of the act." Radcliff also noted that the price Van Voorst and the lessee, Fisher, had negotiated for Fish was equivalent to the full value (or price) of such a slave. And further, the duration of the lease term was so long as to constitute for a twenty-five-year-old African American "a period beyond the ordinary calculation of such a life." The terms of the lease granted the lessee "absolute and irrevocable" power over Fish. Therefore, Radcliff concluded, the lease was in effect a purchase. What Van Voorst and Fisher had done after Fish's escape into New York met the conditions that the New York legislature had set for Fish's liberation from slavery. Fish would be freed.[68]

In a second 1805 New York case, the published headnote read, "The sale of the services of a slave is the same as a sale of a slave." A New Jersey owner had brought a male black child into New York. Nine years later, in 1803, when the child was eighteen, the putative owner had leased out the "services" of the child for twenty years "by a regular indenture, containing a clause of manumission at the expiration of that time." In April 1804, the lessee assigned the remainder of the lease term to someone else. Soon thereafter, the young man deserted, "claiming to be free." The New York court agreed that he was not bound to his twenty-year term. In the words of one lawyer, taking twenty years out of the life of "a man of 18 . . . would exhaust all the valuable portion of his existence." If it were not violative of "the strict letter of the law," it was "clearly . . . a pretext" and an "evasion" of the act. In his opinion, Chief Justice Kent emphasized that one had to look beyond mere form.[69]

In New Jersey, by way of contrast, the courts avoided any presumption in favor of freedom. In 1808, in *State v. Quick*, William Pennington, New Jersey's chief justice, shook his head rhetorically at what he took to be the craziness of New York's judicial practices. Dick, whose continued enslavement was in question in the case, had been the slave of Sir James Jay, the Loyalist brother of John Jay. Sir James owned land in Bergen County. In the mid-1790s, having returned from exile in England to the new United States, he split time between a New York City house and a New Jersey "plantation." Around that time, Sir James moved Dick from New York to New Jersey. For reasons that were not explained, Sir James soon put Dick into a New Jersey jail, and then he sold him. Dick passed through several hands;

eventually he was "owned" by William Quick. At that point, Dick claimed his freedom.

According to Pennington, if Dick were free, it must be because he was made free before he got to New Jersey, since the state of New York could not "extend into this State and attach itself to any act done here, in order to give him his freedom." He rejected the notion that the New York courts or legislature could possibly have meant to challenge New Jersey's jurisdictional autonomy. And he regarded as irrelevant the 1798 New Jersey prohibition on moving a slave into the state for the purpose of sale. He read the New York statutes as offering Dick's freedom as a remedy only if Sir James Jay had moved him to New Jersey with intent to sell him. The fact that Sir James had "kept" Dick for two years before jailing him countered that implication. He did not sell him until there was "a difference of opinion between Sir James and the negro." Pennington acknowledged that the New York courts had held that taking a slave out of state offered presumptive evidence of an illegal intent to sell. (One guesses he was looking to the New York cases we have just described, although he provided no citations in his opinion.) But to him, such holdings seemed inexplicably "strange" and "wholly incomprehensible." The New York courts had, he implied, misread the New York statutes. But, since New York law, whatever it was, did not run in New Jersey, it didn't matter. New Jersey's courts remained free to make the correct decision. Dick lost and remained enslaved.[70]

By 1812, the New Jersey legislature renewed its weak commitment to preventing slaveholders from moving slaves out of state. It increased the monetary penalties for those who violated the law by not obtaining the consent of slaves before moving them. As before, and unlike the situation in New York, the penalties did not include freedom for the slave moved without her or his consent. And there remained provisions that told slaveholders how they could get out of those penalties. Little in the revised law suggested that the legislature had much hope of capturing fines or punishments from those slaveholders (or slave traders) who took slaves out of New Jersey and did not return to the state. It must have been obvious to any reader of the legislation that the penalties remained entirely inadequate to the "problem." At best, the commitment to limiting the movement of slaves into or out of the state was a qualified one. Indeed, it may be that the 1812 law regularized the terms under which slaves could be moved to the South. One may imagine that the revised law helped create a cost structure and a set of practices, a field that defined both what could be done legally and a field for strate-gizing about how to avoid injurious legal consequences.[71]

To put it differently, the 1812 law needs to be understood less as an ef-fort to achieve freedom for New Jersey's slaves and more as a response to the booming demand for slaves in the Deep South. As several historians have detailed and explored, the revised law came about at a moment when both the market had exploded for slaves—particularly in Louisiana (in the midst of a sugar boom) and the Southwest (cotton)—and the international slave trade had been recently banned (1808). Those who serviced the intense de-mand for slaves had to look to the internal trade. Like a few other northern jurisdictions, New Jersey was a site where slave prices were relatively cheap—and becoming cheaper.[72]

Several elite New Jersey families had connections to plantations in the South. It is apparent that some of those families conspired with slave trad-ers to profit from the opportunities that New Jersey law presented. Grad-ual emancipation, combined with what one might label a contractualist legal culture, had led to plummeting prices for New Jersey slaves. New Jersey slaveholders—at least those not committed to abandoning their property to manumission and freedom—would sell cheap. Slaves were becoming a los-ing investment. By contrast, for slave traders and the agents of Louisiana plantations, the opportunities were great. If one could get New Jersey slaves to New Orleans or to other Deep South slave markets, they would fetch high prices. All one had to do was obtain or establish slaves' consent to be moved.

The incentives to fabricate consent must have been overwhelming. The story of the work of Judge Jacob Van Wickle became notorious as exempli-fying this situation.[73] Judge Van Wickle had a son and a brother-in-law in the trade and with a plantation in Point Coupée, Louisiana. His position in the Middlesex Court of Common Pleas situated him to serve their needs and the needs of other slave traders for movable slaves. Apparently it be-came his particular job to manufacture the slave consents that were neces-sary to move slaves out of state. From February to May 1818, he and an associate on the court, John Outcalt, produced well over a hundred releases, or consent agreements, from slaves who agreed to "remove" to Louisiana to "serve" his son, Nicholas Van Wickle, and his brother-in-law, Charles Morgan.[74]

In each release, a slave of a specified age (and sometimes, if a woman, along with her infant child) consented to being "removed" to work "for life" on a sugar plantation in Louisiana. Each such slave, to take the modal language found on each form, "being by us examined seperate [*sic*] and apart from her [or his] Master[,] declared that she [or he] was willing and . . . freely consented to remove and go out of this State to Point Coupee . . . to the State of Louisiana and there to serve Colonel Charles Morgan & Nicholas Van Wickle . . . jointly or severally."

These consent forms were, of course, entirely fraudulent. We can be absolutely confident that the enslaved men and women (and their children) about to be moved to the South were never asked if they were willing to serve "for life" on sugar and cotton plantations. Judge Van Wickle's acts became emblematic of a kidnapping conspiracy said to be centered in Perth Amboy, which was covered at length in newspaper articles in both New Jersey and New York and reprinted elsewhere. A conspiracy to gather and move New Jersey slaves necessarily involved many others, including those who negotiated with slave owners, the slave owners who sold their slaves, those who held and housed the slaves while groups were gathered, ship captains, and those who owned dock sites.

It was also a law-bound conspiracy. The gradual emancipation regime shaped the behavior of the participants. Instead of just taking the slaves onto boats and shipping them South, purchasers and sellers abided by the legal form, including the production of a record of a separate examination for each slave to establish her or his consent to be moved. Why would a record of the consent of the slave property have been important when slaves reached New Orleans? Recent work by Rebecca Scott suggests that officials there only occasionally paid much attention to the legal status or the paper records of apparently enslaved peoples when they arrived.[75] But still, these were careful criminals who wanted their property to have the proper papers, a provenance, and a record of ownership and sale. (Perhaps such a record would be necessary if one intended to borrow using the property as collateral.) To get to the Deep South by land they would have to pass through several free (or freer) jurisdictions, possibly including Pennsylvania and New York. If they went by boat, they would risk being stopped by federal cutters and would need to occasionally dock in "foreign" and possibly hostile jurisdictions. Everywhere they went on the way, certainly until they reached the lower South, they might have needed certifications for consent.

The fictional legalisms—the apparent desire to abide by the rules as given, even if founded on obvious fraud—went deeper. Reading the forms that Van Wickle and Outcalt produced reveals that they were not particularly good lawyers or readers of law, or perhaps they were just rushed, as they drafted one release after another. In any case, throughout the months of February and March 1818, many releases produced the consent of young women who had agreed to go to Louisiana or Alabama with their children. But by 1818, those children whose consent had been incorporated into their mothers' consent were not enslaved at all, even if their mothers still were, as all of them had been born after the 1804 gradual emancipation statute.

At some point, someone must have noticed the problem and mentioned it to the two judges. Charles Morgan, the junior Van Wickle and other slave traders, and the southern plantation owners might have worried about what would happen as the traders moved their commodities South or once they reached Louisiana. Would anyone notice the discrepancy? Would anyone know or care that the children of New Jersey slaves were not slaves? Perhaps not, but why take the chance?

The legal answer to a defective piece of paper is another piece of paper. And so, on April 23, 1818, Van Wickle and Outcalt drafted a new form for the "removal" of "Harriet Jane, Susan, Mary, Augustus, Rozinah, Deanah, Hercules, Dianah, & Dorcas." This was the first of a series of revised documents that recognized the presence of emancipated, or non-enslaved, children. This chaotically framed form worked to produce an approximation of consent to move free children to Louisiana. It noted that on February 10, 1818, James Brown of Middlesex County had brought "his female servant named Harriet Jane aged three years four months and twenty eight days child of Lidia" before Van Wickle and Outcalt. In addition, on February 26, Nicholas Van Wickle, the judge's son, had brought "his female child named Susan aged Seven Months child of Florah and Mary aged two years and Augustus a male child aged four years the said Mary and Augustus children of Hager—and Rozinah aged six weeks child of Rachel." On February 12, the document continued, Nicholas Van Wickle had also brought Dianah, aged seven months, the child of Sarah, and on March 9, Hercules, a male child of Clarissa, aged two years, ten months, and seven days—and Deanah, aged nine years, and Dorcas, aged one year, the children of Christeen. All those "above named" children, who had presumably been purchased from various New Jersey slave owners over the previous days, had been "privately examined separate and apart" from their owners (though with their mothers present, the form acknowledged). Amazingly enough, all the children, including the seven-month-old and six-week-old infants, "declared their willingness and the said respective mothers declared their desire that there [sic] said children should not be separated from them, but should with them remove and go out of this state to Point Coupee . . . and there to serve Colonel Charles Morgan and Nicholas Van Wickle . . . until they [the males] arrive to the age of twenty five years and the female[s] to serve until they arrive to the age of twenty one years." Just as the 1804 gradual emancipation law specified.[76]

Over the next two months, every consent form Van Wickle and Outcalt drafted in which a woman with an infant consented to move with a child included a separate sentence acknowledging that the child would be free when she or he turned twenty-one or twenty-five, respectively. In theory, for them, the legal duration of service in Louisiana would be limited by the terms of New Jersey's gradual emancipation statute.

But to repeat the obvious, each such consent form must have been a fraud. And to continue with the obvious, the redrafted fraud would not change what would happen to those children were they to arrive in Louisiana or Alabama. Once there, they would be slave children. There is no evidence that anyone in Louisiana or Alabama took any notice of the existence of the freedom of New Jersey–born black children. They were not freed on their twenty-first or twenty-fifth birthdays. They would not become free until the Union Army arrived in Louisiana and Alabama between 1861 and 1865.[77]

And yet it is worth contemplating for a moment the legalisms of these criminals—their willingness to follow legal formalities in order to achieve particular ends. And it is also worth noting how the statutes and the regime moved slave traders and others toward contractualist fictions of consent.

ALTHOUGH ONE IMAGINES that Van Wickle and his associates would have liked all of this to have happened quietly, without public attention, they did not get their wish. For a moment, during the summer of 1818, the New Jersey and New York papers were filled with the kidnapping scandal. The papers published reports of the delight supposedly taken in New Orleans at the expected arrival of shipments of more New Jersey slaves. On May 10, 1818, the brig *Mary-Ann* had been searched in New Orleans and the manifests for the thirty-six black people on board challenged, and all of them, the property of Charles Morgan, were impounded. All the enslaved people were identified with the "formalities" produced by and before Judge Van Wickle. An ironic New Jersey article that reproduced material from New Orleans noted that "Jersey negroes appear peculiarly adapted to this market, especially those who bear the mark of Judge Van Wickle." The consent form had become the equivalent of a branding. If the newspapers are correct, there was a trial in July at which the New Orleans jury brought in a verdict for the defendant, slave trader and plantation owner Charles Morgan. However, according to one article, the black people remained "in custody of law" and were not (at least for the moment) returned to the defendant.[78]

Allowing slave traders to gather slaves together and outfit ships that would leave from New Jersey ports reflected badly on New Jersey. The newspapers regarded the illegality formalistically, as being about violations of explicit prohibitions in New Jersey law. They did not consider the issue of re-enslavement, nor did they pay any attention to the fictitious consent forms drafted to move free children.

Probably in response to this kidnapping scandal, the New Jersey legislature soon copied New York and added a sanction that slaveholders who moved slaves for purposes of sale or transfer would lose their property. As before, exemptions were included for slaveholders who wished to move with their personal property and for "sojourners." But New Jersey's kidnapping scandal was almost at an end.[79]

In early 1819, the very active New York Manumission Society helped Jane Wilson, a young married woman from Middlesex County, escape from Thomas Raburgh, another law-bound slave trader. It is not entirely clear how she got to New York City, as the case report in the *New-York City-Hall Recorder* tells several stories about how she came to the city.

Jane Wilson and her husband had earlier brought a habeas corpus case in New Jersey.[80] According to Barent Gardenier, Raburgh's attorney, she had become a fugitive, and Raburgh had chased her to New York City. The case report notes, in the alternative, that Raburgh had purchased a number of New Jersey slaves, intending to move them to Alabama. He had been stopped in Pennsylvania, where, under Pennsylvania law, all the slaves were declared free. Raburgh followed four of them, including Jane Wilson, back to New Jersey, where he recaptured them. Then he hired a boat and transported them to New York, en route to Alabama.

Raburgh must have known that his right to his property was at risk when he arrived in New York. He had prudently gone before Justice Brockholst Livingston of the U.S. Supreme Court, sitting on circuit in the city. Livingston had provided him a certificate under the 1793 federal Fugitive Slave Act that warranted his right to "remove" his "property"—that is, Jane Wilson—back to New Jersey. It is hard to imagine why he would have wanted to return to New Jersey; given the passage of the 1818 law, it would have suddenly become more difficult to remove Jane Wilson from New Jersey to Alabama. In addition, Jane Wilson was no longer enslaved. Whether under Pennsylvania, New York, or New Jersey law, she was a free woman.

Or, to be more precise, by moving her out of New Jersey, Raburgh lost ownership of his property (just as Hornblower's clients lost their rights over Leah or Elsie). And Jane Wilson's enslaved status would not be reinstated when she returned to New Jersey. But one should assume that all Raburgh cared about was that the certificate asserted the primacy of federal law over that of New York. He needed to get his "property" out of New York. New Jersey was likely an easier place than New York to escape from with his "property."

One way or another, Jane Wilson was in New York. There, she and her supporters moved for a writ of habeas corpus before Cadwallader Colden, the mayor of New York City, who was sitting as judge of the municipality's court of general sessions of the peace. At trial, Gardenier, Raburgh's attorney, first tried to get Mayor Colden, at the same time president of the state manumission society, to recuse himself from judging the case. George Griffin, Jane Wilson's attorney, insisted that the manumission society was not the prosecutor in the case, even though they were "guardians of the rights of society." There was thus no reason for Colden to withdraw from judging. The mayor agreed. To be a member of the society was not to have an "interest" in this case; rather, it was to share in sentiments that arise "in the mind of every honorable man." But the crucial point for Colden was that a proceeding under the habeas corpus act was not a discretionary act from which a magistrate had the right to withdraw. There was, he concluded, "no principle upon which he ought to decline acting." He would not recuse himself.

Gardenier next argued that Justice Livingston's certificate under the federal statute was "conclusive," leaving nothing for the mayor to do. The mayor disagreed. No proceeding *"before a single magistrate,"* even a hearing before a justice of the U.S. Supreme Court, could possibly be *"conclusive"* on a question of personal liberty. The proposition that it might be so was, he thought, "a monstrous absurdity." "Personal liberty," of anyone either apparently enslaved or free, should not be "affected or concluded" by an ex parte application to a single magistrate. The certificate could be no more than prima facie evidence of the facts it contained. A federal judge in this regard was no different than a justice of the peace.

Having disposed of federal power by establishing its near irrelevance, the case continued, leaving open the question of what would be the relevant law. In Griffin's version of how Jane Wilson came to be in the city, Raburgh had come from Alabama to New Jersey, where he purchased Jane and "exported" her with the intent to bring her back to Alabama, "after the passage of an act prohibiting such exportation." Griffin then read into the record the New Jersey statute, enacted November 5, 1818, that declared that if a slave like Jane Wilson were "exported," the person doing the exporting would be guilty of a misdemeanor and the slave would be freed. End of story.

On the other side, Raburgh's witnesses described how Jane Wilson and three other slaves (including her husband) had been purchased on November 2, 1818. On that day, three days before the new law went into effect, Jane Wilson had supposedly appeared before one of the Middlesex County judges (not Van Wickle or Outcalt) and given her consent to be moved to the Alabama territory with Raburgh. Raburgh had complied with the formalities for moving slaves as defined under the previous 1812 law. What he had done and what he wanted to do were all legal (even if surely founded on a fictional consent).[81] But unfortunately for Raburgh, misadventure and accident, as well as the mobilized opposition of Pennsylvania abolitionists, had kept him from leaving New Jersey with his "properties" until November 6, 1818, after the new law was in force. Or in Gardenier's words: "He met with several impediments, the particulars of which are not necessary to be detailed." He was himself imprisoned in Pennsylvania, and he had to move Jane and the others back to New Jersey, where he put them in the New Brunswick jail for a few days. Then he found boat passage for them to New York City. Once in the city, he tried to get the captain of another sloop "to carry *some baggage or goods* to Sandy-Hook" in New Jersey ("when asked what goods, [he] replied it made no difference" if the captain "could *keep a secret*"). But before the "baggage" could be removed from one boat to another, it was discovered.

According to Jane Wilson's attorney, the 1818 New Jersey statute was conclusive on the question of her freedom or enslavement. She had been moved from one state to another without her consent. Thus, she became free by operation of law. According to Gardenier, Raburgh had complied with everything in the older 1812 statute. In doing so, Raburgh had acquired a "vested" right to his property. He could not be deprived of it by a subsequent legislative act—except, perhaps, with just compensation. Insofar as it was interpreted to deprive Raburgh of his vested rights when it replaced the 1812 act, the new 1818 New Jersey statute violated the contract clause of the U.S. Constitution. That is, it violated the provision prohibiting state legislatures from passing laws that impaired or destroyed existing private contracts.

Griffin was going to respond, but Colden stopped him. The mayor did not need to hear any more, and he offered an extended opinion—an opinion that spoke for Jane Wilson and her attorney. He began by reasserting his obligation to decide the case in spite of Raburgh's certificate from a federal court. The question of whether Jane Wilson was or was not the slave of Raburgh was, he thought, a question that must be decided under New Jersey state law, without reference to federal law. Under the principle that later law supersedes earlier law, the 1818 New Jersey statute replaced the 1812 New Jersey law. And under that new law, Jane Wilson became a free woman when she was moved out of state without her consent.

Mayor Colden then turned to the counterclaim: that the later law violated the "private vested rights" that Raburgh had acquired when he "relied" on the 1812 law, including the right to transport his slave. Had the New Jersey legislature the power to divest him of that right by passing a later law? There was, Colden was confident, "no such limitation" on "legislative power." State legislatures were supreme except as to explicit constitutional restraints. A New York judge (or, for that matter, a U.S. Supreme Court justice) had no more right to declare a New Jersey law void just "because it is unjust or impolitic, or violates private rights" than he did to do the same for a New York law. Any other decision would make void all laws that "prohibited or restrained the transportation of slaves." None of them could be enacted without affecting previously legal and established private rights.

From there it was easy for the mayor to reject the claim that the 1818 New Jersey law violated the contracts clause of the U.S. Constitution. The contract of sale between Raburgh and Jane Wilson's previous owner was the only contract involved in the situation. That contract remained a valid contract, even as it was, like all contracts, subject to "all regulations, or restrictions," which a state legislature "might see fit to apply." The 1818 statute was an ordinary exercise of the state's police power. That it happened to destroy the value of the transaction was legally or constitutionally irrelevant. On the other hand, there was no contract between Raburgh and the state of New Jersey, certainly none that he should have a vested right to transport his slave.[82]

Here, of course, the mayor was moving on to murky constitutional terrain. By the 1840s, the Taney court would have declared the mayor's understanding of New Jersey law incorrect and unconstitutional. Already by the 1830s there were articulations of another view, certainly with regard to the rights of slaveholders to transport and to recapture their enslaved properties. But all that lay in the future.[83]

In New York City's City Hall in 1819, on the other hand, the mayor refused to recognize the salience of federal power as affecting either New York or New Jersey law. General laws, like the 1818 law forbidding the movement of slaves out of New Jersey, were not to be considered contracts "which the state legislatures may not alter or modify, as in their judgment the public good may require." The interpretation of the federal constitution that Raburgh and his attorney wanted would have robbed the states of "the greatest part of their power of legislation," since so many laws might be considered contracts. "Such a construction of the constitution of the United States"—that is, a construction that gave slaveholders vested rights against legislative amendments of the slave regime by northern states engaged in the process of abolition—"I do not believe would be received with submission by the states." Enforcing the vested rights of slaveholders against northern law could lead, the mayor implied, to the end of the Union.

And thus Jane Wilson went free, as a consequence of a New York City mayor's construction of New Jersey law and of federal constitutional law.

The Subjects of Gradual Emancipation

By 1820, the number of slaves in New Jersey had declined. Where there had been more than twelve thousand enslaved people in the state in 1800, by 1820 there were less than eight thousand, even as the population of the state as a whole, including a growing number of free people of color, had grown from 211,149 to 277,575.

One might imagine that the regime of gradual emancipation was doing the work it was supposed to do. New Jersey was losing slaves. And over the next two decades the loss would become much more dramatic, so that by 1840, when the New Jersey Supreme Court decided *Force v. Haines*, there would be fewer than 700 slaves in the state.

And yet there were slaves in New Jersey—in 1804, 1820, and 1822, when Mrs. Haines and Mr. Force negotiated for Minna, and in 1840, when *Force v. Haines* was decided. Both slaves and slaveholders would still find their lives and their transactions governed and shaped by the New Jersey regime described in these pages.

As with all such regimes, the law paid much more attention to the rights and duties of slaveholders than to slaves, who were for the most part taken for granted and talked about, but not spoken with. The practices and problems (and occasional opportunities) shaped by the mixed motives and political compromises that produced New Jersey's regime of gradual emancipation were those that white property owners and commercial actors (and reformers) confronted. Slaves, on the other hand, were understood as resources and property, not as agents or participants. They were still enslaved, at least until they became "abandoned." Once they had served their legally prescribed periods of service, in the case of those born after July 4, 1804, or been manumitted or become free by operation of law, in the case of parents and older people, they ceased to matter within the terms of the regime. Until then, they were objects of legal scrutiny, not subjects, though traces of their own strategies, resistance, and accommodations to the regime are everywhere in the legal records.

This chapter has emphasized the chaotic and discordant qualities of the rules as enacted and practiced—the indeterminacies and the incoherence of it all. I think that emphasis is true to how it would have been experienced by white people and black people alike. Indeed, I would suspect that such indeterminacies and incoherence multiplied over the generations of New Jersey's gradual emancipation. One implicit feature of a regime of gradual emancipation would have been a growing awareness—on the part of enslaved men and women as well as slaveholders—of the opportunities and fissures, the contradictions and possibilities, present in the rules and practices. This awareness would have led to exploitation, and exploitation to widening fissures and more manifest contradictions.

The presence of free states both to the north and to the south might have made even more manifest the incongruities of the New Jersey regime. In 1817, New York committed itself to the end of all slavery within its boundaries, and the last enslaved person in that state—putting aside the slaves of "sojourners"—would become free "by operation of law" in 1827. By then, most of New Jersey—certainly the part of the state where nearly all enslaved people lived—was bordered by free states.

At the same time, New Jersey's legislators and judges, as well as local officials like the overseers of the poor, found ways to make the strange and incongruous seem less so. Judges like Gabriel Ford worked to repress the singularities and peculiarities of their local slave law. Ford tried to make Minna's situation look as if it were a reproduction of familiar legal situations, particularly those of poor-relief law, family law, and master-and-servant law. As Ford's survey of the cases demonstrated, problems of the responsibility of "masters" for the costs of dependents were not novel or unique to the master–slave relationship. Like slaves, apprentices, paupers, children, and wives were usually without resources they themselves controlled; yet all of them had the capacity—the power—occasionally to impose costs on those who controlled them, their masters, overseers, parents, and husbands. It had long been a legal question about when those masters, overseers, parents, and husbands would have to pay. In all those situations, the dependent ones were never entirely commodified objects, simply property. Yet in all those situations, much of the law was constructed around the capacities of outsiders—including doctors, good Samaritans, and antislavery advocates—to seduce, entice, or alienate away, or to care for those who were both dependents and resources.[84]

In labor relations, poor relief, domestic relations, and master–slave relations, local public agencies had long played complex roles. Statutes may have created governing norms, yet those norms were always incomplete. Local institutions, like the overseers of the poor or the judges who confirmed manumissions, sometimes enforced those norms, sometimes ignored them. Local governmental institutions often served elite interests by resisting centrally articulated norms—for example, by helping local slave owners move property into or out of the state. More often they made government tools available to constituents who needed them and knew how to use them. It is thus not surprising that Sir James Jay or Thomas Raburgh could use a local jail to hold an errant or disobedient slave (even some who were no longer slaves). As recent work in labor-law history shows, jailings and other public or semipublic punishments were part of the panoply of tools that masters used to discipline laborers across the Anglo-American legal world. And Van Wickle's manufacture of slave consent was only a small step further than the normal discretionary work that a local judge or justice of the peace would have done for those of significance in his local community. Local institutions made private relations possible, helped them work, helped masters achieve their economic and material goals. In particular, local institutions made it possible for masters to sustain authority over—and to "police"—their dependents.[85]

These conventional practices of local elites who mobilized local law in their behalf were coming under siege in nineteenth-century America. Wives, servants, apprentices, children, the mobile poor—none of them still conformed to eighteenth-century expectations. Pervasive mobility made it difficult, eventually impossible, to maintain the traditional "peace"—or the traditional policing—of local communities. Structures defined by what was called the law of "persons" were falling apart. Although Gabriel Ford could still find useful precedents for the question of who should pay for a slave's care by ransacking older cases of marriage law, poor-relief law, and apprenticeship law, doing so must have seemed increasingly incoherent and archaic. Slavery as a doctrinal field was becoming ever more singular, out of step with what were increasingly understood as free relations founded on contract (even as New Jersey slavery was itself inflected by contractual understandings). That must have seemed obvious to the younger Justice Dayton, who argued that *Force v. Haines* should not be decided by looking to the doctrinal fields that Ford relied on.

But it was not just the world of "free" relations that was changing. The regime of gradual emancipation was itself slowly becoming something new and different. In particular, lurking behind the structures and practices that the cases and the statutes reveal was a question that would become increasingly pressing as the number of enslaved black people in New Jersey declined: Who was a slave, and how did anyone with authority or responsibility know that any particular black person was enslaved? Before gradual emancipation, that question had lived at the farther boundaries of the law of slavery as it was practiced and experienced throughout the early modern world. In North America, it appeared at odd moments—for example, when white women gave birth to black children.[86] But for those with power in the white world, racial presumptions ordinarily made conclusive their "knowledge" of who was a slave.

However, as places without slave regimes began to proliferate from the early 1790s on—first in Saint-Domingue, then in some northern jurisdictions—and as free people of color and abolitionist societies became a public presence, even jurisdictions like New Jersey, where a slave regime was still established, had to confront situations in which the status of a person of color came into question. This was especially true as men and women of color moved—and were moved—from jurisdiction to jurisdiction; even more so as laws were enacted that forbade the movement of enslaved people into and out of their jurisdictions allowing advocates to insist on freedom for those moved in violation of the law; even more so as an increasing number of free children were born to slaves and grew to adulthood.

By the early 1820s, when Minna was leased by Elizabeth Haines, it would not have been obvious that an African American living within a white household or working for a white man or woman was necessarily enslaved. This would have been true even in the case of an adult black woman born well before 1804, as there were many ways that actions by a putative master—some conscious and voluntary, some unconscious or accidental, some criminal—might have turned slavery into possible freedom.

CHAPTER THREE

Who Is Enslaved?

Arson

There once was a house on the beach at Long Branch. A reporter described it as wonderfully situated, "grand and majestic . . . on the margin of the ocean, about ten miles south from . . . Sandy-Hook." Unlike the bays and marshes that "indented" most of the coast, here, "along the Jersey shore, . . . the ocean boldly approaches." And here, "the temperate breezes from the sea contribute equally to destroy the influence of the chilling blasts of winter and allay the fervent heat of summer." The reporter imagined a fully formed vacation business. "Strangers of delicate health, or those bent on an excursion for pleasure, resorted to this place in great numbers, from a great distance," he wrote, with some exaggeration. "Wandering on the extensive beach, in full view of the boundless prospect towards the rising sun, they felt the salutary influence of the seabreeze by day and at night were lulled to repose by the distant sullen roar of the ocean."[1]

Victorine Du Pont Bauduy, the recently widowed oldest child of a gunpowder company's founder, spent ten days in August 1814 at the house by the beach. At least at first she would not have shared the reporter's enthusiasm. "I now know what bathing-in the sea is!" she wrote her sister. "Let me tell you for your comfort it is the most shocking thing imaginable." Long Branch she described as "the most disagreeable place in the world." She found herself unable to adjust to the rhythms of vacationing. "We spend our time here rather in a monotonous manner, bathing is the chief & grand business with every person, the rest of the time we stay in our chambers." She found "no pleasure in doing always the same things." The house was full. There were persons going and coming every day, some of them quite eminent, including President Madison's secretary. But "all the people here" seemed "quite stupified and most of them look as if they had forgot to bring their brains with them as if they were useless in such a place as this." They "flit by us like shadows." She had to rely on fish wagons for transport.

By the end of her stay, though, she had come to appreciate the pleasures of the place, and she regretted leaving. Her last letter to her sister acknowledged, "How changeable is human nature! It was with extreme reluctance that two weeks ago I consented to bathe in the sea and it was with regret that I went out of it yesterday morning! Upon the whole I had become quite [pleased] . . . with the . . . place I abused so much in my first letters to you . . . the truth must come out."[2]

The beachfront house where Victorine Du Pont eventually learned the art of vacationing was managed and in some sense owned by Joshua Bennet, and it was called Bennet's Hotel. The original building, which had once belonged to General James W. Green, was in the shape of an "oblong square," and faced the shore. There were also two wings, apparently added by Bennet in 1811 or 1812, about seventy feet long and thirty feet wide. One wing had a large hall on the first floor, with lodging rooms above; the other consisted entirely of lodging rooms. There may have been as many as twenty bedrooms. And the property as a whole also included farmland, woodland, an orchard, stables, and a barn, "all in good fence, . . . and in pleasantness of situation . . . inferior to none," to quote a real estate advertisement. That it was located right on the shore meant that sea sand was available as a "permanent source of manure, . . . equal if not superior to ashes, in improving and fertilizing the quality of the soil." It was, the advertisement continued, "unnecessary to attempt to enumerate the many valuable privileges and advantages attached to the situation of this property."[3]

"Such a situation, so retired, so beautiful, so sublime," ought, according to the journalist quoted earlier, "to have escaped the rude grasp of crime and avarice."[4]

JOSHUA BENNET HAD PURCHASED General Green's property at public auction from the estate of Henry Green, the general's brother. Henry had died in 1810, one year after his brother. John Quay, Bennet's business associate, was the administrator of General Green's estate; Joshua Bennet was the co-administrator of Henry Green's estate. Bennet had also purchased ten acres of neighboring property.[5]

By 1814, probably earlier, Bennet was in financial trouble. He owed John Quay and Jacob Wyckoff $8,000. In the words of Bennet's wife, Catherine, John Quay had "become responsible for him in the Orphan's Court." It is not entirely clear what she meant or what had happened. It may be that Quay and Wyckoff had put up security to cover for Bennet's failures as an administrator of estates. In any event, on September 16, 1814, the Monmouth County sheriff executed a judgment on Bennet's Long Branch property, taking it from him in favor of Wyckoff and Quay and other creditors.

Then, on March 7, 1815, John Quay purchased the beach property for $1,005 at a sheriff's sale. Quay received a sheriff's deed, one "subject to all incumbrances." Just what sort of title Quay acquired for his money was unclear. It appears that some of the ground on which the building stood was still owned by others. Quay probably assumed Bennet's two mortgages; he also apparently promised Bennet that he and his family could pay rent and stay in their lodgings on the property.[6]

John Quay was a controversial and litigious figure in Monmouth County. Early in his life, he had lived in Abbeville, South Carolina, and he had served as a lieutenant in the Revolutionary War, although in New Jersey he affected the title of colonel. In the 1790s, he had been involved in the efforts of Citizen Genêt to raise troops to make war on England in Florida on behalf of France. Soon thereafter, he moved to New Jersey. For some time he ran a dry goods and grocery business in Middletown, and he bought and sold real estate. He became a figure in the Jeffersonian Party, the leader of what hostile newspaper articles called "the Colts Neck men." And when the Jeffersonians took power in New Jersey, he became a justice of the peace and a judge in the Monmouth County Court of Common Pleas.[7]

Throughout the early years of the nineteenth century, Quay both owned and manumitted slaves. He also advertised in the newspapers, offering rewards for the return of slaves who had escaped from him. His name also appears regularly in the Monmouth County records as one of the judges certifying that a slave about to be manumitted was competent and able to earn her or his own way in the world.[8]

On April 15, 1815, Quay purchased a $10,000 insurance policy on the house and property he had just acquired. His application to the Eagle Fire-Company of New York City claimed the additions alone had cost $15,000 when they were built three years before. The policy required that the applicant furnish an accurate description of the property. If there was damage from a fire, anyone insured by the company was required to give notice to the company "as soon after as possible," including a "particular . . . Account of . . . Loss or Damage." According to the policy, the claimant had to make an oath and provide "Books of Accounts and other proper Vouchers" and procure a signed certificate from a Magistrate, Notary Public, or Clergyman who lived "contiguous to the Spot where the Fire happened, and not concerned in such Loss." That certificate had to speak to the "Character and Circumstances of the Person or Persons insured." The certificate also had to affirm that the applicant for compensation "really, and by Misfortune, and without Fraud or evil Practice," had "sustained . . . such Fire, Loss and Damage." Any fraud or "false Swearing" would lead to forfeiture of a claim to compensation.[9]

A few days later, John Quay arrived at the house to tell Joshua Bennet and his family to leave. He had, he told them, sold the property to his nephew, a Captain Reed from Philadelphia, who intended to take immediate possession. Bennet was ill, and he soon became more so. He was "thought to be a dying man," but Quay was adamant. On the following Sunday, Bennet received a letter from Quay, "brought by a black man." The letter ordered him to quit the property. Bennet was too sick to reply, so his doctor wrote a response for him.

Bennet soon recovered. Several days later, when he was well enough, he left Long Branch to look for a place his family could move to. While Bennet was away, on a Saturday in early May, Quay returned to the house. There he told Catherine Bennet that he had completed the sale to his nephew and that they must now move. Mrs. Bennet told him that she could do nothing until her husband returned. Quay insisted that they had to be out of the house within a week, whether or not her husband was back. Mrs. Bennet asked if they could move into a few rooms of the house, where they would not be in the nephew's way. But Quay demanded "an entire removal." He then offered her one hundred dollars if she and her family would leave within a week. She told him she would if she could.

Over the next few days, she packed up all their things. Her husband returned. They moved, on a Tuesday, ten days after her last meeting with Quay. They left behind straw mats and a number of old bedsteads in the lofts. The keys were left with a neighbor.

Two nights later, on May 18, 1815, the house burned down. The property stood alone on the beach, far from other houses. By the time anyone got there, it was too late to stop the fire. As three men arrived, several roofs fell in.

It rained the next morning. Since the roads were sandy, the wagon tracks filled up. By evening, all that a witness could see were the prints of a single horse.

Thomas Chandler, who kept a store two miles away and had once owned some of the land on which the house stood, testified at trial that Quay came in a day or two later. Quay wanted to know if Chandler had seen a man and his horse go past his store on the night the house burned down. Chandler said he had not but that he had heard a horse being ridden very fast. Until he heard of the fire, he had assumed someone was fetching a doctor; he then asked Quay if the person on the horse was the arsonist. According to Chandler, Quay then answered either "undoubtedly it was" or "in my opinion it was." According to Chandler, Quay continued: "Any person who would do such a thing, would not be too good to stick a sword in." Quay asked Chandler who local opinion thought was responsible for the fire. Chandler answered "that the opinion of the people was, that he [Quay] . . . was the cause of it." Quay replied that "he did not care what they thought, but they must take good care how they talked, or he would make them pay for it." (Quay was then in the midst of a slander suit against someone who had once called him a "damned red headed Irish horse thief." Thus, this was not an idle threat.) Chandler replied, "No doubt of that; if he [Quay] was bad enough to have the house burned, he would be bad enough to make a person pay for their talk." Quay acknowledged that he should not have left the property alone. He told Chandler that he had said to his wife, right after news of the fire came out, that he would be suspected, "as it was so uncommon a thing to insure houses in the country." Chandler asked Quay if he thought he would have trouble getting the insurance proceeds. "Not at all," Quay replied, "the people in New-York know me very well."[10]

Quay apparently spoke in misleading ways to several people about the amount of insurance he had placed on the property, telling them that it was worth four or five or six thousand dollars. He also told them that he had suffered "a great loss, which would ruin him." And people heard various things from him about the nephew who had bought the property. Mary Crawford, to take one example, reported that Quay came to her house at Long Branch the day after the fire. He seemed much agitated and shed tears. He was ruined, he declared. Hadn't he sold the property to his nephew? There were no writings, he replied, "as there was the most perfect understanding between his nephew and himself." The loss would fall on him. Wasn't he insured? "For a mere trifle." According to Crawford, when she asked how much he was insured for, "he hesitatingly replied, . . . 'for 5,000 dollars.' "[11]

By September, the insurance company had refused to pay on the policy. Instead, the company hired an investigator, who made inquiries around New Jersey. Quay published a letter in a Trenton paper defending his name against the "report" circulating that he had a part in setting the fire. Boyd, the investigator, had "used gentlemen's names living in Monmouth to prop up his cause." But "at a proper time," Quay would prove his honor. He had initiated an action against the Eagle Fire-Company on his policy, which was, he wrote, valued at "less than the buildings were worth." Quay concluded the letter with a "certificate" from various prominent Monmouth men who knew him and who had "never known any act of his life [that] . . . would justify a suspicion of his being guilty of so monstrous an act of Moral Turpitude."[12]

THE TRIAL OF John Quay versus the Eagle Fire-Company of New-York began more than a year later, on Friday, December 6, 1816. William Van Ness, a justice on New York's Supreme Court of Judicature, presided in the New York City Court of Common Pleas.[13] Each side had retained eminent New York City counsel.

Quay's attorneys began by establishing the value of the property lost, Quay's title by way of the sheriff's deed, and the insurance policy. They also produced depositions that asserted that Quay's reputation for "truth, honesty, and probity was unexceptionable."

The insurance company's lawyers, John Wells and Thomas Addis Emmet, began by introducing several witnesses and depositions that detailed Quay's behavior in the days before and after the fire. They also raised questions about whether the property had been overvalued in the policy.[14]

They then put Peter Brewer, who was a fishmonger, on the witness stand. On the night of the fire, Brewer was driving a covered wagon filled with fish from Spotswood to Long Branch. He saw light coming from the building that had been Bennet's Hotel. A while later he passed a man on horseback traveling toward Freehold. The horse had been going at a run, but when it got close it slowed down and passed at a trot. Brewer recognized the man riding; it was "Adam, the black man of the plaintiff." Brewer knew the man well. Adam was a fiddler, and he had played at parties and other events that Brewer had gone to. There was good moonlight that night, and it was just a little cloudy. Brewer met no one else on the road that night. In cross-examination, Brewer added details that gave credence to his story: "The night was light, and the moon was on the right side, the road was level, and the woods cleared on each side" when he met the black man. The horse the man was riding "was one of the two" belonging to Quay, and Brewer "thought it was the smallest [sic] one. The black man was dressed in a different dress" from that which the fishmonger had seen him in before. "He wore an old great-coat," and Brewer "wondered what the negro was doing there so late. After the black man passed . . . and he had proceeded four or five miles, it rained hard."

Over the next few days, Brewer told his story to several others, who were then called as corroborating witnesses. However, he apparently stopped recounting what he had seen after he heard from his sister that Quay threatened to prosecute anyone who implicated him. And when asked later on about what he knew, he answered that he knew nothing.

One of the corroborating witnesses added that he lived two miles from the building that burned. He had been up during that night with a sick child, and he had heard a horse and rider racing up the road. Another witness, Charles Haight, who had testified earlier on behalf of the insurance company about the value of the property (he claimed that Quay had offered it to him for $1,005) and who had been "at the Branch" until May 17, was recalled to the stand. He reported that he had noticed that no preparations had been made on the insured property "for gardening." (Presumably, that was odd, because it suggested that no one planned to use the house during the summer and fall.)[15]

At this point in the trial, counsel for the insurance company called Adam Wyckoff to testify. Quay's lawyers objected. Adam Wyckoff was John Quay's slave.[16] Under New Jersey or New York law, indeed under the law of all American jurisdictions that practiced slavery in any form, no slave could testify in a civil matter involving white people, certainly not in a matter involving the slave's owner. To prove Adam Wyckoff's status as a slave, Quay's lawyers produced a bill of sale from William Wyckoff to John Quay, dated May 1, 1812. The price had been $250. The insurance company's lawyers objected that an 1812 bill of sale provided no proof that Adam Wyckoff was still enslaved in 1815 or 1816. But the court overruled the objection.[17]

The insurance company then set out to prove that Adam Wyckoff had become a free man by the time of the trial. The company's lawyers produced a piece of paper that Adam had kept in his possession. The paper was dated April 10, 1816, and was signed by John Quay: "Adam, the bearer hereof, is my servant, and has my liberty to work for himself, to any [one] willing to employ him; provided he pays me sixty-four dollars per year, for four years. Adam has served me five years as a slave, and has been a faithful, obedient servant."

The insurance company then attempted to prove that $256 had been offered to John Quay, presumably by agents of the insurance company. That was, of course, the sum that Adam had promised to pay to Quay over those four years. According to the lawyers, once that money had been offered, Adam Wyckoff had become a free man.[18]

To this, Quay's lawyers objected. Neither the document nor the tendered amount proved that Adam Wyckoff was free.

The scene was now set for a full-scale debate by counsel on what constituted a valid manumission, a performance the court reporter described as "one of the most splendid exhibitions of talent, on both sides, perhaps ever witnessed in the [City] Hall."

Quay's lawyers, David Ogden and Cadwallader Colden, went first. (This is, of course, the same Cadwallader Colden who, while serving as both mayor of New York City and head of the state's manumission society, would free Jane Wilson in 1819. In this trial, however, he and his co-counsel were arguing that a slave owner could keep a possibly enslaved person from testifying in a civil matter.)[19] Ogden and Colden moved in four directions to challenge Adam Wyckoff's competence as a witness.

First, they read the contract Adam Wyckoff had made with his master literally. It did not promise him freedom; all it did was grant him permission to work for himself for a limited term. There were slaves all around New Jersey and the northern United States who worked and lived under similar arrangements. Second, even if one understood this contract as promising freedom after four annual payments, that is not what had occurred. The insurance company had offered Quay a single lump payment, ostensibly on behalf of Adam Wyckoff. There was no reason why Quay was obligated to accept a lump payment as equivalent to four annual payments. (One might note that Quay's lawyers implicitly acknowledged that contracts between enslaved people and their masters were enforceable.)

Third, the question of whether or not Adam Wyckoff was a slave was a matter to be decided under New Jersey law, not New York law. Under standard choice-of-law rules, a contract should be interpreted under the law of the jurisdiction where it was made (called in legalese the *lex loci*). In New Jersey, where the paper was produced, there was both a clear statute and a clear case precedent that together settled the question of what was and what was not a valid manumission.

Quay's lawyers then described the New Jersey law that established that Adam Wyckoff was still John Quay's slave. As we have seen, the 1798 statute that enacted a close to comprehensive slave code for New Jersey required an unvarying set of practices to produce a valid manumission. The slave had to be between the ages of twenty-one and forty, sound in mind, and free from any "bodily incapacity." An owner who wished to emancipate such an eligible slave had to make a formal written declaration of intent to manumit, in the presence of at least two witnesses. That document had to be accompanied by two certificates: one made by two justices of the peace and the other by two of the local overseers of the poor. And all three documents had to be recorded in the county clerk's books. These sections of the 1798 law were, as the court in *State v. Emmons* (1806) had explained, enacted to stop earlier practices of more informal manumissions, practices that had become common in the years following the end of the Revolutionary War. Many of those late eighteenth-century manumissions had resembled what Quay and Adam had apparently done, marked by an informally drafted piece of paper. And those early informal manumissions, according to Quay's attorneys, had produced a confused legal understanding, one that distinguished "emancipation, as it respects the owner, and emancipation as it respects the State": although a slave might be freed from duties of labor or obedience to a master, the master might still be responsible for the care of the slave if the slave required poor relief or other forms of public care. The 1798 law undid what Justice Pennington in 1806 had called this "unintelligible" understanding. Essentially, those early manumissions had come close to the creation of an in-between status, in which a "slave" would be free of the control of a master, yet the master (and the overseers of the poor) would not be free of potential responsibility for the slave's care. To avoid that result, a manumission after 1798 had to be done in precise ways in order to be effective.[20]

According to Quay's counsel, that meant that Adam Wyckoff was still enslaved. He had not been manumitted using the forms that the New Jersey courts and the New Jersey legislature required. And New Jersey law was the only law that was relevant.

Fourth, even if, as Quay's lawyers implicitly recognized, New York law was different and would have given effect to a less formal manumission, this New York court had to acknowledge that New Jersey law governed on this question. The Constitution of the United States and a variety of acts of Congress, in particular the 1793 Fugitive Slave Act, all held that a slave in one state did not become a free man in another state. Adam Wyckoff's status remained as it was defined under New Jersey law. That meant Quay was free to reclaim him as a fugitive slave. And likewise, Adam's "slavery . . . followed him into this state, and here as well as there disqualified him from being a witness."[21]

The response by Thomas Addis Emmet and John Wells, the insurance company's lawyers, answered Quay's lawyers' arguments and reframed the question of Adam Wyckoff's status. They conceded that Quay's agreement with Adam had "artfully" omitted any direct promise of freedom. But questions of slavery or freedom should not rest on a master's syntactic cleverness. Even read as drafted, they insisted, the document made Adam Wyckoff a free man. They read that document in light of a presumption "in favour of liberty." That lens allowed them to understand the text as granting Adam permission to work for himself for life if he paid the four annual sums of sixty-four dollars. Similarly, he had the right to tender the full amount at any time, "especially as the effect of it would be in favour of liberty, by producing a speedier emancipation."[22]

At the heart of the insurance company's case was what we might call a performative argument in favor of freedom. Those who acted free became free. Thus, when a master permitted his slave to work for himself for life, the master–slave relationship "dissolved." Why? Because "all" that a master was entitled to was a slave's service. Once a master "parted" with service, there was no property left. The effect was "virtually" a manumission. Indeed, the very act of contracting with a slave contradicted the existence of a continuing slave relation. Quay's agreement with Adam Wyckoff "amounted to a contract on the part of the master with his slave, touching his liberty, which, upon general principles, independent of any particular statute, made him free."

The performative argument for freedom that the insurance company's lawyers mobilized reflected an emergent understanding in New York and elsewhere in the North of the moral and existential significance of contractual language. To contract meant that one was necessarily free. Whether that understanding had any resonance in the New Jersey courts at that time is less clear, as we will see. Even in New York, the performative presumption was of uncertain legal significance. Indeed, Thomas Addis Emmet— the insurance company's lead lawyer, whose practice included representation of many early corporations, some slaves, and some slaveholders, and who served as the attorney for the New York Manumission Society—had made exactly the opposite argument in a New York City murder case just one week earlier. In that case he had represented Diana Sellick, a black woman of ambiguous legal status, who had been accused of poisoning the child of a free black woman.[23] The prosecution had wanted to hear the testimony of Benjamin Johnson, the husband of the free black woman whose child was dead. But before Mr. Johnson was allowed to testify, Emmet and his co-counsel had questioned his competence as a witness: "Have you ever been a slave?" they asked him. "Yes, but I am now free." "How did you become free?" "Mrs. Alexander purchased me of Mr. Curtis, and I lived with this lady after her marriage with Mr. Jaques. She always told me that after her death I should be free, and that Mr. Jaques had nothing to do with me.— After her death I became free, and left the house. I have often seen Mr. Jaques since, and he spoke very friendly to me, and has never made any claim of me." But did Benjamin Johnson have a formal manumission paper? He did not. Emmet objected to Benjamin Johnson's testimony. That Benjamin Johnson had lived as a free man—had "performed" freedom—did not make him free and competent to testify. Mere words combined with behavior did not make a man free. On reflection, the court agreed; the testimony of Benjamin Johnson would not be heard. "Though, in effect, he may be free, yet, in contemplation of law," he remained a slave.[24]

In the Quay case, Emmet and Wells ignored what Emmet had argued a week earlier in the same building and constructed an opposite claim. The New Jersey rules that required a formal manumission did not, they argued, apply to "prospective" or "conditional" manumissions. These rules were concerned only with immediate decisions to manumit and thus would have no relevance to Adam Wyckoff's situation. In effect, the lawyers read the "contract" between Wyckoff and Quay as an enforceable promise to make a manumission. Once Adam Wyckoff had complied with the conditions in the contract, he had the right, in equity, to enforce a specific performance against his master and to compel him to make good the manumission by doing exactly what the New Jersey rules required of him. Without such a right, Quay would be unjustly enriched at Adam Wyckoff's expense.

One might note that this argument violated a central premise of most slave regimes, as interpreted in innumerable southern decisions. According to that premise, a slave existed for the profit of—to enrich—a master. A notion of the unjust enrichment of a master at a slave's expense stood in fundamental contradiction to that premise. And one should certainly note that if Emmet and Wells's understanding of conditional manumissions had become everyday law in New Jersey (or in New York), it would have thrown the practices of many slaveholders into confusion. As we have seen, it had become routine to frame manumissions as promises to occur at the end of limited or conditional terms. (Perhaps that is what Quay thought he was doing when he wrote the note that Adam Wyckoff had in his possession.) No court or other legal authority in New York or in New Jersey, best as I can tell, ever assumed that a slave conveyed by will or by contract had a preemptive right to purchase her or his freedom at any time during the duration of a continuing, though delimited, term of "service."[25]

In any case, the insurance company's lawyers went on to say that the capacity of a witness to testify in a court was always to be determined by the law of the jurisdiction in which the court stood (called the *lex fori*, in contrast to the *lex loci*). Thus, the question of Adam Wyckoff's competence to testify as a witness must be settled according to the laws of New York State. Under New York law, according to Emmet and Wells, an agreement coupled with payment of the money on which the agreement was conditioned amounted to an emancipation, making Adam Wyckoff a competent witness. And, to turn the issue in one further direction, Adam Wyckoff's offer to pay his master the money owed under his agreement was, under New York law, an act of a free man (or rather an act that revealed that he was a free man). Once he made that offer, he had a right to go where he pleased. If he found himself in New York, he was then entitled to the full protection of its laws, as a free man. Quay retained no right to reclaim him as a "fugitive slave" under the U.S. Constitution or federal law because he wasn't a fugitive: "The plaintiff [Quay] could not, either under the constitution or act of Congress relative to slaves, reclaim Adam in this state as a slave, and take him back to New-Jersey, because none but *fugitives from labour* could be so reclaimed. Adam could not be considered a fugitive from his master's labour, when his [former] master had given him permission to work for himself."[26]

Justice Van Ness agreed almost entirely with the insurance company's lawyers. He characterized the paper in Adam's possession as a "contract" for a "conditional emancipation," one that left Adam Wyckoff a free man—at least "as between himself and his former master"—once he had complied with its terms. In this way, Van Ness repressed the issue that the New Jersey legislature and court in *State v. Emmons* had tried to resolve; in effect, he reinstated the pre-1798 New Jersey understanding of an informal manumission as undoing the power relations between a master and his slave without necessarily freeing the master from public responsibility for the no-longer-enslaved person if he or she became dependent or on poor relief. Speaking as a New York judge, he determined that old New Jersey law was better than new or newer New Jersey law. Second, he held that Adam Wyckoff had the right to tender to John Quay the full amount that he owed (or have the insurance company do it for him). He did not have to wait four years. And third, he ruled that New York law was determinative of Adam Wyckoff's status. (On the other hand, he had no doubt that even in New Jersey Adam Wyckoff would be able to enforce this contract against his master by compelling him to emancipate him.) Thus, Adam Wyckoff would be free and admissible as a witness, as soon as it was shown that he had offered to pay Quay "according to the condition of the instrument"—that is, according to the terms of the piece of paper that he had brandished.[27]

The insurance company lawyers quickly put two witnesses on the stand. Each of them testified that he had tried to give Quay $256 on behalf of Adam Wyckoff (presumably each was an employee of the insurance company). Quay had refused the money each time it had been offered. According to one of the two, Quay "did not pretend but that the [purpose of the] paper was to make Adam free."

Adam Wyckoff was then called to the witness stand.

At that moment, according to the court reporter, the face of John Quay, "covered with drops of sweat which burst from every pore, suddenly changed to a deadly paleness—his whole frame was convulsively agitated, and he retired with difficulty and tottering steps from the court-room; and, as we have understood, actually fell at the outside of its door in the hall." He did not return to the courtroom until after his former slave's testimony.[28]

ADAM WYCKOFF'S TESTIMONY went as follows:[29]

In March 1815, he was at work in Quay's barn. Quay came and told him he had a "particular business" for him. But he had to be sure that Adam could keep a secret—even from his wife, "because a woman could not keep a secret." Quay wanted him "to go down and burn some buildings at the Branch." Wyckoff told him that he did not know the way, as he had not been there for twelve or fifteen years. Quay said he would send him to Long Branch with a letter for the Bennets. While he was there, he must look up in the lofts and see where there were good places to set fire to.

Wyckoff did as he was told, although he had not consented to set any fires. At the house, he delivered the letter to Mrs. Bennet. Her husband was sick in the room, with the doctor attending him. She told him to wait, and Wyckoff found the Bennets' young son, whom he asked to show him the property. In the "garrets of the south and west wings of the building" he found straw mats and bedding, which would burn easily, and he saw that much straw was lying in the barn. Back in the kitchen, he was given a letter for his master and for a Mr. Haight (probably Charles Haight), who lived about ten miles away, on the road to Freehold.

When he came home, Quay asked him if there were flammable materials around. There were, Wyckoff answered. Did he know the way now? He did, and "he could go there at any time of night." Quay then told him that he wanted him to go down at night and burn the buildings. Adam told his master that "it was a dreadful thing—state-prison work." If he were caught, people would "throw him into the fire and burn him up." Wyckoff undoubtedly knew that slaves were feared by whites throughout early America as potential arsonists.[30] But Quay said he would protect him: "They sha'nt hurt you." And in another conversation, he told Wyckoff that if he would do it, he would have his freedom and $100. Wyckoff said nothing.

Some days later, on a Tuesday, Quay and his wife took the ferry at Middletown Point to New York City. Wyckoff drove them to the ferry. When Mrs. Quay got out of the wagon and walked to the boat, Quay stayed behind and asked Wyckoff if he had made up his mind. Again, Wyckoff did not answer. Mrs. Quay was going to stay in New York, and Wyckoff should come pick him up on Friday. They would talk further then. On Friday, as they rode back to Freehold, Quay sweetened his offer. If he would do it, Wyckoff would get $100, and he and his wife would both get their freedom. Further, their child (already free because of the 1804 law) would be taught to read and write (as we have seen, this was actually already an obligation under the 1798 slave code, although it was rarely complied with), and be taught "to get her living by her needle." Quay added that Wyckoff and his family should stay with him, in apparent service, for two years (obviously, this was to provide cover and to avoid suspicion), but Quay promised to pay him $100 a year for those two years. So, after two years, Wyckoff would have his family, his freedom, and $300; "he would have a good beginning."

At that point, Wyckoff consented to burn the buildings, telling Quay "he would do it."

Quay gave him detailed instructions, told him "to make a tinder-box and steel, and procure a flint." Wyckoff said he knew how to do all that, and that he had those "instruments" at his former master's house. He went to the house of his former master, but he could not find the materials. Quay then told him to get a steel from a blacksmith, but Wyckoff objected, saying that "people would know." He told Quay he would get an old rasp, grind off the edge, and try that. He practiced trying to make fire with those tools in his garret, and it worked. Then Quay told him to make brimstone matches of cedar. But Wyckoff, who clearly had a much better sense for such things then Quay, disagreed. The matches would break. Instead, he proposed to roll rags in melted brimstone. And that is what he did, at night, when all the family was in bed.

By Thursday the 18th, Quay had received a letter that the Bennets had moved out. Quay was going to see the sheriff that day (presumably on judicial business), and Mrs. Quay was going to see a Mrs. Conover. Alibis were in place. Meanwhile, Quay told Wyckoff to get ready to go to Long Branch that night. He should put his old clothes in the barn and hide the old saddle and bridle. Quay returned about sundown. All was ready, and Adam must go and burn all the buildings, including the barn. He should leave at 9 P.M.

After eating his supper, Adam Wyckoff went to the barn and changed clothes. He followed Quay's directions and took back roads for the nineteen miles or so between Freehold and Long Branch. Quay had told him to put his horse in a nearby shed, but Wyckoff feared that if he were discovered, "he might be cut off from his horse." So, after looking around, he moved his horse to an even more secluded spot in the woods. He then took his "fire works" and walked to the buildings. As he had been instructed, he wandered through all parts of the house, making sure no one was there. Then he set fires throughout the building, using the bedding that had been left in the eaves to start the fires. He walked over to the barn, but by the time he got there, the fire in the main building was beginning to crackle, and flames were beginning to show, and the wind blew out his candle. He became frightened and decided "to quit the horrid business." He ran back to his horse. The horse became frightened at the sight of the flames and set off at full speed, jumping the fence. As the reins of the bridle were old, Wyckoff "was afraid to hold in the horse hard; and for the purpose of managing him, lay over his neck, reaching both hands as near the bits as he could, and sawed them in the mouth of the horse." After a mile and a half or more, the horse finally slowed down. He remembered passing a fish wagon on the way back.

Once home, Wyckoff put his horse in the stable, cleaned him, and thoroughly cleaned his hooves, so that no one would know that he had been out. He changed his clothes, went into the house, and lay down on a bench by the kitchen fire.

At daybreak, Quay came to ask how things had gone. He wanted to know if he had cleaned the horse well. Wyckoff said that he had, but Quay wanted him to do it again. Wyckoff went back to the stable and did as his master wanted. While there, he saw a Mr. Stilwell, who asked for Quay and went to look at the horses. Wyckoff then went to bed.[31]

Later that day, Quay came again, worried that Wyckoff "had not done the business." Why had he not yet heard about the fire? Wyckoff replied that it had rained very hard later in the night. The next day, Quay rode down to Long Branch, purportedly "to see how Bennet had left the house." He returned a day later and told Wyckoff to put a letter for "Capt. Reed" in the post office at Trenton.

A few days later, Quay pressed him again about what had happened. Had he met anyone on the road? Wyckoff mentioned the fish wagon. Quay told him that it was Peter Brewer's. Obviously concerned that Wyckoff might confess, Quay told him that if he ever did, Wyckoff would be put in the state prison. Wyckoff replied that there was no danger that he would. Quay "thereupon renewed his former promises."

In June or July, Wyckoff met an Irish waiter in Trenton, who asked him if he knew anything about the fire. The waiter said that "the Philadelphians" were offering $5,000 to anyone who gave information about who had burned the building. They suspected Quay. Adam replied that Quay "would not do such a thing, as he was a nice man, *and a judge*."[32]

Over the winter, Wyckoff drove Quay to the Perth Amboy ferry to New York "to get his money." Quay again "cautioned him" to keep silent. Wyckoff promised that he would, although he told Quay that "the Philadelphians" had offered him $5,000 if he would talk. Quay reemphasized that the result would be that Wyckoff would end up in the state prison.

Adam Wyckoff first confessed to Charles Haight. Haight asked to meet him at a tavern in Trenton. There, he took him into a private room and told him that if he did not confess he would be taken to New York, that Peter Brewer had sworn that he had seen him on the road that night. Wyckoff "at first denied it, then hesitated, and walked the floor for some time." Haight told him that he was not in danger "because he was a slave, and bound to do what he was bid." Wyckoff said that whether he confessed or not, "state-prison would be his portion." Haight then gave his word that if he told the truth, he would not be punished. Wyckoff then confessed. He "had been very much troubled in his mind, had no rest, and was always afraid."

Haight, who apparently did not yet know about the paper that Quay had given to Adam Wyckoff, here played the other side in the question of Adam's enslavement. Wyckoff was no slave when it came to whether he could testify, at least in New York, but he was a slave in terms of his own liability, certainly as compared to Quay. As a slave, he was nothing but an instrument of his master's will.[33]

At a second meeting, Haight asked Wyckoff whether he was free. He answered that he was, that he had a paper that made him free. Haight asked him to get it. According to Wyckoff's understanding, "by the paper given him by his master, . . . he was to go once a year, as if to pay money to his master, yet he need not, in fact, do so, but that the plaintiff would pay him the money, as he had promised."

At a third meeting, Haight asked Wyckoff to go with him to New York, which he did.

And so his direct testimony ended.

During a "long, minute, and critical" cross-examination, Adam Wyckoff repeatedly insisted that he "thought he was made a free man . . . by means of the writing given him by his master." Little else changed. Charles Haight was recalled, and he too confirmed the testimony he had already given.[34]

What happened to Adam Wyckoff in the period between his "confession" to Charles Haight and the trial is not clear. One later witness on Quay's side, William R. Trotter, reported that Wyckoff had told him that if he went to New York he would have his freedom and $800. He did not say from whom he was to receive that money. Trotter had known Wyckoff in New Jersey, but the conversation he testified about took place in the New York City jail, where Trotter was being confined for debt. Why Adam Wyckoff was in the jail was never spelled out. Perhaps he was being held there as something like a material witness.[35]

In giving his charge to the jury, the judge noted that he'd found Adam Wyckoff's account "plain, connected, [and] consistent," although the jury should "receive and weigh" the man's testimony with "great caution and deliberation." It was Justice Van Ness's conviction that there "remained no reasonable doubt of his truth." And the jury, after retiring for ten minutes, agreed and decided in favor of the Eagle Fire-Company.[36] John Quay would receive no insurance proceeds.

WHAT HAPPENED AFTER the New York verdict? For the court reporter, this was a story about the importance of fire insurance and about the need to expose fraud in order to protect the integrity of insurance: "When fraud, coupled with crime, is dragged from its dark and secret recesses to the glaring light of day, the example is solemn and highly interesting to the community." The transcript of the case was widely advertised in newspapers around the northeastern United States.[37]

Why had John Quay done it? A month after the verdict, in January 1817, a sheriff levied an execution on the goods and property of John Quay, Joshua Bennet, and Jacob Wyckoff. The sheriff took four beds and bedding, six hogs, twelve sheep, and twelve cattle; the farm on which Jacob Wyckoff was living; a house and lot at Middletown Point, then in the possession of a William Little; and "the house and lotts in which John Quay" was living.[38] Presumably, the land on which Bennet's Hotel at Long Branch had been located was taken as well.[39]

What was the nature of the enterprise that had bound Joshua Bennet, Jacob Wyckoff, and John Quay? Quay and Bennet had served as administrators of several estates. Had they taken funds from those estates? Whatever had transpired, Quay, Bennet, and Wyckoff had accumulated a large enough debt that they would lose all their real estate, including their homes and most of their personal property. One might speculate that the possibility that this execution was in the offing had led Quay, in desperation, toward arson and a fraudulent insurance policy.

Was Quay disgraced by the insurance verdict? One might assume so. Yet in November 1817, he still served as a justice in endorsing the manumission of a slave belonging to someone else. And he never faced criminal charges, either in New York or in New Jersey.[40]

In 1818, John Quay brought suit in South Carolina against John McNinch, a South Carolinian. McNinch had hired a black man in Philadelphia, an apparently free man, to serve as his coachman and to drive him back to South Carolina. The free man was, Quay asserted, actually his slave—another slave—who had run away to Philadelphia. Quay wanted damages for McNinch's wrongful appropriation (his "conversion") of his property. Quay sued in trover, the common law action to recover the value of personal property. In doing so, Quay made it clear that he did not want his property returned to him, only money damages. Presumably, he no longer had the means or the desire to keep a slave; yet his escaped slave might be a means of extracting funds from the former slave's new master or employer.

The South Carolina trial court judge disagreed and ruled that the action could not be maintained. When Quay appealed, the South Carolina Constitutional Court agreed with the trial court judge: McNinch had done nothing wrong. According to the court, "He had honestly and fairly hired a man, reputed to be free, in a country [that is, in Pennsylvania] where all men are free, to attend to his lawful business."[41]

When Quay died nine years later, at the age of eighty-seven, he left his "beloved wife," Agnes, an estate valued at only $115, $99 of which came from what was still due him under his Revolutionary War pension. His clothes were valued at $4.[42]

The consequences of the trial lingered on in other ways. Charles Haight, whose testimony had been crucial in establishing Quay's fraud, sued Jonathan Morris, who had testified for Quay. One day in 1819, at breakfast (in the home of the man who had once been sued for libel by John Quay for calling Quay a redheaded Irish horse thief), Morris had evidently declared that Haight "was a rascal and a rogue—that he had taken a false oath, and was a damned perjured rascal." According to one witness to the breakfast, they were at the time "talking something about the burnt buildings and some trial at New York," though the witness couldn't go into specifics. Morris's particular complaint turned on how Haight had described the road back from Long Branch to Freehold, and the presence or absence of a particular black walnut tree in a particular place, as well as that Haight had "drilled or trained a negro to swear against Quay." Haight lost in the Monmouth County lower court, and he lost again before the New Jersey Supreme Court. Evidently those courts thought that there was plausible evidence that Charles Haight had perjured himself in New York City at the trial of John Quay. But in 1824, those decisions were unanimously reversed by the Court for the Correction of Errors. And what happened next is unknown.[43]

As for Adam Wyckoff, I long assumed that after having testified, he would have quickly disappeared into the free black community in New York City. He had obviously played a most dangerous game, one that could have ended in a long prison term—or worse. He had come out unscathed, and he had established his freedom. He wouldn't press his luck and would probably just disappear, perhaps changing his name.

What of Adam Wyckoff's wife and daughter? When the sheriff executed on Quay's property in early 1817, he did not take slave property, presumably because there was none. Certainly by the time of Quay's death, both of them were gone from Quay's household, and they were no part of his estate. Perhaps Quay had quietly let Wyckoff's wife and daughter go away, sometime in the period just before or after the verdict. Maybe they left on their own, and Quay no longer had the legal or social wherewithal to pursue them. Quay never formally manumitted them, although he obviously knew how to carry out a proper manumission. Slaves might no longer have been much use to him once he had lost his house.

And yet the 1830 census reveals that an Adam Wikoff, spelled with an *i*, a free black man over the age of fifty-five, lived in an exclusively black area of Freehold, in Monmouth County, with three children—two boys and one girl—all under age ten, and a wife who was between the ages of thirty-six and fifty-five. Because we don't have the 1820 census records for New Jersey, it is impossible to guess when or whether Adam Wyckoff had reconnected with his wife or when he had moved back to New Jersey. And since the names of household members were not given in the 1830 census, we cannot know if this wife was the same wife he had in 1816 and 1817. But if this was in fact the same Adam, then we might infer that, by 1830, his daughter from 1816 would have left home. Perhaps the three young children in the household were grandchildren, or perhaps his wife (or a different wife) had new children. These are all plausible possibilities. In any event, if Adam

Wikoff was indeed Adam Wyckoff, then in 1830 he was living as a free man within a few miles of where he and the rest of his family had been the enslaved property of John Quay.[44]

Libel, Kidnapping, and Cruelty

In November 1816, just before the beginning of John Quay's arson trial, an article appeared in the *New-York Evening Post*. (William Coleman, a lawyer, was the controversial editor of the paper at the time.)[45] The article described how John C. Hatfield (sometimes Hetfield), an Elizabethtown-based proprietor of ferry sailboats, had arrived in the city on a Saturday afternoon.[46] Hatfield, accompanied by two city marshals, had waited by the Whitehall slip for the arrival of one of the boats owned by Thomas Gibbons. The ferryman managing Gibbons's boat was a "free black man" named Cato Richards. As soon as the boat docked, Hatfield and the two officials boarded it. They beat up the ferryman, forced him out of the boat, and pushed him across the slip. Then, according to the article, they threw him headfirst, "like a dead dog," into Hatfield's boat, and Hatfield immediately set sail for Elizabethtown Point.

All this happened in front of a crowd that watched as "the black man" was "forced along, all covered over with blood." Many might have interfered, but the presence of two officers made it seem as though it were "being done by authority." And so they had been "deterred."

The article continued. It described how years before, Hatfield had purchased Cato Richards from his owner in New York. Hatfield took Richards to New Jersey, "where he received his services" for five or six years, at which point Cato Richards realized that Hatfield had no claim on him, since under New York law (not yet under New Jersey law) he had become free as soon as he had been sold out of the state. Richards left Hatfield's service and went to work for Gibbons and Cornelius Vanderbilt, Hatfield's competitors, "taking charge" of one of their boats. He was "regarded as a very honest, sober man, and perfectly competent to his business." Hatfield, according to the article, had accepted the fact of Richards's freedom.

Why, then, did Hatfield act as he did on that November day? A "P.S." was appended to the article in the *Evening Post*, drafted "since the above was in type." It explained that Hatfield had secured a warrant for Richards's arrest from the governor of New Jersey, requesting the assistance of New York officers of the peace, which explained why the two marshals were in attendance. Cato Richards had been charged with a felony for having stolen or kidnapped his wife from Hatfield. According to the *Evening Post*, although Hatfield and the New Jersey officials surely disagreed, Mrs. Richards was in exactly the same legal position as Cato Richards. She, too, had become a free woman when she was moved out of New York State. She had, however, remained in service with Hatfield apart from her husband. The P.S. concluded: "This gives the transaction a somewhat different, though I do not think a more favourable complexion, except as to the officers who assisted, for to commit an act of cruelty under the colour of law, is only to add another and a heavier thong to the lash of oppression and injustice."[47]

Hatfield sued Coleman for libel, both for accusing him of kidnapping and for accusing him of cruelty.

Why Hatfield brought suit is mysterious. The case would not seem to have been winnable in New York City. Perhaps Hatfield, who was a small-time operator in the world of Hudson ferries rather than a participant in the new technology of steam, thought that the article might drive him out of business. In any case, this is what happened anyway, and the trial did not help him restore his reputation.

The trial began in April 1817. Hatfield's lawyer began with a reading of the article. The defendant admitted publication, and Hatfield's lawyer rested.

Coleman's defense (he represented himself) began by asking that the first count of the libel cause of action—that he had charged Hatfield with "kidnapping"—be retracted. The P.S. he had written acknowledged that the events occurred under the guise of a state warrant. Thus, the article, read as a whole, did not accuse Hatfield of having kidnapped Cato Richards.

On the other hand, with regard to the other allegation contained in the article—of "cruelty"—the defense intended to repel any allegation of malice—a necessary feature of a charge of libel—by presenting a witness. The witness, William Curtis, explained that he was the source of the facts that Coleman had printed. Curtis was an officer of the New York Manumission Society, who had fortuitously been present on the dock that day. Implicitly, Coleman was claiming that he had simply reproduced what someone else had reported.

Hatfield's attorney rejected both "moves." Coleman had assumed responsibility for the contents of the article, and that also precluded him from retracting the charge of kidnapping contained in the piece. And malice was beside the point when a libel was published. Coleman disagreed, and he then worked to distinguish a civil action in libel from criminal libel. In the latter, the absence of malice was no defense, but it was different, he claimed, in a civil action for damages. Coleman also wanted testimony introduced about the truth or falsity of the accusation of "cruelty," as truth repelled the suggestion of malice.

The court decided to admit the testimony.

Several witnesses described how roughly Richards had been treated when he was taken from "Vanderbilt's boat." One thought he had seen Richards spit blood and his hand being stamped on.

Hatfield's attorney introduced a New Jersey warrant requesting the help of New York's "constables and marshalls" to deliver Cato Richards as a fugitive from justice. Hatfield, Richards, and the officers all testified on behalf of the prosecution. (Note that in putting Cato Richards on the stand, Hatfield's lawyer was acknowledging that Cato was a free man. One might wonder, though, how uncoerced his testimony could possibly have been understood to be.) All, including Cato Richards, denied that any more "violence" had been used than was necessary to prevent his escape. Richards had left the one boat voluntarily and gone to the other. He "was treated with some liquor on the way." He was not thrown into the hold, but he was kept in the hold until they reached the Jersey shore. Later testimony revealed that Richards had recently "induced his wife to leave" Hatfield's service, and that "she took away her bed, and the clothes which her child wore, and came with Cato to this city."

Why had Hatfield gone to the grand jury in New Jersey? He had done so, his lawyer explained, in order to "regain possession of his property." What property? For "stealing the woman and the other property." It is impossible to conclude from the transcript whether Hatfield actually believed that Mrs. Richards was still his slave, yet he had evidently been able to convince a New Jersey grand jury that she was.

After they returned to Elizabethtown, Hatfield had put Richards into the local jail and told him that "unless he would serve him for four years, he would put him in the state prison for five years." Richards might "take his choice." Richards then "chose" to serve Hatfield for four years longer, and he "executed" a writing that bound himself.

Coleman's defense insisted that this narrative proved undue and excessive cruelty in the "seizure." All that the *Evening Post* had done was report facts, and reported facts negated malice. An essential element of the charge of libel was not present. Hatfield had no right to seize Cato Richards; he was a free man, and his wife was a free woman. The application to the state was fraudulent. Richards had not stolen his wife; the only things Hatfield lost that were his were, perhaps, "the trifling articles which were hers." "Under such pretence[,] to obtain a warrant backed by the executive of this state, was a flagrant abuse of justice." Hatfield's subsequent conduct was "infamous in the extreme." Coleman presumed that a New York jury would agree with him that Hatfield's conduct was "base, cruel, infamous." Were these facts presented to him again, he would print a similar article immediately.

The mayor gave a charge that leaned heavily to Coleman's side. The question resolved itself, he believed, into one question: had Coleman published the article with malicious intent. If not, the jury should acquit—which the jury did, after about five minutes. In his article on the case, Coleman crowed that one member of the jury had told him that although he differed with Coleman in politics and did not like his paper, "he would have set three days and three nights before he would have consented to come in with any other verdict."[48]

NOTHING ABOUT THIS libel case should seem surprising. Here again we see the interconnections between New York and New Jersey; here again we watch New York City legal actors shaping and being shaped by the New Jersey regime of gradual emancipation; here again we can observe the uncertain and fraught situation of a freed individual like Cato Richards. Indeed, he was free, but burdened by a racist culture that presumed the legitimacy of a white master's power.

What did freedom mean for Cato Richards? Or, rather, what did it mean to be bound to service? Evidently, John C. Hatfield had thought about that question and about how to articulate such terms in legal language. When he and Cato Richards "executed" the writing that bound Richards to service while he sat in that New Jersey jail, the writing Hatfield drafted (or had drafted) went as follows:

> This Indenture . . . [w]itnesseth that Cato Richards, a free black man aged about twenty-six years, formerly a slave belonging to John C. Hetfield . . . hath of his own free will and accord, . . . placed and bound himself a servant unto the said . . . Hetfield . . . to dwell with & serve him for and during the full term of four years from the day of the date hereof during all which term the said servant [for] the said master will & faithfully shall serve, his secrets keep, his lawful commands everywhere readily obey, hurt to his said master he shall not do nor willingly suffer it to be done by others, but of the same

forthwith give notice to his said master. The goods of his master he shall not embezzle or waste nor lend them without consent, from the service of his said master he shall not at any time absent himself without leave, but in all things as a good and faithful servant shall & will behave and demean himself towards his said master & all his. And the said John C. Hetfield doth hereby agree to and with the said Cato that he will during the term aforesaid find & provide him with competent & sufficient meat, drink, washing, lodging, clothing, and all other necessaries fit and convenient for such a servant.

Richards gave his X. Hatfield signed. There were two witnesses.[49]

Richards was free, Hatfield acknowledged. Like any other free worker, his service would be rooted in his own agreement, in a contract. And his service was for a delimited term. But the form and the content of his service replicated slavery. While in the style of an employment contract, it said nothing about pay. It was nothing but a contract to avoid imprisonment, a Hobbesian bargain. We should note as well that the agreement said nothing about Richards's wife and child. When Richards was captured and brought back to New Jersey, they may have been left in New York, where he had brought them. Or did they also return to Hatfield's household?

We don't know what Cato Richards knew, how he had calculated his own and his family's interest in this situation. Was the contract even read to him? Did he realize that his wife was as free as he was? Was he making the best of a bad situation, knowing or believing that Hatfield had the means to send him to state prison? Or was he just biding his time, waiting for escape or for new opportunities? Did the form of the contract hide other understandings and unformalized agreements?[50]

As for Hatfield: One suspects that Hatfield wanted Cato Richards not to be working for Gibbons and Vanderbilt, his competitors.[51] Or perhaps Hatfield knew he was going to be leaving the ferryboat field soon, and he wanted to maximize his assets. By binding Cato Richards, by contractually re-creating a slave-like relationship, he would force anyone who wanted Richards's labor and skill to deal with him first.

In fact, this is exactly what occurred. On July 17, 1817, just three months after the end of the libel trial, John C. Hatfield sold his boat, the *Industry*, to Gibbons for $750.[52] Around the same time, he sold Gibbons the remainder of Richards's term of service for $300. The assignment of the term occurred "with the consent of the said Cato."[53]

Gibbons owned rice plantations in Georgia and in South Carolina, and he knew all about slavery. Apparently he did not want to mimic slavery in his relations with his employees in the New Jersey to New York ferry trade. He certainly did not want to have to care for an employee. After he concluded his transaction with Hatfield, he drafted a new agreement with Cato Richards. He would not provide meat, drink, washing, lodging, clothing, and the other necessities that Hatfield had bound himself to offer Richards. In exchange, Richards would receive "a commutation" of ten dollars a month. Gibbons's papers show him paying Richards a regular salary for the next several years.[54]

"Harboring or Assisting to Convey Away"

By 1817, Thomas Gibbons had invested heavily in steamboats, as well as in sailboats (like the *Industry*). He was engaged in a world-changing struggle with his hated rival, Aaron Ogden, for control of the steamboat ferry trade across the Hudson. After having moved from Georgia to Elizabethtown around 1802, Gibbons had purchased the space that constituted Elizabethtown "port," including the dock from which many boats set out for New York City. At first Ogden had rented dock space from him (or from the family trust that Gibbons controlled). He and Ogden were partners, of a sort. But Gibbons and Ogden had a dramatic falling out in 1816. By then, Ogden was relying on a license from John Livingston to use the steamboat technology that had been developed by Robert Fulton and Robert Livingston. In 1808, Fulton and Livingston had received an exclusive franchise from the New York legislature that covered all steamboat traffic to and from New York on the Hudson River. Ogden's license in that exclusive franchise would eventually, in 1824, be defeated in the U.S. Supreme Court in the famous case of *Gibbons v. Ogden*. However, that defeat—or Gibbons's victory—lay in the future.[55]

In 1817 and 1818, Gibbons and Ogden were trying to destroy each other—both legally and by other means. At the same time, each was trying to build up a ferry business for himself, which meant working to drive out other competitors along the way, men like John Hatfield.

On July 4, 1818, Thomas Gibbons offered free passage on his boats. That day, Harry—a slave owned by a Dr. Isaac Morse of Elizabethtown—took advantage of that widely advertised opportunity. He got on the *Nonpareil*, one of Gibbons's boats (not a steamboat), which was captained by Cato

Richards, who by then went by the name Cato Williams. Then he disappeared.[56]

Why Harry traveled on the *Nonpareil* that day became a matter of controversy. Of course the simple answer would be that he took the opportunity that Gibbons had offered of free passage to get to New York and freedom. But because Dr. Morse's family may have been involved in gathering up New Jersey slaves for sale to southern plantations (the kidnapping controversy was at the center of public debate and attention during the summer of 1818), other possibilities were raised during the trial. Dr. Morse's attorney argued implicitly that a boat captained by a free black man was a kind of "attractive nuisance" that would have drawn enslaved people to it. Gibbons and his attorney, William Halstead, suggested that Harry had been paid by Dr. Morse to run away, that Harry was a difficult and unsalable piece of property—"a worthless fellow," according to Zadock Tooker, a free black man and a witness for Gibbons. According to this line of argument, Dr. Morse had encouraged Harry to escape, concluding that he could get more for Harry—or out of Harry—by suing Gibbons than in any other way.[57]

In any case, enslaved Harry took passage on the boat. Forty passengers had crowded into the small boat that day, taking advantage of Gibbons's offer. As a result, so Cato Williams claimed, he had not seen Harry, at least not until they had arrived in New York City. Zadock Tooker testified that Cato Williams and Harry were on opposite sides of the boat throughout the passage, and he did not see them converse with each other. Indeed, he saw nothing that indicated that they knew each other. But when they landed, he may have heard Williams call Harry "by the name of Harry Morse" to help him "make fast the boat." Williams disagreed; he had called to Bill Morse, another black person on board, not to anyone named Harry. He did not know Harry. In any case, after they landed, Harry, Cato Williams, and Zadock Tooker went off with a large group to get a drink to celebrate the holiday. Harry then disappeared.[58]

Harry's owner, Dr. Morse, sent his son-in-law, Jonas Marsh—a slave trader and later a southern plantation owner—to New York and to Long Island to look for Harry. Marsh failed to find him.

Dr. Morse then sued Gibbons for Harry's value ($400, he claimed). He sued under one provision of the 1798 New Jersey slave code, one that reproduced a much older New Jersey colonial law: "Any person . . . found guilty of harbouring, entertaining, or concealing any slave, or conveying or assisting to convey away such slave, and if such slave should be lost, die, or be otherwise destroyed, or should be disabled or rendered unserviceable, the person . . . so harbouring, entertaining, concealing, conveying, or assisting to convey away such slave to the owner or owners, to be recovered by action of debt or trespass on the case."[59]

Dr. Morse was represented by William Chetwood, who was Aaron Ogden's brother-in-law. After an elaborate trial in Elizabethtown before Chief Justice Andrew Kirkpatrick, the judge gave detailed jury instructions that supported Dr. Morse's claim. The jury then awarded Dr. Morse $250 plus costs.

Gibbons, no stranger to slavery or to litigation, was furious about being sued. He drafted detailed notes for his attorney (Gibbons was legally trained and a sophisticated reader of legal texts). It is not entirely clear when those notes were drafted. I suspect that he sat down to write them at the conclusion of testimony at the trial, before concluding statements by the attorneys for both sides. If so, he was making suggestions (given his disposition, more like instructions or demands) for what William Halstead, his attorney, should include when providing jury instructions to the court in his closing arguments.[60]

Gibbons began by emphasizing that no ferryboat operator had ever been charged under the section of the 1798 code that created a cause of action for owners whose slaves had been conveyed away. That section reproduced the content of statutes enacted by the New Jersey provincial and colonial legislatures. The cause of action had existed for more than a century, yet no slave owner had ever recovered against any boat captain or owner. The theoretical liability of the ferry owner was, Gibbons thought, countered by the general obligation of a common carrier to take all passengers who wished to travel. Even as "hundreds of slaves" had "been conveyed out of the State" in the twenty-two years since the 1798 law had been enacted, no suit had ever been brought.

Others agreed. Richard Adams, a former boatman, testified that it had long been the "general custom" to carry slaves on board boats without a pass. He had worked on the boats of John C. Hatfield and those of a Mr. Wilson, and he had sometimes been on Colonel Ogden's boat, though he had never worked for Ogden. In his experience, passes were never required on any of their boats. Another witness agreed, noting that Ogden did not require a pass from slaves. In his brief for Gibbons, William Halstead argued that because the statute at issue was a "penal" statute and an abridgment of the common law, it ought to be construed narrowly—that is, only to knowing and intentional acts.[61]

Gibbons's notes flogged the complex and much litigated question as to whether he, as an employer, should be liable for the acts of his servants. The statute made someone who aided or abetted in the escape of a slave liable. But who could be held liable? Gibbons believed he had delegated responsibility to Joseph Periam and William Price, his agents and employees (by the time the Morse case had come to trial, Gibbons was in litigation with Periam, and Periam testified against him). According to Gibbons, he had forcefully told his employees not to take slaves on board: "When Mr. Periam informed [me] of the Law in the same breath I ~~ordered~~ told him to stop all people of colour." That statement demonstrated, at least in his mind, that responsibility should be placed on their shoulders. On the other hand, Gibbons admitted at another point that he had told his employees that free people of color should be allowed to take passage on his boats. How to distinguish the free from the enslaved? Gibbons did not have an answer. But he noted what must have seemed odd to someone raised in Georgia: that there was no law in New Jersey requiring that a slave must have a pass when out and about, away from the control of a master.[62]

Gibbons's former agent Periam claimed that when Gibbons had said that all should travel free on the third, fourth, and fifth of July 1818, he had made no exception for slaves, had said "nothing respecting them." Price, who was the ticket taker and the manager of Gibbons's dock, agreed. Gibbons had said nothing before July 4 "respecting blacks." After July 4, Gibbons had instructed him "not to let any black person go on board his boats." Still, until Dr. Morse sued, Price had no idea that it was against the law to let slaves go as passengers on boats. On cross-examination, Periam admitted that when he had first been hired by Gibbons, he had warned him that if he carried any slaves he might be made liable if any escaped. Gibbons had then told him that he must not permit "negroes" to go in the boat. But some time later, Gibbons had told Periam "that he might let free blacks go in his boat, for their shilling was as good as the shilling of any other person."[63]

What of Cato Williams (or Richards)? Did Gibbons think he was responsible or liable, like Periam or Price? In his notes for his attorney, Gibbons's first answer was no. "Cato cannot read. The boat never went from dry dock without Mr. Periam or Mr. Price being there[,] and they both read." At a later point in his notes, he returned to this point: "Cato the servant is not liable because Harry hid himself from Cato and therefore Cato [is] not liable, for certainly the Statute cannot mean that if a slave is hid . . . from the captain on [board] the boat and is conveyed away, that he is liable—in such case there is no knowledge—and it will be an outrage . . . to make Cato liable when this slave hid away in his boat." And further: "Cato says I had ordered [him] not to carry any but what he knew free or what had papers." But who would examine the papers? "Was it not Mr. Periam or Mr. Price?" It was their duty to check, and they had not done so. And still further on: "Cato will prove his orders have always been to obey laws . . . that he does not [k]now this boy, but he knew all slave blacks that he saw on board, and he did not see a stranger[;] therefore he did not carry Harry knowingly."

In his own testimony, Cato Williams testified that he had always worked to keep enslaved people from using Gibbons's boat to escape from New Jersey. Gibbons had told him not to carry slaves "without a pass." All the "coloured people" he saw on Independence Day on board had been free. Price confirmed Williams's testimony. He had "turned" slaves out of Williams's boat more than once, but not often. On the other hand, he had "turned away hundreds from" ferryboats managed by others. The reporter for the case report added, "Cato appeared to be very candid, and did not manifest a disposition to carry away negroes or conceal them more than any other boatman," and he "can prove" that one of them "was landed in N.York on Col. Ogden's sail boat."[64]

But at another point in his notes, as he contemplated various strategic possibilities, Gibbons considered the possible advantages of arguing for Cato Williams's liability: "Can a free black be sued[?]—he is hired at $10 a month—paid monthly." Various precedents provided authority for this possibility. "If my servant without my notice puts my beasts in another's land[,] my servant is trespasser, and not I"; "If my servant sell[s] an unsound horse, I am not liable, unless I warrant the horse sound—look for this case"; "The acts of a servant shall not bind his master unless he acts by the authority of the master." And more, including, "If a Master is liable for the wrong[,] his servant may burn a house, and the master would be made liable," which surely was not the case. And on new sheets, on which he summarized the case with citations in the margins: "We say the suit, if any suit can be maintained[,] should be against the boatman—a free man hired at $10—a month."[65]

Whoever might be held liable, Gibbons believed that it could not be "pretended" that he had personally aided or abetted in Harry's escape: "You all know me better." If there were a cause of action available on this unused provision of the statute, it should not be mobilized against him as the employer and the owner of the boat.

On this question, however, Chief Justice Kirkpatrick would give clear instructions to the jury, instructions that entirely rejected Gibbons's sense of his innocence. The owner of a passage boat should be the only one held responsible. Gibbons was the owner, the "advertiser of the terms," and the "receiver of the profits." He should not be able to "exonerate himself" by claiming to have given contrary orders to his servants, his employees. It was he who had "the ultimate government, direction, and contract." Could it be tolerated, Kirkpatrick continued, with a racist flourish and probably pointing to Cato Williams, that Gibbons could "employ a black man, perhaps a slave, to navigate his boat," and then excuse himself from liability by demonstrating that he had instructed that "black man, perhaps a slave . . . to do no unlawful act[?]" The owner of the boat, Gibbons, might have a cause of action against an employee who had been "the immediate wrong-doer," but Gibbons could not put an employee in his place as the party responsible for Dr. Morse's loss.[66]

During the trial, there was a great deal of indirect and suggestive testimony about the circumstances that might or might not have led to Harry's departure from Dr. Morse's household. What was going on there? Zadock Tooker's testimony focused on his conversations with a white man named Van Ort who boarded at Dr. Morse's house. Van Ort had tried to convince Tooker, who was free, "to go with him to the southward." It was, Van Ort assured him, "a fine place for one to go if he did well, for he could make five dollars a day there, where he could [make only] one here." Obviously Tooker was not taken with this possibility, which would probably have led to his re-enslavement. Tooker said that he had seen numbers of black people at Morse's house, people who were "strangers." A white witness described a man named Morris, "a coloured man" who was Van Ort's companion. Morris dressed well, and "he sometimes said that he was free." Van Ort used him "as a kind of stool-pigeon, to decoy or persuade other blacks to go south with him."[67]

The white witness testified that he knew William Stone, Jonas Marsh's brother-in-law and the partner of Jonas Marsh's brother, John C. Marsh (Jonas Marsh was Dr. Morse's son-in-law, who had gone looking for absent Harry in New York City). That season, the summer of 1818, Stone and John C. Marsh had been purchasing "negroes" for plantations in Louisiana. The witness had seen nearly fifty on board a vessel and on shore waiting to board. He had watched the vessel leave. Was Morse involved? The witness testified that Dr. Morse had given him a check for $350 for a slave he had sold to Van Ort. And Van Ort had apparently turned his money (the money Van Ort used to purchase slaves) over to Morse to hold for him. There were, the witness testified, two or three cargoes of slaves sent off that season, on their way to plantations in the Deep South, the last boat leaving from South Amboy in October 1818. Before their departure, those "negroes" were "kept" in several places, including Isaac Morse's house in Elizabethtown.[68]

And what of enslaved Harry, who had disappeared? The witness had heard Dr. Morse describe Harry as a "gentleman" and that "it took him all the time to watch Harry, and Harry all the time to watch him, and that he had better do his work himself." What that meant, whether it suggested that Morse had encouraged Harry to free himself by escaping, was left unexplained. In his notes, Gibbons suggested an alternative: Harry would be worth quite a bit if he were shipped South, but he was worth very little as part of Morse's household. (But did that mean that Morse allowed him to escape in order to save him from a life in a southern plantation, as an alternative to selling him? That possibility was not raised by either side.) Another witness described Harry as a "lazy fellow" and often drunk. He had seen him the worse for liquor seven or eight times. He would be worth $150 or $200 drunk in the morning. If he had been industrious and sober, he might be worth $300. The implication all this left was that Morse had concluded he was better off suing Gibbons. The 1798 law became a kind of insurance policy that covered for Harry's defects.[69]

Toward the end of Gibbons's notes, he tried out a summary paragraph: "Plaintiff [Morse] is one of those men, who contrary to Law—and contrary to habit, and custom, has been . . . aiding and abetting in trafficking in human flesh." It might be wondered, he continued, why he, Thomas Gibbons, "a man from the South" and a slave owner (someone who owned several rice plantations in South Carolina and Georgia), would speak in this manner. (One assumes that here his notes were rehearsing his own potential testimony at trial.) The answer, wrote Gibbons, was that he had adjusted to the social and legal circumstances he found himself in. One acted differently in "different countries." "In one country a man will nourish his aged Parents, in another he will knock their brains out, and all equally lawful." There was "a wide difference, in respect to this matter, between a Virginian, a Carolinian, and a Jerseyman,—because Laws[,] customs and habits in the one country warrant slavery, and allow the practice, [where] in the other it is expressly forbid[den]." The contrast he was searching for—between a "free" New Jersey and an enslaved South—drifted off into incoherence: "The man of the North who would be aiding and assisting kidnapping and dealing in human flesh, that man in the South would be willing to murder." But then the notes he was drafting returned to the kidnapping controversy of 1818: The existence of "the very combination of the Plaintiff, his son in law Marsh," and others "obliged our Legislature in a late Session, to pass a highly penal law making this traffic [a] felony."[70]

Chief Justice Kirkpatrick's jury instructions entirely rejected Gibbons's intimations. Indeed, he criticized Dr. Morse's attorney, William Chetwood, for not having objected to Gibbons's introduction of evidence of the kidnapping controversy. As we have already seen, Kirkpatrick ruled that Gibbons was the proper person to be sued. Then, in response to the unarticulated but implicit problem of how to distinguish free blacks from enslaved people in a state committed to gradual emancipation, he introduced a presumption that became the core holding in this case. In New Jersey, he wrote, "all black men, . . . are *prima facie* slaves, and are to be dealt with as such. The colour of the man was sufficient evidence that he was a slave until the contrary appeared. All our laws . . . upon this subject are founded on this principle, and all men of this colour are to be dealt with upon this principle."[71]

Sixteen years after gradual emancipation had been introduced, at a time when the number of free blacks in the state was already substantially greater than the declining number of slaves, New Jersey in 1821 established a presumption that black people were slaves. (The 1820 census identified 7,557 enslaved people and 12,460 "free non-white" people in New Jersey.)

Ferry operators had no excuse if they allowed black people passage on their boats and slave owners then sued them for the loss of their property. The presumption simplified the legal process, which is what presumptions were supposed to do, and it constituted something of a gift to slave owners. The burden of proof was now on the ferryboat owner, who would have to show that he knew who was free and who was enslaved. And more: "All men of this colour" were "to be dealt with" on the "principle" that they were enslaved. To be free did not free one from the presumption. Only proof of freedom, presumably a valid deed of manumission, would do so.[72] (One can only wonder what this would have meant for Adam Wyckoff if Quay's case had been tried in New Jersey after *Gibbons v. Morse*.)

In the context of New Jersey's regime of gradual emancipation, what Kirkpatrick had done was radical and reactionary. It countered Gibbons's apparently naive faith that New Jersey's rules and legal culture differed from those in the South and that New Jersey was increasingly like its neighbor New York. Indeed, when Jacob Wheeler, a New Yorker, published a short treatise on the law of slavery to serve the needs of southern lawyers, he pointed to *Gibbons v. Morse*, along with a number of older southern cases, for the rule that presumed the enslavement of black people.[73]

Gibbons, of course, appealed. However, one suspects that he did so without much hope of success. Halstead's brief to the New Jersey Court for the Correction of Errors flailed around, trying to find a point of entry to counter Kirkpatrick's presumption. He introduced a contrary long-established evidentiary presumption: "It is a rule of law that no man is presumed to do an illegal act. To take a slave, knowing him to be such, is an illegal act; therefore if a man takes one, he is presumed not to know until it is proved against him." One presumption, Halstead argued, was as good as another. Why choose one presumption over another? But that was, as Halstead must have known, a relatively weak counter. Implicitly, Kirkpatrick had already made that choice. Why would the rest of the court disagree? Beyond that, Halstead acknowledged, "this doctrine"—the presumption that all black people were slaves until the contrary was shown—had been laid down "at the circuits," by which he meant the federal courts that enforced the federal fugitive slave law. But, he insisted, the circuit courts had never gone as far as the New Jersey court had gone. They had used the presumption only in situations in which the capacity of a black person to testify as a witness had been put into question.

Halstead hoped that the New Jersey court would instead choose laws that suited "all the changes and exigencies of our . . . progress." A principle like this—one without "foundation in the moral stability of justice"—should, if it continued at all, "be confined within the very letter of authority and precedent, and not be extended." He hoped that an "enlightened court in this age" would not adopt it to cover situations like the one in this case, that it would not "extend a principle so hostile to the feelings of freemen—so repugnant to the feelings of humanity."[74]

But of course he was wrong. The court silently affirmed Kirkpatrick's jury charge. The presumption had become ruling New Jersey doctrine.

Stages in the Life of a Presumption

Two years later, in 1823, a slave owner sued Henry Moore for the loss of his slave. Moore was the captain of the *Olive Branch*, a steamboat owned by Robert M. Livingston. A Middlesex County court found for Moore, holding that there was no evidence Moore was responsible for the slave's escape. The slave owner appealed, relying on *Gibbons v. Morse*, and the New Jersey Supreme Court reversed the decision. According to Chief Justice Ewing

(Kirkpatrick had been forced into retirement in the interim), *Gibbons v. Morse* settled the matter. The only difference between the two cases was that in this case the captain, rather than the owner, was sued. According to Ewing, that only made the case an easier one. A captain took responsibility for whomever was on board his boat; that was a matter beyond dispute.[75]

IN APRIL 1824, an attorney in New Brunswick wrote Thomas Gibbons a short note: "One day last week a valuable negro belonging to Mr. George Boice near this City—was carried to New York from this place in the *Steam Boat Bellona* [one of Gibbons's boats]. Mr. Boice has directed [me] to take legal steps in his behalf. I have addressed you a line to say, that I shall be compelled to do so unless the negro is returned to him the beginning of the week."[76]

The "valuable negro" was not returned. Soon thereafter, the attorney initiated suit in the Middlesex County court.

Gibbons's attorneys demurred to the charge of having allowed Boice's slave to escape. Chief Justice Ewing, sitting as judge in the county court, sustained the demurrer. In effect, the case was thrown out. Why? The lawyer had made an error. Boice's complaint, as drafted, had alleged that Gibbons and his agents "wrongfully and illegally" conveyed "away the said negro man Tom, the slave of the said George Boice." That phrasing was much too broad. The language made it seem as if all that would be necessary for Boice to prevail was evidence that the slave had traveled on Gibbons's boat. It read the presumption as if it conclusively directed liability against those who owned or were in charge of a boat whenever an enslaved person used that boat to escape.

According to Ewing, the complaint ought to have required Boice to demonstrate the "knowledge and intention" of Gibbons or of his employees. Ewing believed that proof of guilt—which could mean negligence or inattention, as well as active participation in a slave's escape—should be necessary to sustain an action under the 1798 statute. Slaves had will and capacity. Not every escape by boat could be blamed on the boat's captain or owner. It was certainly imaginable that an escaping slave might use a boat without making her- or himself known to the captain or owner of the boat. Gibbons should not be held responsible if there was no "knowledge and intention" on his part or on the part of his employees. Thus, the case was thrown out.

But even as Ewing sustained the demurrer and narrowed his predecessor's presumption by requiring more precise language in the pleadings, he also reiterated the court's commitment to Kirkpatrick's understanding of the significance of racial identity. The result in *Boice v. Gibbons* did not suggest any change in that regard.[77]

AT ABOUT THE SAME TIME, however, in the case of *Fox v. Lambson* (1826), Ewing acknowledged that he hoped that the presumption would not have a long life. This was not a case about an escape by ferryboat. Rather, it concerned a challenge to the competence of black people to testify at trial. In one part of his opinion, Ewing surveyed cases dating back to 1789 that had ruled in favor of the testimonial capacity of black people. He noted an 1813 case in which one side had insisted that nothing short of a paper record of manumission should be sufficient to prove capacity. But the court in that earlier case had rejected that rigorous standard. Instead, it had held that proof that a black person had been "considered and reputed by his neighbors to be free from his childhood" was sufficient to admit that person as a witness. So would it be in this first part of *Fox v. Lambson*. Over time, "our act of 1804," the gradual emancipation statute, would, Ewing hoped, "speedily wipe out the stain of slavery and leave us only the reproach that it once polluted the statute book and the soil of New Jersey."

For Ewing, the analogy to adverse possession of real estate solved the problem of how to prove freedom (and how to counter the presumption of black enslavement). The "quiet, peaceable and adverse possession of real estate for twenty years" raised "a presumption of title." Likewise, "the unquestioned and uninterrupted possession of freedom for more than that period is . . . sufficient to overcome the presumption arising from color." With the increasing number of black people living freely in an emancipating New Jersey, Kirkpatrick's presumption would over time become a nullity.

But not yet. Another challenge in the appeal that was *Fox v. Lambson* went again to the competence of a black person to testify, in this case a female black witness who had evidently lived as a free person for nearly thirty years. Was her manumission in 1797 sufficiently proven by the introduction into evidence of the Salem County manumission book, an official county record book that contained copies of the records of the deed as well as the acknowledgments by the county judges and the overseers of the poor? Ewing reviewed the legislation and formalistically concluded that it was not. The actual manumission documents had to be brought in to prove freedom.

Otherwise, this former slave—or apparently former slave—was held not competent to testify.[78]

OGDEN V. PRICE, decided the following year, in 1827, brought together many of the themes and issues that had colored the gradual emancipation regime for nearly a generation. Many repeat players, the lawyers and judges who have shaped our story, appeared as well. Smith Scudder, who would later represent Henry Force in the 1840 appeal of *Force v. Haines*, and Joseph Hornblower, who was still practicing law, not yet appointed to the New Jersey Supreme Court, together represented Oliver W. Ogden. On the other side, William Halstead, who had recently been Thomas Gibbons's attorney, appeared for the brothers Price, who believed they were entitled to the services of the child of a slave. Chief Justice Ewing and Justice Gabriel Ford each wrote opinions in the case.

A "black girl," Betty, had been born to enslaved parents, Prime (or Priam) and Jude (or Judah). All three of them belonged to Oliver Ogden.[79] In 1816, Ogden sold Betty and her parents to Thomas Morrell, a former Revolutionary War soldier who had become a well-known itinerant Methodist minister. The price Ogden received from Morrell for the three of them was $450. At the time of the sale, Prime and Jude—sold "forever," as slaves typically were—were thirty-three and twenty-seven years old. Betty, who was around five in 1816, was sold on terms that gave Morrell her "service . . . agreeable to the Acts of the Legislature in such case made and provided for those born under and provided for by said Acts." That is, she would be entitled to her freedom when she turned twenty-one. But until then, her status was unclear.

In 1817, Morrell sold all of them to Phineas Moore for $525. And in 1824, Moore sold the three of them, along with "three younger ones[—]one boy and two girls" (children born to Prime and Jude in the intervening years)—to Elihu Price. At that time, Moore received only $100 for the package.

In 1816, soon after he had purchased Prime, Jude, and Betty from Oliver Ogden, Reverend Morrell had drafted and signed a separate "promise." If Prime would serve him or his "assigns" "faithfully and diligently" for the next six years and four months—that is, until just before Prime's fortieth birthday—Morrell would manumit him, as long as Prime would "do and perform such labour and work as shall reasonably be required of him, as an obedient and faithful servant ought to do." Likewise, Prime's wife, Jude, would be freed after eight more years of "faithful and obedient" service. Morrell obviously understood the restrictions that New Jersey's legislature and judicial interpretations had placed on a slaveholder's freedom to manumit. He wanted to avoid any risk of having to support Jude or Prime after manumission. The document conditioned his promise on the "health and bodily ability" of Prime and Jude—that is, their capacity to earn their own way and not end up as dependents needing care from the overseers of the poor of a locality. He would be discharged "from any subsequent liability to maintain and support them or either of them" after emancipation. Clearly, the minister did not want any responsibility for care.[80]

When Morrell sold the three a year later, he apparently did not tell the purchaser, Phineas Moore, about his "promise." Or, as the agreed-upon statement of facts in the case put it, Moore "did not hear or understand that any instrument of writing had been given by Morrell promising to manumit Prime and Jude." But Prime knew the promise Morrell had made to him and to his wife. Or at least he understood its rough terms. And he told Moore that Morrell had agreed to make him and his family free at the end of seven years from the time of the bill of sale from Ogden to Morrell. Moore agreed to abide by that understanding. He promised to manumit Prime and Jude at the end of seven years.

But Moore didn't do as he had told Prime he would do. Instead, he sold the family to Price. When Moore sold them, he told Price that "he had better manumit Prime before he reached forty." (By then, Prime was probably already forty, at least if the ages given in the trial record are accurate.) And Price resolved to do it "immediately." One might guess that the much reduced price they fetched by 1824 reflected both the general decline in the prices of New Jersey slaves and the limited term they were expected to serve.[81]

But Elihu Price did not end up manumitting Prime or anyone else in his family. Soon after the purchase, Price went bankrupt, and taking advantage of a provision of New Jersey's "insolvent act," he assigned "all his estate real and personal" to his brothers Robert Price and Joseph D. Price. Prime, Jude, and Betty were "mentioned and included in the inventory attached to the . . . assignment." That is, they were understood as still movable and marketable property.

At that point, Prime and Jude disappear from the narrative constructed by agreement by the lawyers who litigated *Ogden v. Price*. This became a case about who was entitled to Betty's services, and for how long. It may be that Prime and Jude were manumitted, informally, offstage. Perhaps because Prime was already over forty, the best way for him to be freed, from the standpoint of his former owners (whomever they were), was for him to take a ferry to New York or to travel to Philadelphia and just disappear. He and Jude may have established a new life with their younger children else-where. On the other hand, Betty, their oldest child, who was thirteen by then, apparently moved back to the household of her first "owner," Oli-ver W. Ogden of Elizabethtown. That is why the case became *Ogden v. Price* when Elihu's brothers sued because they could not lay their hands on Betty, whom they regarded as their property.[82]

In any event, thirteen-year-old Betty was "received and taken into" Oliver Ogden's household, where she had lived eight years earlier. When the brothers Price, who had purchased Betty along with her parents, asked Ogden "to give up said Girl," he refused to do so, even though, according to the complaint, he was well aware of the assignment of Betty from Elihu Price to them. The brothers then went to a small claims court in Essex County to sue for the loss of their property. There, the local justice of the peace ruled that Ogden was guilty of "harboring" Betty and gave the brothers a token judgment for one dollar, plus costs.

The case was then appealed to the New Jersey Supreme Court. One as-sumes that the appeal was brought solely because of the uncertainty of Betty's legal status, and that of other similarly situated children of slaves. But it is not clear why Ogden pursued the appeal; presumably, he could have paid his one-dollar fine and kept Betty.

The question, as the lawyers framed it, was a simple one. Was Betty a kind of assignable property? To answer that question required the court to decide what identity—what analogy—fit her situation best. Was she like a slave, although one whose term of service could last only until she turned twenty-one? Or was she like an apprentice, who would be bound to service for the duration of her minority? In either case, she would not be free until she turned twenty-one. If the latter, the dominant (but not uncontrover-sial) understanding was that such an "indented servant" could not be assigned or sold.

According to Chief Justice Ewing, the 1804 statute left no doubt that Betty was a movable asset of Elihu Price's estate. The assignability of such servants—the children of enslaved people—was explicitly established using unqualified and familiar legal language. Scudder and Hornblower had coun-tered that the implicit understanding of the gradual emancipation act was to tie the assignability of the child to the assignability of her still enslaved mother. The only person who could retain possession of the child was the owner of her mother. And that led them toward the inference that the "death or manumission of the mother would at once discharge the child." (Though it remained unspoken, they assumed that Jude, Betty's mother, had been manumitted.) Once a child's mother was dead or free, they believed the child was free as well and not assignable as property. But Ewing thought that reading found "not the slightest support in the act." Indeed, it was clearly "repudiated." It made no sense, Ewing continued, that the legislature would have "cut off" owners "from all remuneration" after "the expense of nursing and maintaining the child during the helpless years of infancy." Owners should not lose their right to the services of a child through the happenstance of a "premature decease of the mother" or even because of "a liberal and generous manumission of its [sic] parent."

On the other hand, the legislature had introduced some ambiguity into the 1804 act by also writing that the child was to "remain" a servant just as if she or he had been "bound to service by the trustees or overseers of the poor." That is, the legislature also used the metaphor of the bound-out apprentice characteristic of early modern poor-relief and labor relations. Apprentices, Scudder and Hornblower had argued, could not be assigned and were not, for the most part, considered assignable property. So, according to the lawyers, on like principles, no assignment could be made of Betty.

Again, Ewing thought that a misreading of the statute. (He also noted that it was not "so perfectly clear" as Scudder and Hornblower assumed it was that "indented servants"—apprentices—could not be assigned.) This particular kind of servant—the children of slaves—had been made explicitly assignable. The analogy in the statute to indented servants described how the child was to be treated by her master, not whether that master had the right to transfer her. In any case, Betty remained a "species of property"—at least until she reached the statutory age of twenty-one. That was the law as established by the New Jersey legislature. "With the question of abstract or original right to such property, we have here nothing to do; nor with its policy."

Ewing concluded by dismissing Scudder and Hornblower's "vivid" portrayal of the abuses that resulted from allowing such assignments. What they projected might be true. "Much, too, was said, and just[l]y, in reprobation of personal and domestic slavery in every form; and . . . we may yield as men and as citizens to the truth of the remarks which did honor to the head and heart of the counsel who submitted them." But he assumed that they knew as well as he did that a court could not "refuse obedience" to an explicit legislative act.

The published case of *Ogden v. Price* also included a concurrence by Gabriel Ford. He retold the facts in order to emphasize that Betty had remained "the servant of the *owner of the mother*" as long as there was any such owner. But what happened if and when, as Scudder and Hornblower had evidently argued, Prime and Jude became free at the end of seven years, according to the terms of Morrell's written promise? Was there still anyone Betty could be compelled to serve? Ford allowed the premise that Jude, the mother, might have become free, even though he also noted that the question whether "verbal promises of freedom, without any act or record of manumission," could be effective remained "to be proved." (Remember this when we return to *Force v. Haines* in chapter 4.) But a mother's acquisition of freedom had no "influence" over her child's condition. Betty's status "resulted from being born of a *slave*." The consequence, thanks to the legislature, was that she was separated from the "fate" and the "destiny" of her mother. Until she turned twenty-one, she also remained an assignable piece of property. According to Ford, the legislature had given her the benefit of not suffering her mother's enslaved fate, but in exchange, the legislature had also denied her the ability to share (at least immediately) in the happenstance of her mother's freedom.

Ford then restated the analogy to poor relief. Just as overseers of the poor had the ability to "bind out" the child of a poor or dependent adult, and that transaction was not negated by the future status of the parent, even if the parent left the poorhouse, so it was in this case. Betty's owners' rights to her service were independent of wherever her mother now lived. "If the mother's freedom could unbind the child and discharge it from service, it would paralize [sic] that entire clause in the statute which declares that such child shall remain and *continue in such service till she attains the age of twenty-one years*." Scudder and Hornblower had evidently suggested that one result of this explicit statutory language might be that Betty could be sold at auction by the Price brothers or by later assignees, and they took the possibility of such a consequence as "an outrage upon humanity." Ford was unperturbed. He was unwilling to do away with slavery "by an act of the *court*." And he thought the lawyers were being hyperbolic.[83]

NINE YEARS LATER, in 1836, the New Jersey Supreme Court officially abandoned the presumption of slavery. Or so it seems. The case, *Stoutenborough v. Haviland*, involved the failed attempt by William Stoutenborough to trade "his boy," named John Smith, for Amos Heavilan's wagon (the published case report misspells Heavilan as Haviland). Both Heavilan and Stoutenborough lived in Shrewsbury in Monmouth County. They were neighbors or near neighbors. John Stoutenborough negotiated for his brother, William.

The deal Stoutenborough and Heavilan made on Saturday, September 20, 1828, was that William was to transfer the boy plus twenty-five dollars to Heavilan in exchange for Heavilan's "light Dearborn" wagon. William "wanted the waggon to go to church the next day." The exchange took place immediately. The boy and the money went to Heavilan; Heavilan helped John Stoutenborough fasten his brother's new wagon behind his own.

But two days later, Heavilan met up with John Stoutenborough, the brother, and asked about John Smith's legal status. He obviously wanted a paper record of his right to the boy. The two Stoutenborough brothers went to Daniel Ellis, who had been John Smith's previous master. Ellis gave them the indenture that was the foundation for William's right to John Smith.

Unfortunately for them, that indenture was not an assignment of the child of a slave. Rather, it was an 1821 apprenticeship agreement that bound John Smith out from the Monmouth County poorhouse. At that time, John Smith was just three years old, and he was bound out to John Dey to become an apprentice farmer and to remain in Dey's service until he turned twenty-one. (Nothing was said in the indenture about his parents except his father's name, Majer Smith. Apparently the father was free and had given up his child to the local overseers of the poor. Perhaps John Smith's mother had died.) On the back of the indenture, two further transactions were documented in separate freestanding paragraphs: In January 1826, a sheriff's auction conveyed John Smith from Dey to Daniel Ellis. That probably meant that Dey had become insolvent. And then in January 1828, William Stoutenborough purchased "all" the "right, title & interest" to "the boy" from Daniel Ellis. That was basically a quitclaim deed, one that gave William whatever it was that Ellis had, without specifying what Ellis's rights or interests actually were, or if Ellis had any rights or interests at all. There was no warranty of title.

Now a third paragraph was there as well, on the back of the indenture, dated September 20, 1828. It declared that William Stoutenborough "hereby assign[s] & transfer[s] to Amos Heavilan all my right title & interest to the . . . within mentioned boy." (We might suspect that this last paragraph was actually written on Monday, September 22, after Heavilan's request for evidence of Stoutenborough's title to the boy, but predated and added to the back of the indenture.)

Heavilan refused to accept the indenture. He did not want a "bound boy," that is, an apprentice who would go free at twenty-one, rather than an assignable male child of a slave, who would serve until he was twenty-five. He may also have suspected that John Smith was no longer bound as an apprentice after the assignments that sent him from Dey to Ellis and then to William Stoutenborough. Whatever title he had received to the "use" of John Smith was not a secure one.

In any case, Heavilan brought John Smith back to Stoutenborough's place, where William refused to receive him. Then Heavilan, probably after a fight, took the wagon he had given Stoutenborough back to his own home. In February 1829, Stoutenborough went to a local justice of the peace.

In one of several trials that followed, John Stoutenborough, the brother, testified that he had negotiated with Heavilan without any idea that John Smith was anything other than the child of a slave. There had been no deceit or trickery in the negotiations. He had "traded him under expectation that he belonged" to his brother. He had traded him "as William[']s property." Indeed, it is altogether possible that William himself had no idea at the time that John Smith was not his assignable property—that is, until he went to talk to Ellis. It may be that he was less than fully literate; it may also be that Ellis had lied to him when he had first "purchased" the boy.

Stoutenborough won a one hundred dollar judgment from the justice of the peace for the loss of the wagon he had purchased. That judgment was appealed to the Monmouth County circuit court, which affirmed the judgment after rejecting Heavilan's attorney's efforts to introduce evidence about the legal status of the "boy" who had been traded for the wagon.[84] Heavilan appealed, and the New Jersey Supreme Court granted certiorari and reversed the judgment in 1833. The case then went back to a different justice of the peace, who heard the case in November 1833. This second justice of the peace gave judgment for Heavilan for sixty dollars, plus costs. Since Heavilan already had his wagon back, it is not clear what he was being compensated for—what the measure of damages were. That judgment was appealed first to the county Court of Common Pleas, which affirmed it. Then Stoutenborough appealed to the New Jersey Supreme Court, which in February 1836 again affirmed the judgment for Heavilan. By the time the case was appealed for the second time, William L. Dayton—a young attorney who would soon be promoted to the Supreme Court—had become one of Heavilan's counsel.

Justice Ryerson, who wrote the opinion in the appeal (with the agreement of Ford and by then Chief Justice Hornblower), thought the "most important question" was whether the law held Stoutenborough to "an implied warranty" that he had a right to dispose of the boy until he reached the age of twenty-five, as defined by the gradual emancipation statute. Ryerson continued: "It was once the doctrine of this court, that every colored person was presumed a slave till the contrary was shown." That meant that anyone who sold such a "person" in his possession was taken as having the right to do so (this is what an implied warranty of title would have meant in this context). Heavilan should have been able to rely on that presumption when he traded his wagon for the services of the boy. When he later discovered, after the transaction, that the boy he had purchased was not a child born of a slave but had been bound out from the Monmouth County poorhouse in August 1821, Heavilan had the right to negate the sale and re-take possession of the wagon, as he had. He had discovered "that the said negro boy was a free boy, and that the defendant [Stoutenborough] had no right and title to him, and [decided] to dispose of him." John Smith was no longer of value to Amos Heavilan. The boy was not what he was warranted to be—that is, a purchasable child of a slave. He was, instead, merely a bound-out apprentice (and more, he was probably a formerly bound-out apprentice, whose binding out had been negated by one or more illegal conveyances).

Was the presumption of slavery still the doctrine of the court? Ryerson had, he said, long believed that it was not: "This presumption ought no longer to be admitted, both from the notorious fact, that the generality of persons of this description in this State, are not in truth held as slaves *now*, as well as from the natural consequence which must be supposed to follow our statute for the gradual abolition of slavery." Perhaps this ended things, as in no published New Jersey case thereafter is this presumption explicitly raised. Still, what Ryerson wrote was really just dictum, since the case concerned a transaction involving a boy and a wagon, not a slave. And Ryerson conceded that there remained an implicit presumption (or an implied warranty) that a young black man was subject to service until he was twenty-five. He thought that one was much stronger than presuming that an "aged man of color" was still enslaved. Indeed, he needed something like this second presumption to explain why John and William Stoutenborough ought to have disclosed John Smith's status immediately. Or, as Ryerson put it: "The presumption, and of course the implication is, not that he is such an *indented* servant, but as it were, a special apprentice under our act of assembly." Because a presumption founded on racial identity existed, Heavilan had been misled.

The last question the case raised was whether Heavilan had been right to retake possession of his wagon immediately, rather than waiting until he had been "lawfully dispossessed" of the boy. If John Smith were an ordinary chattel, exchanged for another chattel, Heavilan would have been required "to rest contented with the possession of the thing in question, till his right was questioned and disproved." Not in this case, though. Ryerson raised the possibility that if the assignment of the poorhouse indenture had given Heavilan a positive and clear right to the "possession and services" of the boy until he reached the age of twenty-one—that is, until his majority—then perhaps it would have made sense to require him to wait for a prosecution or a challenge to his possession. But in this case, where it was unclear whether any assignment was legal, where there were "unknown damages, not the subject of calculation, before he could have an action for a breach of warranty," the "hazard" was too much. Heavilan should not have to wait.

What of John Smith, the pauper apprentice who had been traded for a wagon? John Stoutenborough, on the witness stand, described how on Monday, February 22, 1828, after having seen the indenture, Amos Heavilan brought "the boy" back to William Stoutenborough's place. Or, more precisely, Heavilan brought the boy and "turned him out in the road," presumably a road leading to or by William's house. At that point, "the boy went away." Ten-year-old John Smith had no reason to stay, and there was no one to stop him. He walked away, and he was gone.[85]

IN THE LATE 1820s and 1830s, William Jenkins captained one of Cornelius Vanderbilt's steamboats, the *Thistle*, which carried passengers from New Brunswick to New York City. Vanderbilt had bought out William Gibbons, who had inherited Thomas Gibbons's steamboat enterprises after Thomas died in 1825. Jenkins was evidently a popular figure, the subject of several positive news articles in local papers. Before captaining the *Thistle*, he had captained another one of Gibbons's early steamboats.[86]

In 1833, Ephraim, the seventeen-year-old "bound" and "colored" servant of Edward T. Stille of Piscataway, was "received and harbored" on Jenkins's boat, the *Thistle*, and "conveyed" to New York. As a result, Stille "lost" his "servant." Like John Smith, Ephraim was an apprentice; and like John Smith, he was supposedly being trained in "farming." His term of service would end in 1837, when he became twenty-one.

Everything about the case that resulted is weird, as if there must be an alternative story, one unarticulated in the legal record. Stille's attorney, James Schureman Nevius, who would soon be named to the New Jersey Supreme Court (and who would dissent with Hornblower in *Force v. Haines*), knew not to frame the case as a property loss. Instead, it became an enticement case about the loss of an ordinary servant, a common law tort. The pleadings emphasized William Jenkins's knowledge and intent. Captain

Jenkins had intended to "injure" Stille, had intended to deprive him of the "profits, benefits and advantages" of Ephraim's service. He had "received" Ephraim on board; he had "harbored, detained and kept" him; and then he had carried him beyond Edward Stille's reach. Nevius asked for damages of $1,000 for the loss of Ephraim's labor as a farm hand for at most four years. This was an extraordinary sum, given that slaves were then selling for a small fraction of that amount, farm labor was relatively cheap, and the only losses were of prospective future damages (the additional cost of purchasing replacement labor for the farm).

The Middlesex County Circuit Court jury awarded Stille $120, considerably less than he had asked for but still a significant amount. And when that award was appealed, the New Jersey Supreme Court affirmed. Justices Ford and Ryerson both wrote in support of affirmance. Chief Justice Hornblower angrily dissented.[87]

Ford's opinion simply agreed that "harboring" and carrying away an escaping apprentice constituted a compensable injury. Just because "the boy" might return didn't mean the loss was not "total," justifying the jury award.

Ryerson offered a more elaborate opinion, one that could be read as yearning for the continued existence of a presumption of slavery. He acknowledged that prospective damages were discouraged by many older cases, but noted that those cases had all occurred before the technological transformations of the past few years, "before the modern facilities for removing from place to place, from province to province, and from State to State" existed. Steamboats had "changed the habits . . . and propensities of the people, especially of the class . . . which [produce] the lower order of servants." Meanwhile, "pursuit and recovery" had become "much more difficult and precarious"—even more so in an America, "where the propensity and the facilities for change have always been greater, and the perpetual movements of its inhabitants have become in some measure a national characteristic." Deprivation of someone's servant was a serious injury that deserved an adequate legal remedy.

Ryerson wrote, almost wistfully, that if Ephraim had been a slave, a jury could have considered his price in the market. They would have been able to "measure" an "adequate compensation." He thought the court ought to be able to fashion an equivalent remedy for Ephraim's loss to Stille.

Ryerson acknowledged that the remedies for the loss of a slave were ordinarily considered solely statutory, not founded in the common law.

Those remedies were, he knew, inapplicable to this situation, which was not about slavery. But he tried to imagine how to re-create remedies that had been lost. The remedies the legislature had enacted for the loss of slave services were, he claimed, implicitly rooted in the principles of the common law. Thus, they could be generalized to the new situation of an absconding (black) apprentice. He wandered back and forth between remedies for slave and non-slave servant losses, looking for points of connection. He noted that a master who lost a slave could sue in trover for the "conversion" of his property, and thus he could recover the full value of what he had lost. An apprentice, not "strictly" property, was not the object of an action for trover. But a master, he thought, ought to be understood as able to receive equal protection and be compensated for his loss.

Hornblower, in dissent, found these ruminations ridiculous. He regarded the notion that Stille should get damages for prospective losses for Ephraim's departure as a "non sequitur." He thought the form of the cause of action both "grammatically inaccurate" and "mathematically untrue." He noted that the statute regarding slaves (the 1798 statute) gave the value of the slave to the owner against the person who conveyed the slave away. But the cause of action here was not founded on that statute because Ephraim was not a slave. And there was no equivalent remedy for the loss of an apprentice.[88]

It's hard to know exactly what was going on. What lay between Captain Jenkins and Edward Stille remained offstage. An article in the *Philadelphia Inquirer* in August 1836, about the tumult that came about when a slave catcher tried to apprehend a man who had lived as free in Burlington, noted in passing that a Captain Jenkins (who may or may not be the same Jenkins) had been charged $300 for the loss of a slave, and that steamboat captains were becoming loath to take African Americans on their boats. Although advertisements for Jenkins's boats were ubiquitous in the newspapers of the time, and there were several admiring articles about his courtesy as a captain and his skill, I have found little other information about him. And of Ephraim, whose last name is never mentioned, there is, as so often, nothing.[89]

But it may be that William Jenkins was African American himself. The only William Jenkins in New Jersey of approximately the right age was, if the 1830 census is correct, a free black man who lived in North Brunswick with his wife and no children. Is it possible that Ephraim was a relative, perhaps a child of William and his wife? That would make a certain sense of the enticement action. We might speculate, then, that perhaps this was not really about servants escaping on boats but about families reconstituting themselves. And perhaps it was really the case that William Jenkins, or someone close to William Jenkins, had enticed Ephraim away from employment with Stille and brought him onto his boat.[90]

BY THE TIME *Stille v. Jenkins* was decided, the presumption of slavery was gone from the law of the state—or so it seems, but for two small pieces of evidence: First, in an 1838 federal trial in Trenton, Justice Baldwin of the U.S. Supreme Court delivered a jury charge while sitting on circuit. A slave catcher had been "obstructed" by a group of Salem County Quakers. "No one," Baldwin intoned, "must harbor, conceal or countenance a colored person after notice that he is claimed as a slave." Why? Because "the laws of New Jersey presume that every colored person is a slave till the contrary is shown!!" As Baldwin read New Jersey law, the presumption remained, though it is clear that by the mid-1830s, Baldwin's colleagues on the court thought of him as erratic and probably mentally ill. Nevertheless, Baldwin's reading would have been seconded by the Quaker journal, *The Friend*, which in 1840 concluded an editorial with the following (our second piece of evidence): "Even the evidence of a *free* coloured person cannot be received, unless he can prove his freedom. A black skin being held presumptive evidence of slavery!!! Is New Jersey a *free state?*"[91]

Still, by then it is impossible to find direct invocations of the presumption anywhere in the New Jersey case reports or in legal commentary on New Jersey state law. General legal opinion would have rejected Baldwin's reading of New Jersey law. Kirkpatrick's 1821 experiment had failed, even as the racist underpinnings remained that had brought his holding in *Gibbons v. Morse* into being.

Over the previous twenty-plus years, gradual emancipation had been muddied and confused by cascades of contradictory legal decisions, as well as by the mobility that Ryerson had recognized as the central feature of the time. Jurisdictions overlapped. Doctrinal fields—labor relations, poor relief, domestic relations, the conflicts of laws—offered competing analogies and analytic frames. And foreign jurisdictions seduced.

Over the course of more than forty years of gradual emancipation, the core questions of gradual emancipation had lost their salience: Who was enslaved? Who was free? How were slaves to be recognized? How did enslaved people become free? What did public agencies, including overseers of the poor, owe to those who had once been enslaved? What did freedom cost—for the public and for those who had once owned slaves? What rights and what duties did those who had once been or were still slaveholders have? What did it mean to possess slave property? These questions—once crucial, once constitutive of a regime—apparently no longer mattered much in New Jersey's legal culture.

By the late 1830s, there was little profit, perhaps even little honor or prestige, in keeping slaves in New Jersey. Unlike jurisdictions defined by plantation economies, few New Jersey whites depended on slave labor. Others—Irish immigrants, for example—would serve as domestic "help." And many of those who had once been enslaved were long gone. The number of black people in the state, free or enslaved, had declined sharply.

Even so, gradual emancipation survived, residual but real. That is, there were still New Jersey slaves, at least a few, and the terms of their enslavement—of their relations with masters and with other whites—continued to produce legal issues.

And that brings us back to Minna and the case that revolved around her, *Force v. Haines*. Who was she? What can we infer about the world she inhabited? And how had the legal culture of gradual emancipation shaped her life?

CHAPTER FOUR

Inferences and Speculations

Once again: On September 2, 1822, Elizabeth Haines of Elizabethtown, New Jersey, rented a slave from Henry Force. Force lived about eight miles away, in Woodbridge, along the Rahway River. Haines paid sixty dollars for the "services" of Minna. The lease was supposed to continue until June 19, 1826, when Minna turned thirty-three. At that time, Minna was to be returned to Force—at least according to William Pennington, the powerful lawyer who represented Haines when the case went to trial in 1836.

Part of the freedom that came with being a white person in New Jersey in 1822 was the freedom not to explain one's actions. Thus, it is not surprising that we don't really know why Elizabeth Haines rented Minna. Unless she had wanted to publicize her reasons, they would remain private, her own. And so it was for Henry Force. Like anyone else with disposable income and assets, each was free to make consumption choices for her or his own unexpressed reasons. The law did not require any public acknowledgment or explanation for the lease of a slave.[1]

But we can speculate about what might have led to this transaction, relying on what we do know. We might assume, for example, that Elizabeth Haines leased Minna in order to work her. Since Minna slept in the kitchen, Mrs. Haines probably wanted domestic labor, perhaps cooking. Nothing in the records suggests that she expected to take care of Minna.

But that is not the only possibility. It is at least possible that Haines and Force agreed to the lease so that Minna could be united or reunited with a man, perhaps a husband. There was one man of color, roughly Minna's age, living with Haines, at least according to the 1830 census. And by 1824, Minna would have given birth to a child, although no father was ever identified.[2]

Further, the duration of the lease went for a period of about three years and nine months, to end on Minna's thirty-third birthday. Why make a lease for the labor of a slave that ended on the slave's birthday? In general, no one except apprentices and slaves who had received or negotiated defined and limited remaining terms of service were the subjects of leases that ended on birthdays. Thus, if we put aside the claim that there was an expectation that Minna was to be returned to Force, a statement that Pennington, Elizabeth Haines's lawyer, would make without supporting evidence more than fourteen years later—a claim made legally necessary by the form the case would take in the 1830s—perhaps Minna had previously negotiated a manumission agreement with Henry Force, which stated that Minna's enslavement was to end when she turned thirty-three. And no one ever expected that Minna would return or be returned to Henry Force, which would be consistent with the terms of other agreements to manumit, agreements that often ended on birthdays. We might imagine that Elizabeth Haines had bought from Henry Force the last years of Minna's bondage, and the lease was a form of private emancipation by Force. Its implicit terms: you, Elizabeth Haines, pay me to take my former or soon-to-be former slave off my hands for a period that will end with Minna's freedom.

Why would Henry Force have done that, given that he had apparently acquired Minna less than a year earlier? Again, the documents reveal little, but that little allows for some inferences. Force had bought Minna just after the death of his second wife, when he was left with several small children. He would have needed help, and so he bought a slave. But then Minna had not worked out, as help often doesn't work out. Perhaps she was careless or disobedient. Perhaps she drank. Perhaps he found it awkward to have a slave in a community where almost no one else did. In any event, he soon found someone else to help him, a white woman who was willing to become his third wife. (By the time of the 1830 census, his household would include two more very young children.) Once he had found a wife, perhaps he had no need for a slave. Or perhaps his new wife did not want a slave around. Perhaps she disapproved of slavery, as many New Jerseyans did by the 1820s.

But Force could not simply fire Minna, as he could have fired a free employee. He could not simply send her away. She was his slave, which meant that he was responsible for her. If he abandoned her and she were needy, his local community, through the overseers of the poor, could require him to pay for her care and maintenance. She was his property, and that meant he had to "alienate" her in some way if he no longer wished to own her. In theory, he could have sold her. But perhaps there were no buyers. His problem was how to abandon slavery once he had entered on to its terrain.

It may be that the unknown person who had sold Minna to Henry Force in the first place had placed a term limit into the deed, something like "I give Minna to you, Henry Force, as your slave, for a term that will end on her 33d birthday." (By the 1820s, this was routine language in New Jersey slave transactions.) Or perhaps the unknown person only told Force that he or she had negotiated with Minna for her promised emancipation at age thirty-three. That, too, would have been a common occurrence. If it were the latter, if there were only an oral promise to manumit, it would likely have been an unenforceable promise, and Force could have safely ignored it and sold Minna without a term limit. But perhaps Force was scrupulous, thought of himself as ethically bound. And so, when Henry Force leased Minna to Elizabeth Haines, motivated by whatever reasons had led him to rid himself of Minna, he did so in a way that he thought would give effect to that preexisting promise.

One might speculate how he should have formally manumitted Minna. Could he have alienated her freedom to her? Doing so would have been complicated, and it almost certainly would have required him to underwrite her support to his local community. Perhaps he had tried manumitting her and failed—or, more likely, he realized he would fail if he tried. If Minna was already disabled (at least in the eyes of the white community), already known to drink to excess, the overseers of the poor and the local judges would have rejected his petition to manumit Minna, at least without payment of a large bond to protect the overseers from future costs. She would have been exactly the sort of enslaved person the statutes warned the local white community to protect itself against.

On the other hand, Elizabeth Haines lived eight miles away, perhaps far enough away not to know of Minna's "defects." Or perhaps she did know and had taken them into account in the negotiations. Or perhaps there were no defects apparent as yet. In any case, by doing it this way, he made a little money, recouped some portion of his earlier investment, and got rid of her. Perhaps that is what happened.

If Henry Force had really wanted to make sure that Minna was freed at the end of the lease term, there was, at least in theory, a right way to do it, assuming she was in 1822 a manumittable slave—an enslaved person eligible for manumission. That would have been to name Elizabeth Haines as his "attorney" to free his slave at the end of the term. Aside from ignorance or lack of legal advice, it may be that Henry Force would have found it difficult to give Elizabeth Haines, a woman, his power of attorney. And in any case, he didn't.[3]

Enough about what may or may not have been intended when Elizabeth Haines rented Minna from Henry Force in 1822. In June 1836, fourteen years later, Elizabeth Haines sued Henry Force for the costs of maintaining Minna from 1826 forward, from the end of the lease term. Minna was or had become or was revealed to be a drunk, so much so that she became blind in one eye. Thus, she was of no value as a laborer in the household. In 1824 she had given birth to a boy named Jesse. By 1836, she was either already or would very soon turn forty. Minna had never been taken back by Force. Instead, she had for the most part continued to live in Elizabeth Haine's household, and Force had not provided for her, as he was legally and morally bound to do. (Could Minna's looming fortieth birthday have been the impetus that moved Haines toward litigation? Perhaps she had been advised that once Minna turned forty, she would never be rid of her.)

Elizabeth Haines was represented by William Pennington, the son of a former judge, also named William Pennington, who had served on the New Jersey Supreme Court between 1805 and 1813 before becoming governor for a term and then going on to act as judge for the U.S. District Court in New Jersey. (We have seen several of the senior William Pennington's opinions in earlier chapters.) The junior William Pennington had been his father's clerk for many years before setting out on his own successful political and legal career, one that concluded with him serving as Speaker of the House of Representatives in the early years of the Civil War. On the other side, Henry Force was represented by a very young and less elite attorney, Edward Y. Rogers, the only attorney in Rahway at the time. Rogers would later be a founding member of New Jersey's Republican Party and, in the 1860s, would serve as public prosecutor for the new Union County, which was hived out of the existing Essex County.[4]

At trial, James Brown, a carpenter, testified in support of Elizabeth Haines.[5] He first saw "the black woman called Minner" in 1823 or 1824. She was not blind then. In 1828, he was doing work for Mrs. Haines, putting a roof over the kitchen where Minna slept. It did "not appear then as if she could see." Whenever she wanted anything, she looked to a little boy, who appeared to be her son and who was "smart and active." The habits of this black woman were "intemperate," and "she was of an ugly disposition." He assumed that she was "a great charge" on Mrs. Haines, "that she would want more waiting on than she would be able to wait on others." He thought her board would be worth twelve to fourteen shillings per week.

James Whitfield of Rahway testified that six or seven years before the trial he had been asked by Mrs. Haines's son (who had died in the interim) to take a black woman whose name he did not know to Henry Force's house. He did so, and he left her there. Force was not "about" the property. The black woman appeared to be blind.

Mary R. Cross—Elizabeth Haines's recently married daughter, who had lived in her mother's household throughout nearly all the years in question—testified that doctors believed that Minna's blindness was caused by intemperance. (Mary Cross had herself married a medical doctor.) According to Cross, Minna had become blind about one year before "her time was out," by which Cross apparently meant the end of the lease term. "She will drink whenever she can get anything to drink.—For about a year she was entirely helpless so that she had to be fed—after that she was better." Like Brown, Mrs. Cross believed her mother needed "to keep quite as much help as if she [Minna] did not live there."

Mrs. Cross remembered that in 1826, when the lease term was over, she and her mother took Minna in a gig to return her to Henry Force. But Minna came back with them. Two years later, around May or June 1828, her mother told Minna that she could not keep her any longer, that she must leave. What it meant to send someone away who was still enslaved was not explained. Neither attorney asked Mrs. Cross whether her mother regarded Minna as still enslaved. At that time, or sometime soon thereafter, Minna did leave. She moved in with Anthony Morse, who owned several slaves and lived in Rahway. While she lived in the Morse household, according to Morse's son, she was temperate in her habits. He also described her as "at his father's on a visit." So, evidently he did not understand her stay as a permanent move. After six months, Morse sent her back to Elizabeth Haines's household.[6]

In the spring of 1830, Mrs. Cross again went with her mother to return Minna to Henry Force. Force again refused to take Minna. According to Mrs. Cross, Force "said he never would receive her unless obligated to by law." If Elizabeth Haines "recovered any thing of him[,] he would put his property out of his hands." So, back home they went with unwanted Minna. Around the same time or a little later, James Whitehead, another witness, was asked by one of Mrs. Haines's sons (a son who had died by the time of the trial) to take Minna once again to Force's house. He took her there and left her. No one was around when he left "the black girl" at the house. But apparently Minna soon found her way back from Woodbridge to Elizabethtown, to Elizabeth Haines's house (about eight miles). And as far as the record of the trial reveals, she remained in the Haines household for the next six years, until 1836, when Elizabeth Haines filed suit for compensation for the care she had provided.

In cross-examination, Mrs. Cross conceded that her mother had not offered to return Minna's son to Henry Force. At the time of the trial, Jesse was about thirteen years old. He was, reported Mrs. Cross, still "in the habit of waiting on his mother." But he was also a "smart active boy," and he would, she thought, "be better [off] without his mother." He helped both in and out of doors; clearly, Elizabeth Haines did not want to give him up.

The theory of the case: After more then a decade of care, Elizabeth Haines had gone to court because Henry Force refused to compensate her for doing what he was legally and morally obligated to do: take care of his slave. The 1798 statute that codified New Jersey's slave law was clear: "Every owner of any negro or other slave not manumitted . . . shall be obliged, at all times, to support and maintain such slave." From 1826 on, Elizabeth Haines had "always" been "ready and willing to deliver up" Minna to Force, and she had "frequently offered so to do," but Force had "wholly refused to take her [Minna] into his custody and possession." Meanwhile, Haines had "provided . . . meat, drink, washing, lodging, clothing, and other necessaries" that were his responsibility and that indeed he had promised to pay for. (The evidence for this last claim in the chain of claims—that he had promised to pay for such necessaries—is nonexistent.) She had cared for what was his, and he should pay for her work. And so she sued for $2,000, plus costs.

Henry Force, through his young attorney, Edward Rogers, asked that Mrs. Haines be nonsuited. Force denied that he had ever made any promises to pay Elizabeth Haines for Minna's support. He denied that Haines had ever returned Minna to him "according to the condition contained in the Bill of sale." And finally, he insisted that whatever Elizabeth Haines had expended in the support of Minna was "a voluntary support . . . for which no action will lie." Force never denied that he had a legal obligation to "support and maintain" Minna, that he was still her master, and that she was still his slave. But his public obligation to care for Minna did not translate into a debt owed to Elizabeth Haines.

The judges of the Middlesex County Court of Common Pleas rejected Force's attorney's motion for nonsuit, and they gave the case to the jury, which awarded Haines $312, plus $50 in costs. To them this was a worthy suit by someone who had a burden wrongfully thrust upon her. Henry Force was responsible for the support of Minna from the end of the lease term in 1826. He had to compensate Elizabeth Haines because she had been put in the position of having to assume his legal obligations. Although the parallel may seem forced, she was in roughly the same position as someone who provided care (at law, the term is usually providing "necessaries") to a child or a wife who had been wrongfully thrown out of a husband's or a father's household. Minna was Henry Force's slave and remained Henry Force's slave; thus, he should be supporting Minna. If he did not do so directly, then others who provided support and care—Elizabeth Haines in this case—would be able to sue for compensation.

The actions—or inactions—that produced Henry Force's apparent liability might make a certain sense if we imagine them as having been framed by a belief that he was no longer responsible for Minna. Did he think that Minna was now free, or at least that she should have been free? And it may be that Elizabeth Haines also thought—at least some of the time, before she went to see a lawyer about initiating suit—that Minna was no longer enslaved. When the census taker came to her house in 1830, Elizabeth Haines, as the head of the household, identified no one as a slave. He found four free people of color living at the house, including one woman approximately the age of Minna (between twenty-four and thirty-six, assuming that Minna had not yet turned thirty-seven when the census taker came by) and one young African American boy the age of Jesse (under ten). In that all of them were identified as free, perhaps Mrs. Haines did not, at least in 1830, consider Minna a slave.[7]

On the other hand, when the census taker came to the Haines house in 1830, was Minna part of her household? Perhaps she was then part of Anthony Morse's household. (No one gives the date when Minna left the Morse household. Everybody who testified in the trial was fairly vague about dates that had occurred six to eight years earlier. And the census record does not indicate when the census taker came to the Haines household.) If one looks at the 1830 census records for Anthony Morse, it turns out that the fourteen members of his household included an enslaved woman between the ages of thirty-six and fifty-five. Since Minna would have been thirty-seven in June 1830, it is possible that the female slave of that age in Morse's household was Minna. (On the other hand, Mary Cross, Elizabeth Force's daughter, had testified that she and her mother had tried to return Minna to Force sometime right around then.)[8]

In the end, one should probably not rely on census takers for clarity, as they probably reproduced whatever the household head told them. Nor was the testimony at trial fully consistent. Nobody was precise about the ages of enslaved people. No one challenged the dates recounted in testimony. In any event, does it make sense to imagine that Minna would have been told by Elizabeth Haines that she must leave, that she could no longer keep her (in part because she was no longer enslaved), and that Minna would have then wandered off on her own to assume voluntarily the position of a slave in Anthony Morse's household? (It should be noted that the census taker also marked Morse as having three free people of color living in his household, but only one of the three was a woman, and she was between ten and twenty-four in age, certainly too young to be Minna.) If Anthony Morse considered her his slave, could she then have made her way back to Elizabeth's household a few months later? What was her status then?

By contrast, Henry Force's household in 1830 included no slaves and no free people of color. Minna was, not surprisingly, not part of his household. But was she still his slave at all? In a sense, that question underlay the case. But the question was never presented. Instead, lawyers and judges all found it more convenient to take her status as his slave for granted.

One can only conclude that the judges on the appeal must have assumed that she was unable to be manumitted because she was disabled and because, by the time of the appeal, she was well over forty. By then, certainly, she was exactly the kind of dependent enslaved person that the New Jersey legislature believed should not be freed, because she would have been likely to become a charge on the local overseers of the poor. Her owner, Henry Force, should not be able to escape liability by abandoning slavery—that is, he should not be permitted to make her a "public charge" through manumission.

Still, we can reconstruct the story behind the case as a very different one from how it was presented. Perhaps, from Henry Force's perspective, Minna was no longer a slave after her thirty-third birthday. This would explain his refusal to take her back. And it would make sense of his language to Elizabeth Force when she tried to return Minna. On the other hand, why, then, had Minna's freedom not been raised at trial? It may be that Force had promised Minna freedom in 1822 and, having mistakenly thought that his promise was sufficient, had not actually manumitted Minna. And by the later 1830s, given Minna's age and apparent disability, he could no longer do so. He and his lawyer were stuck by his inaction.

Meanwhile, Elizabeth Haines refused to give up Jesse, the child born to Minna in 1824. Remember that when Haines recorded Jesse's birth in the Essex County registration book for children of slaves born after 1804, she carefully described the birth as having occurred "during the term of service of my woman Minna." She avoided calling Minna a slave, unlike the language used in recording nearly all the other births of children born to slaves. On the other hand, by registering Jesse's birth, she apparently became entitled to his services until he turned twenty-five. She was gaining the use and the control of Jesse, even as she was denying or rejecting the slavery of his mother. Or that may be what she believed.

But what, then, led her to believe that she ought to be compensated by Henry Force for the costs of maintaining Minna? Was she suing in order to remove Minna as a threat to her desire to keep Jesse? Did she hope to coerce Force into taking Minna back? Was her underlying goal to separate Minna from Jesse?

Henry, Elizabeth, and Minna on Appeal

By the time that *Force v. Haines* came before the New Jersey Supreme Court of Judicature in 1840, more than three years later, Elizabeth Haines and Henry Force had each changed attorneys. Haines had hired Benjamin Williamson and Smith Scudder, both eminent members of the bar, to replace William Pennington, who was by then serving in the dual position of governor and chancellor of the state. Fifteen years earlier, Scudder had worked with Joseph Hornblower to represent Betty in *Ogden v. Price*. Along the way, they had tried without success to turn that case into a test of the continued legality of New Jersey slavery. In 1838 and 1839, Scudder was also the mayor of Elizabethtown. Williamson was the son of a former governor and chancellor and would a few years later, under the 1846 New Jersey constitution, become the chancellor of the state of New Jersey. Force had brought in Amzi Armstrong, a somewhat more senior attorney, to replace young Rogers.[9]

We don't have the briefs that were filed in the case, but from the arguments that the four judges who wrote opinions worked through, and the precedents they struggled to distinguish or analogize, it is relatively easy to figure out how Armstrong built his appeal. He must have emphasized that Elizabeth Haines's claim lacked proof that the care and support she had offered Minna had been at the direct request of Henry Force. Without such evidence, the action (in assumpsit) could not be maintained unless it fell into a very small number of exceptional circumstances in which an underlying agreement could be implied. He then raised a number of New Jersey, New York, and English cases that he interpreted as establishing the presence of sharp and clear boundaries on any notion of an implied obligation on an owner to pay a "stranger" for care of a dependent slave or servant.

The cleverness of Armstrong's argument lay in his ability to reframe the issue away from the wrongdoing of Henry Force and on to what one might call the legal character of Elizabeth Haines. The judges joined and divided around the questions of who she was, who she was like, and whether the law ought to reward conduct by people like her. Henry Force's legal character remained offstage except in Chief Justice Hornblower's dissent.

As so often happens on appeal, the facts in the case were radically simplified. No one challenged Minna's status as a slave; no one even mentioned her son. This was not a case about her life, her capacities, her needs. Her care became a financial cost assumed by Elizabeth Haines that either would or would not be reimbursed by Henry Force. Those who wanted Force held liable for Minna's care viewed Minna as his dependent. Those who wanted Force freed from liability portrayed Minna as belonging to his private sphere, as property subject to his continuing disposal (within the limited boundaries of the police power). Along the way, both the judges in the majority and those in the minority tried to treat the case as a routine problem of private law rather than as one that raised issues about the legitimacy and continuing viability of the New Jersey slave regime. The legitimacy of that regime would not be permitted to come into question (thirty-six years after gradual emancipation had been formally instituted). Anxieties about abolitionism, fugitive slaves, and poor relief leaked into the language of the judges, but the case on appeal became a problem in contract theory—or, more accurately, what legal scholars would later call doctrines of quasi-contract. The issue was whether services rendered by Elizabeth Haines required compensation by Henry Force. Was there a contract that bound Force to pay Haines—implied by the relationship of Force to Minna, by his duty to support Minna, or by his knowledge that Elizabeth was caring for Minna? Or, to put it in the terms that the three-member majority on the court imposed on the case, was there anything about the situation that Haines and Force found themselves in that made her conduct anything other than a "mere voluntary courtesy"? Was there anything that demonstrated that she had been anything more than a "mere volunteer" or, to use the more pejorative term, an "officious intermeddler"?

Three of the judges—Dayton in his concurrence, and Hornblower and Nevius in their dissents—emphasized Henry Force's moral and legal responsibility for Minna. Hornblower, in particular, went on at great length about what Force should have done. His dissent focused on Force's inescapable responsibility for the care of Minna. He had to pay the costs of her care. "The law has not left it to the humanity, the avarice, or the caprice of the master, to say, whether he will or will not, support his helpless slave; nor yet, whether he will do it himself, or compel the public in the first instance to furnish such support and then look to him for remuneration."

When he wrote in this way, though, Chief Justice Hornblower was obscuring Force's actual situation, which was one of total and absolute insolvency. In 1830, Force had been able to plausibly threaten to put property out of his hands when Haines tried to make him take Minna back. By the late 1830s, Henry Force had no property to put away—or anywhere else. In between, a number of creditors had obtained judgments against him. Once, in February 1835, and again a month later, Abraham Cruden, the sheriff of Middlesex County, had levied an execution on Force's goods and chattels after he had confessed judgment in the twin cases of *Southwick v. Force* and *Clark v. Force*. The sheriff took

an eight day clock, one side board and contents, two bureaus, one desk, four beds and bedding, bedsteads, three carpets, looking glasses, three dozen chairs, eight tables, pots, kettles etc. in kitchen, casks in cellar, four horses, two sets harness, one single harness, one yoke of oxen, three cows, two calves, two farm wagons, one small wagon, ploughs and harness, one barouck [*sic*], one gig, lots of rails and posts, lumber, locust posts, boards and plank, mahogany wood, manure, tools in blacksmith shop, bees, three ox chains, grain and hay, straw and flax, ox cart, tanning mill, and corn shiller, carpenters tools, two sleds, forks, shovels, spades, etc. and one small farm [and] saw mill[,] containing 70 acres more or less situated in the township of Wood-bridge.[10]

Four years later, Sheriff A. W. Brown levied an execution again on Force, after he confessed judgment in the case of *Wing v. Force*. Most everything Henry Force had left was taken in this second sheriff's levy. This time the sheriff took

two horses, four cows, four hogs, three sets harness, two harrows, three ploughs, two farm wagons, one barouck [*sic*], one gig, one hay fork, rakes etc, one tanning mill, one corn shiller, two sleds, a small lot of building timber, a lot of hickory and other plank, . . . locust posts, shift spokes[,] . . . old and new mill[s,] . . . a lot of mill irons, three . . . french burr mill stones, . . . lot of chains and second hand irons, two lots of blacksmiths tools, one eight day clock, one side board, two bureaus . . . other tables, two boston rocking chairs, twenty four sitting chairs, five beds and bedding and bedsteads, four carpets, three looking glasses etc., lot for cooking, one lot of china, one dozen knives and forks, kitchen furniture etc.[,] lot of meat and other casks in cellar, etc. and eighty acres of land more or less situated in the township of Woodbridge . . . adjoining Benjamin Smith and others.[11]

By 1840, by the time Hornblower was writing his dissent, Henry hardly had anything. And what little he had left was about to go in a third (or fourth) sheriff's levy.[12] He probably couldn't have taken responsibility for a slave if he had wanted to. He had no means to do so.

For our purposes, though, what is most important is that Chief Justice Hornblower knew perfectly well that Henry Force was insolvent, surely judgment-proof. Hornblower was the judge who certified the sheriff's levy in each of those cases (his signature is prominently displayed on all the levies). For all his talk about the state coercing resources out of Force, and of the inescapability of his responsibilities, Joseph Hornblower knew that Henry Force had no resources to be coerced out of.

Indeed, Henry Force's insolvency also meant that the local overseers of the poor might have been compelled to provide support to Minna as a pauper if Elizabeth Haines had turned her over to them, even if Minna were still enslaved. In that sense, Justice Dayton may have been correct in his opinion in *Force v. Haines* when he insisted that the correct thing for Haines to do would have been to turn Minna over to the overseers of the poor, who would have had to care for her—and Hornblower would have been wrong. Ever since 1798, a person enslaved to an insolvent was understood as a pauper potentially or theoretically entitled to relief by a township.[13]

Finally, how can we understand mobile but apparently blind and still enslaved Minna? How "worthless" was she, really? And when had her drunken condition become manifest? Should Elizabeth Haines have known about it when she leased her? And how isolated was she in actuality? The record is amazingly sparse, and all one can do is speculate.

In New Jersey, an enslaved woman born before 1804, as Minna was, had no entitlement to freedom. At the same time, the possibilities for escape (or even just departure) must have been very great, particularly for an enslaved person living in a port city like Elizabethtown, especially in the later 1820s and 1830s, when steamship travel had become routine. Once one reached New York City or even Staten Island, just across the channel from Elizabethtown, it was remarkably easy to disappear into a community of free black people. The presumption of slavery that we saw mobilized in the New Jersey case law would not have been a problem for Minna. One can hardly imagine that either Elizabeth Haines or Henry Force would have contemplated suing any captain or boat owner if Minna had availed herself of the possibilities to leave. The presumption, if it still existed, only mattered if there was a master willing and ready to sue for the value of the slave. Minna, presumably, had little value, and neither of the two white people, who might have claimed a possessory interest in her, wanted her.

The testimony suggests that Elizabeth Haines, Henry Force, and Minna herself all assumed that she could move about as free, certainly by the 1830s. And for a seemingly blind and disabled woman, she moved around ably and competently enough. Haines wanted Minna to leave, and Force didn't care; he had, one might say, released or abandoned his property. From his perspective, indeed, it makes sense to think of Elizabeth Haines as an officious intermeddler, who got in the way of his expectation that Minna should just disappear. To him, Elizabeth Haines was somewhat like Ford's example of the neighbor who insists on repairing one's broken sleigh: she was interfering with his freedom as a property holder. How was she doing that? Presumably, by holding on to Minna's son.

So what, then, did it mean that Minna did not move away, even when encouraged to do so by Elizabeth Haines? It is likely that she did not wish to leave her son, who remained in the household under the control of Haines. Another possible answer might be that Haines did care for her, and Minna knew no one else who would. Perhaps Elizabeth had really been a good Samaritan to her (although this would beg the question of why she would ever go to court). What we know nothing of, on the other hand, is the community of other people of color—slave and free—who lived in and around the Haines household and at Anthony Morse's house. Was one or another of them the father of Jesse? Was it their care that she looked to when she returned to the Haines household?

The records offer us one further mystery: In the 1840 census, presumably based on the visit of a Woodbridge census taker that occurred after the final decision in *Force v. Haines* (recorded as April 1840), Henry Force is listed as having one slave in his household, a female between the ages of thirty-five and fifty-five. Under a separate heading, that enslaved woman is identified as a "blind colored person." The 1840 census, like the 1830 census, lists only the head of household by name. Thus, it is impossible to know for certain if Minna was that female slave. And a census notation can tell us nothing about the actual conditions of life, of who was really living with whom and under what circumstances. But is it possible that, in the end— after Force had forcefully told Elizabeth Haines and her daughter that he would never receive Minna unless forced by law to do so, after securing from the New Jersey Supreme Court a decision that he was not liable for Minna's support while she lived in the Haines household, and at a time when he was bankrupt and completely without resources—he took Minna back and resumed responsibility for her care?[14]

AFTER 1840, Elizabeth Haines lived first with her daughter and her son-in-law in Elizabethtown; then, by 1850, she lived with her stepsons in central New Jersey. Henry Force moved to Virginia, where he lived with his third wife and two younger children. At that point, he called himself a lawyer. By the 1850 census, he owned real estate he valued (for purposes of the census) at $1,500. And he also owned one slave, aged fourteen. He died in 1850.[15]

About the later lives of Minna and Jesse, we know nothing. In the 1850 census, the only black Minna or Mina or Minner of approximately the right age—a Mina Clark, originally from New Jersey—lived in Philadelphia in a largely African American neighborhood with her son, James, who was twenty-seven years old and worked as a seaman. The census did not identify her as blind. Was Minna now Mina Clark? Was her son Jesse now James Clark?[16]

By the 1850s, perhaps earlier, New Jersey had become part of a unified "free" North (see map 2). Still, the detritus of gradual emancipation lingered on, until the passage of the Thirteenth Amendment of the U.S. Constitution—or, perhaps even longer, since the Democrat-controlled New Jersey legislature voted down the Thirteenth Amendment in 1865. As late as 1860, there remained eighteen enslaved persons in the state according to the census records, although state law by then identified them as "apprentices for life."

In 1846, after constitutional challenges to the continued existence of slavery under the new New Jersey state constitution had failed, the legislature passed a law that "abolished" slavery. Those few who remained in the status of slaves were renamed "apprentices." Their children became fully free, no longer bound to service until adulthood. This abolition law was published as part of a general revision of "domestic relations," including new rules for apprenticeships and for the regulation of servants. As a consequence of the new law, servants who "absconded" could be bound to double their term of service. Apprentices who absconded could be charged by their master for the value of what the master had lost. On the other hand, slaveholders or former slaveholders were still understood to be responsible for the care (and the costs) of aged enslaved peoples, who were presumably still ineligible for a settlement in a town for purposes of poor relief. As late as 1857, a pauper who was the child of a slave who had spent his life in the town of Morris was ruled not to have a settlement there, because an enslaved man never acquired a settlement entitling him (or his son) to poor relief (and his free son had not been born in Morris).[17]

By then, though, such law making and interpretation no longer occurred under the heading of slavery or of gradual emancipation. Instead, it had become part of the complex law of a free state, of New Jersey, if not a state of freedom.

Acknowledgments

I first came across *Force v. Haines* more than a decade ago, as a citation in cases where late nineteenth- and early twentieth-century judges and lawyers argued over compensation for elder care. I was hooked by that mysterious phrase "a mere voluntary courtesy." A few years later, when I wanted relief from the stresses that studying elder care raise, I turned temporarily toward the apparently more distant issues of master–slave relations in nineteenth-century New Jersey (the weird R & R of the legal historian). For one summer I gathered material on the legal world of gradual emancipation in northern New Jersey that surrounded *Force v. Haines*. Then I put what I had found aside and returned to the history of old age and inheritance. Then, four years later, in order to distract myself from another project—this one on steamboats and monopolies—I returned to what I had collected about New Jersey gradual abolition and realized that I could see a book in it. And then I started writing.

That is one story about how this book came to be. An equally plausible story of origin would be that I began the work that became this book because I wanted a project I could share with a few close friends and distinguished scholars, including Amy Dru Stanley, Rebecca Scott, and Dylan Penningroth. I wanted to work on themes and materials that they would recognize and that I could talk about with each of them.

I was able to write the first draft of this manuscript because of the extraordinary privilege of a fellowship at the New-York Historical Society in 2015–16. I am immensely grateful to Sidney Lapidus, who funded me as the recipient of the Sidney Lapidus Fellowship at the society; to Louise Mirrer, the president of the society; and to Valerie Paley, the vice president and chief historian of the society. Conversations with my fellow fellows were fruitful, as were conversations with others at the society, particularly Michael Ryan, the director of the library. The fruits of research into the magnificent holdings at the library of the society are visible throughout my notes. The even greater gift that the fellowship offered was time to write.

The support of Princeton University, materially and in all sorts of other ways, has been crucial. As I have so often done over the past quarter century, I leaned on Firestone Library and on the immense number of web-based services that the Princeton libraries make available to members of the Princeton University community.

The core of the research for this book comes from the rich and underutilized holdings of the New Jersey State Archives. I am grateful to Bette M. Epstein, the head archivist. Other collections that shaped this book include those in Firestone Library; Drew University's Gibbons Family Papers; the Carver Collection of Gibbons Family holdings, previously at the Museum of American Finance, now at the Hagley Museum; and the holdings of the Monmouth County Historical Society. I had one productive day at the New Jersey Historical Society; my then research assistant, Farah Peterson, had another. The riches that are located there await anyone with an interest in the legal history of New Jersey and the American nation, and a bright and well-funded future. As is obvious, I have drawn heavily on Princeton University's account with Ancestry.com. I am grateful to Rutgers University Law School's website on the law of slavery in New Jersey for providing an essential starting point for my research into the legislative record.

Early drafts were read by Martha Sandweiss, James Alexander Dun, Sarah Seo, Maeve Glass, Alix Lerner, Tal Kastner, Dylan Penningroth, Michelle McKinley, and Stuart Chinn. I am particularly grateful to the close readings that Amy Dru Stanley and Rebecca Scott each gave twice to the manuscript, as outside readers for the University of North Carolina Press. Also for the careful reading I received from Chuck Grench, my editor at the press. Conversations with Barbara Welke, Emma Rothschild, Laura Edwards, Margot Canaday, Susanna Blumenthal, Wendy Warren, Yaacob Dweck, Matt Axtell, Annie Twitty, Dan Rodgers, Anne Cheng, Desmond Jagmohan, Kellen Funk, Farah Peterson, Risa Goluboff, Kenneth W. Mack, Geneva Smith, Sean Wilentz, Tom Green, Andrew Edwards, Sean Vanatta, Tera Hunter, Ariela Gross, Martha Jones, Natalie Davis, and Nell Painter, among others, were of immeasurable significance.

Research assistance from Farah Peterson in 2010, Sophie Jin and Emily Sung in 2011, and Geneva Smith in 2016 helped enormously. Geneva Smith also provided excellent editorial assistance.

I am thrilled to return to UNC Press, which published my first book and with which I had a productive relationship while we worked together to edit and produce the book series Studies in Legal History for the American Society for Legal History. I am particularly grateful to the work of Chuck Grench and Jad Michael Adkins of UNC Press and Michelle Witkowski of Westchester Publishing Services for their work in moving the book through production.

An early draft of the first section of chapter 3, devoted to the arson case of *Quay v. Eagle Fire-Company*, was presented as a keynote address at the New Jersey Historical Commission's fall conference in 2012. A later version became the 2016 O'Fallon Lecture at the University of Oregon Law School and a 2016 lecture at CUNY Graduate Center. I have talked through portions of the argument in this manuscript to seminars and workshops at the University of Michigan, to the Hurst Seminar at the University of Wisconsin (Madison), to a faculty seminar at the University of Wisconsin Law School, to a history and law seminar at the University of Oregon, to Martha Sandweiss's seminar on Princeton and slavery, to the Legal and Constitutional History Workshop at NYU School of Law, and to the fellows of the LAPA program at Princeton University. A few sentences come from a short essay, "Learning from the Legal Culture of Gradual Emancipation, or Misled by the Thirteenth Amendment," published in *Process: A Blog for American History* (OAH).

I received much encouragement from Jacob Hartog. The first draft was read by the brilliant Nancy Hartog, who subjected it to withering and helpful criticism that saved me from several errors.

My grandchildren—Pearl Blossom Hartog, Naomi Emiko Hartog, Elias Masura Hartog, May Alice Hartog, and Cole Read Hartog—did little to help me with this book but ought to be textually visible. They fill my life with joy and remind me that there are so many more important things than scholarly books. This one is not much of a gift for them. (Cole would rather that it be about the Jurassic period, and both he and Elias would prefer that it be a part of the Lego corpus.) But they should know how grateful I am for their love and occasional attention.

Maps

MAP 1 The slaveholding counties of New Jersey as of 1820–1830.

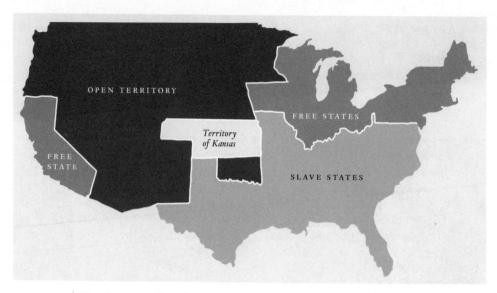

MAP 2 Free States vs. Slave States. Drawn from the Reynolds Political Map of the United States, 1856.

Notes

Abbreviations and Guides for Frequently Used Sources in Notes

Collections, New Jersey State Archives, Trenton, New Jersey (NJSA)
  Supreme Court Case Files, 1704–1844 (Searchable Index Database, https://
    wwwnet-dos.state.nj.us/DOS_ArchivesDBPortal/SupremeCourt.aspx)
  County Government Records (http://nj.gov/state/archives/catcounty.html)
The Law of Slavery in New Jersey, compiled by Paul Axel-Lute (rev. June 5, 2012),
  The New Jersey Digital Legal Library, Rutgers University Library for the
  Center for Law & Justice, Newark, New Jersey (http://njlegallib.rutgers.edu
  /slavery/) (NJDLL)
Collections, New-York Historical Society, New York City, New York (NYHS)
Gibbons Family Papers, Drew University Library, University Archives, Madison,
  New Jersey (GFP)

Introduction

1. See the conversations of Dido and Minnie in Branden Jacobs-Jenkins, *An Octo-roon* (New York: Dramatists Play Service, 2015), 17–19, 27, 34, 44, 57. Michelle McKinley notes in conversation that Mina is a common West African name. On the other hand, Minner was not an uncommon name among the Dutch inhabitants of New Jersey. For simplicity, I will refer to her as Minna.

2. See Simeon Moss, "The Persistence of Slavery and Involuntary Servitude in a Free State (1685–1866)," *Journal of Negro History* 35, no. 3 (July 1950): 289–314; Henry Scofield Cooley, *A Study of Slavery in New Jersey*, Johns Hopkins University Studies in Historical and Political Science (Baltimore: Johns Hopkins University Press, 1896); James J. Gigantino II, *The Ragged Road to Abolition: Slavery and Freedom in New Jersey, 1775–1865* (Philadelphia: University of Pennsylvania Press, 2014); Graham Russell Hodges, *Slavery and Freedom in the Rural North: African Americans in Monmouth County, New Jersey, 1665–1865* (Madison, WI: Madison House, 1997); Alfred M. Heston, *Story of the Slave; Paper Read Before the Monmouth County Historical Association on October 30th, 1902, Wherein is Given Some Account of Slavery and Servitude in New Jersey, with Notes Concerning Slaves and Redemptioners in Other States* (Camden, NJ: S. Chew & Sons, 1903); Arthur Zilversmit, *The First Emancipation: The Abolition of Slavery in the North* (Chicago: University of Chicago Press, 1967); Andrew D. Mellick Jr., *The Story of an Old Farm, or Life in New Jersey in the Eighteenth Century* (Somerville, NJ: Unionist-Gazette, 1889); Frances D. Pingeon, "An Abominable Business: The New Jersey Slave Trade, 1818," *New Jersey History* 109, no. 3–4 (1991): 14–35; Stuart Gold, "The 'Gift'

of Liberty: Testamentary Manumission in New Jersey, 1791–1805," *Rutgers Race and the Law Review* 15 (2014): 1–72.

3. "Table 1: United States Resident Population by State: 1790–1850," New Jersey Department of Labor and Workforce Development, http://lwd.dol.state.nj.us/labor /lpa/census/1990/poptrd1.htm; Susan B. Carter, Scott Sigmund Gartner, Michael R. Haines, Alan L. Olmstead, Richard Sutch, and Gavin Wright, eds., *Historical Statistics of the United States, Millennial Edition Online*, vol. 2, *Work and Welfare* (New York: Cambridge University Press, 2006), 375–76; Gold, "'Gift' of Liberty."

4. I will return to the question of population decline in chapters 2 and 3. For similar reflections on Ohio and other midwestern states, see Anne Twitty, *Before* Dred Scott: *Slavery and Legal Culture in the American Confluence, 1787–1857* (New York: Cambridge University Press, 2016), 38.

5. The moral dilemmas that Robert Cover thought should have shaped the judgments of northern judges with antislavery credentials seem not to have bothered any of the New Jersey judges—in opinions in Force v. Haines, or anywhere else. See Robert M. Cover, *Justice Accused: Antislavery and the Judicial Process* (New Haven, CT: Yale University Press, 1975).

6. See Force v. Haines, Trial Transcript #12912 (NJSA). On the usual rules of responsibility for tenants of leaseholds of land, see Adam Wolkoff, "Possession and Power" (PhD diss., Rutgers University, 2015). On the laws of slave rentals, see Thomas D. Morris, *Southern Slavery and the Law, 1619–1860*, Studies in Legal History (Chapel Hill: University of North Carolina, 1996), 132–60.

7. The reasons that they reduced the award from $2,000 to $300 are not apparent, although some of the care she had offered would have occurred in a period outside the limits of the state's statutes of limitations on causes of actions (occurred too long in the past). *Laws of the State of New-Jersey, Revised and Published under the Authority of the Legislature* (Trenton, 1821), 410–13.

8. Edward W. Hope, "Officiousness," *Cornell Law Review* 15 (Winter 1929–30): 25–53, 205–42; Hanoch Dogan, "In Defense of the Good Samaritan," *Michigan Law Review* 97, no. 5 (March 1999): 1152–1200. One finds the language in *Force v. Haines*, often referenced with a citation to a later case, *Glen v. Savage*, 14 Or. 567 (1887). In *Glen*, the opinion of the court had borrowed phrases from *Force*. On quasi-contract, see William A. Keener, "Contract—Quasi Contract—Tort," chap. 12 in *Selections on the Elements of Jurisprudence* (St. Paul: West, 1896). On the European alternatives, see John P. Dawson, "The Self-Serving Intermeddler," *Harvard Law Review* 87, no. 7 (May 1974): 1409–58; John P. Dawson, "*Negotiorum Gestio*: The Altruistic Intermeddler, Part One," *Harvard Law Review* 74 (March 1961): 817–65; John P. Dawson, "*Negotiorum Gestio*: The Altruistic Intermeddler, Part Two," *Harvard Law Review* 74 (1961): 1073–1129; Jeroen Kortmann, *Altruism in Private Law: Liability for Nonfeasance and Negotiorum Gestio* (Oxford: Oxford University Press, 2005).

9. Oliver Wendell Holmes, "The Path of the Law," *Harvard Law Review* 10 (1897): 457.

10. See cases discussed in Hendrik Hartog, *Someday All This Will Be Yours: A History of Inheritance and Old Age* (Cambridge, MA: Harvard University Press, 2012).

11. Recent writing about the history of abolition in the North tends to read that history as being all about getting to its end point, to a regime of freedom that is fundamentally familiar. Or, in the alternative, it involves a moralistic examination of why emancipation took so long, why it didn't come, or the inadequacies of what it was when it arrived. At least in the United States, what is meant by abolition is fundamentally shaped by the later fact of the Thirteenth Amendment—by the notion of an instantaneous abolition (which was of course a fiction in 1865 as well). For work that challenges that conventional wisdom, see Patrick Rael, *Eighty-Eight Years: The Long Death of Slavery in the United States, 1777–1865*, Race in the Atlantic World, 1700–1900 (Athens: University of Georgia Press, 2015); Twitty, *Before* Dred Scott, 155–57. I am not engaged in this book with the contrast between a "free" North and an "enslaved" South, nor with its converse: the recent efforts to demonstrate that the boundaries between North and South were indistinct, if they existed at all. See Steven Hahn, *The Political Worlds of Slavery and Freedom*, Nathan I. Huggins Lectures (Cambridge, MA: Harvard University Press, 2009).

12. I am grateful to Maeve Glass for this turn of phrase.

13. See Michelle McKinley, *Fractional Freedoms: Slavery, Intimacy, and Legal Mobilization in Colonial Lima, 1600–1700* (New York: Cambridge University Press, 2016); Sidney Chalhoub, "The Politics of Ambiguity: Conditional Manumission, Labor Contracts, and Slave Emancipation in Brazil (1850s–1888)," *International Review of Social History* 60, no. 2 (August 2015): 161–91; Alejandro De La Fuente and Ariela Gross, "Slaves, Free Blacks, and Race in the Legal Regimes of Cuba, Louisiana and Virginia: A Comparison," *North Carolina Law Review* 91, no. 5 (2013): 1699–1756; Douglas Hay and Paul Craven, eds., *Masters, Servants, and Magistrates in Britain and the Empire, 1562–1955* (Chapel Hill: University of North Carolina Press, 2004); Rebecca J. Scott, *Degrees of Freedom: Louisiana and Cuba after Slavery* (Cambridge, MA: Belknap Press of Harvard University Press, 2005).

14. James Alexander Dun, *Dangerous Neighbors: Making the Haitian Revolution in Early America*, Early American Studies (Philadelphia: University of Pennsylvania Press, 2016). But even Haiti eventually was compelled to agree to compensate the French for the loss of enslaved property.

15. The canonical work is Robert William Fogel and Stanley L. Engerman, "Philanthropy at Bargain Prices: Notes on the Economics of Gradual Emancipation," *Journal of Legal Studies* 3, no. 2 (June 1974): 377–401.

16. As in all my writing, I remain fundamentally dependent on, and in conversation with, the insights of James Willard Hurst. J. Willard Hurst, *Law and the Conditions of Freedom in the Nineteenth Century United States* (Madison: University of Wisconsin Press, 1956).

17. The method used in this chapter bears some resemblance to the "surface reading" recommended in recent work in law and literature, particularly in its focus on the "rhetorical effects of the citation of precedent." Bernadette A. Meyler, "The Rhetoric of Precedent," in *Rhetorical Processes and Legal Judgments*, ed. Austin Sarat (Cambridge: Cambridge University Press, 2016), 83–99

18. I draw inspiration from the work of Stewart Macaulay, in particular from his "Non-Contractual Relations in Business: A Preliminary Study," a work that both

initiated a core inquiry of what became known as the "law and society movement" and, at that same time, offered a paradigm of the heterodox study of contract law, typically known as relational contracting. Like Macaulay, I am interested in exploring what competent bargaining individuals—those we call legal subjects and legal actors—actually did. At the heart of the study of relational contracting is the recognition that identities are changed by contracts. Women and men become partners, wives and husbands, masters and servants (perhaps masters and slaves), connected together, joined often in opposition to others. They lose their character as individual, self-seeking dealers. It is inevitably the business of a legal system to decide—to make judgments about—which relational identities to value and sustain. At a second level, the relational perspective understands contract law as being all about responsibility, duty, and care. Voluntarism remains, but it is a voluntarism defined by the decision to assume responsibility for others and for the production and care of public goods. Stewart Macaulay, "Non-Contractual Relations in Business: A Preliminary Study," *American Sociological Review* 28, no. 1 (February 1963): 55–67; Joseph William Singer, "The Reliance Interest in Property," *Stanford Law Review* 40, no. 3 (February 1988): 611–751.

19. Anne Carson, *Eros the Bittersweet: An Essay* (Princeton, NJ: Princeton University Press, 1986). For a focus on the "present tense," see also Stanley Cavell, *Must We Mean What We Say? A Book of Essays* (Cambridge: Cambridge University Press, 2002).

20. Patricia J. Williams, *The Alchemy of Race and Rights* (Cambridge, MA: Harvard University Press, 1991); Elizabeth B. Clark, "Matrimonial Bonds: Slavery and Divorce in Nineteenth-Century America," *Law and History Review* 8, no. 1 (Spring 1990): 25–54; Amy Dru Stanley, *From Bondage to Contract: Wage Labor, Marriage and the Market in the Age of Slave Emancipation* (New York: Cambridge University Press, 1998). The supposed "impossibility" of slave marriage offers the paradigm case. It is one measure of the singularity of New Jersey slavery that marriages between enslaved people were considered legitimate by the 1790s—and probably earlier. Others have, of course, studied slavery through the lens of contract, often focusing on the debt relations and the contracts of sale that shaped the identities of slaveholders. It is as well a long-standing insight of the social history of slavery and of legal anthropology that working relations on plantations and everywhere else slavery was practiced depended on informal bargaining and on what contract scholars would call "reliance interests." Walter Johnson, *Soul by Soul: Life Inside the Antebellum Slave Market* (Cambridge, MA: Harvard University Press, 1999); Ariela J. Gross, *Double Character: Slavery and Mastery in the Antebellum Southern Courtroom* (Princeton, NJ: Princeton University Press, 2000); Dylan C. Penningroth, *The Claims of Kinfolk: African American Property and Community in the Nineteenth-Century South* (Chapel Hill: University of North Carolina Press, 2003); Eugene Genovese, *Roll, Jordan, Roll* (New York: Pantheon Books, 1974).

21. Albert O. Hirschman, *Exit, Voice, and Loyalty: Responses to Decline in Firms, Organizations, and States* (Cambridge, MA: Harvard University Press, 1970). For the conventional focus on the coercive and compulsory law of a state, see William Novak, *The People's Welfare* (Chapel Hill: University of North Carolina Press, 1996).

22. Duncan Kennedy, "The Structure of Blackstone's Commentaries," *Buffalo Law Review* 28 (1979): 205–382; Janet Halley, "What Is Family Law? A Genealogy, Part One," *Yale Journal of Law and the Humanities* 23, no. 1 (2011): 1–109.

Chapter One

1. See Lucius Q. C. Elmer, *The Constitution and Government of the Province and State of New Jersey* (Newark, NJ: M. R. Dennis, 1872), 313–17. Ford's family's money derived from an early ironworks, one that had been worked out by the early nineteenth century. His father and grandfather had built the largest house in the county. Because that house once served as Washington's winter headquarters, it remains a well-known Revolutionary-era historical monument. Jude M. Pfister, *The Fords of New Jersey: Power and Family during America's Founding* (Charleston, SC: History Press, 2010).

2. To complete the domestic circle of the Ford and DeSaussure law firm, Timothy Ford had married DeSaussure's sister Amelia. Sally Hadden, "DeSaussure and Ford: A Charleston Law Firm of the 1790s," in *Transformations in American Legal History: Essays in Honor of Professor Morton J. Horwitz*, ed. Daniel Hamilton and Alfred Brophy (Cambridge, MA: Harvard University Press, 2009), 85–108. See Ford's testimony in Cutter v. Moore, 8 N.J.L. 219 (Sup. Ct. 1825). By the 1830 census, Ford acknowledged the presence of only one woman of color in his household. It looks like the census taker first marked her as enslaved and between the ages of ten and twenty-five, but then, realizing that no one born after 1804 could be enslaved, marked her as free colored (the mark in the enslaved column was remade into a zero). 1830 United States Federal Census for New Jersey, Morristown, Morris, New Jersey, 33–34 of 46 (Ancestry.com). On the correspondence between Timothy and Gabriel Ford, see Konstantin Dierks, "Letter Writing, Gender, and Class in America, 1750–1800" (PhD diss., Brown University, 1999), 199–201, 206–7.

3. Force v. Haines, 17 N.J.L. 385, 386 (Sup. Ct. 1840).

4. By the time that Ford decided *Force v. Haines*, there was a developing legal literature on the distinctive law of slavery. Jacob D. Wheeler, *A Practical Treatise on the Law of Slavery. Being a Compilation of All the Decisions Made on That Subject, in the Several Courts of the United States, and State Courts. With Copious Notes and References to the Statutes and Other Authorities, Systematically Arranged* (New York: Allan Pollock, Jr.; New Orleans: Benjamin Levy, 1837). For the southern law of slavery as a doctrinal field, see Thomas D. Morris, *Southern Slavery and the Law, 1619–1860*, Studies in Legal History (Chapel Hill: University of North Carolina Press, 1996). But see Walter Johnson, "Inconsistency, Contradiction, and Complete Confusion: The Everyday Life of the Law of Slavery," *Law and Social Inquiry* 22, no. 2 (Spring 1997): 405–33.

5. *Force v. Haines*, 386–87.

6. See Jeroen Kortmann, *Altruism in Private Law: Liability for Nonfeasance and Negotiorum Gestio* (Oxford: Oxford University Press, 2005).

7. See State v. Mann, 13 N.C. 263 (1829).

8. See Carol M. Rose, *Property and Persuasion Essays on the History, Theory, and Rhetoric of Ownership*, New Perspectives on Law, Culture, and Society (Boulder, CO:

Westview Press, 1994); William Novak, *The People's Welfare* (Chapel Hill: University of North Carolina Press, 1996).

9. Linda Gordon, *Heroes of Their Own Lives* (New York: Vintage, 1988); Paul S. Boyer, *Urban Masses and Moral Order in America, 1820–1920* (Cambridge, MA: Harvard University Press, 1978).

10. See Morris, *Southern Slavery and the Law*, 137–39, 190–92, 278–80, 364–65, 388, 430.

11. Force v. Haines, at 394.

12. Ford assumed that his perspective derived ineluctably from the common law, that it expressed fundamental truths found through common law legal reasoning. That common law understanding, he would have known, stood in contrast both to lay understandings of moral obligation and, perhaps more importantly, to a Roman law understanding—identified with the Latin phrase *negotiorum gestio*—that began with the presumption that benevolent intervenors were entitled to reward and compensation. We might speculate that his perspective was intrinsic to his professional identity. When as a young man, he would have learned "the law," while clerking for an older lawyer, Ford would have learned the structures and "forms of action" (or pleadings) of assumpsit law and of what was adequate "consideration" for a contract. In learning to "think like a lawyer," he would have learned to bracket off claims to compensation for neighborliness and care as nonlegal or wrongheaded. It is a question deserving further research how questions of compensation for "good Samaritans" and similar ethical conundrums would have been taught at schools like the College of New Jersey (the future Princeton University), where so many of the judges and lawyers had received their early education. Commonsense philosophy could have been mobilized for a variety of positions. See Susanna L. Blumenthal, *Law and the Modern Mind: Consciousness and Responsibility in American Legal Culture* (Cambridge, MA: Harvard University Press, 2016). On an alternative lay understanding that rooted care in the "peace" of a local community, see Laura F. Edwards, *The People and Their Peace: Legal Culture and the Transformation of Inequality in the Post-Revolutionary South* (Chapel Hill: University of North Carolina Press, 2009).

13. John William Smith, *A Selection of Leading Cases, on Various Branches of the Law, with Notes* (Philadelphia: T. & J. Johnson, 1832); John William Smith, *A Selection of Leading Cases on Various Branches of the Law: With Notes*, Law Library, vol. 19, no. 1 (Philadelphia: John S. Littell, 1838–40).

14. Lampleigh v. Braithwait, Hob. 105 (1615). For a recent portrayal of the story of the case as a Siamese folktale, see Siti Suhaidah's YouTube video, "Past Consideration" (2015).

15. Francis Buller, *An Introduction to the Law Relative to Trials at Nisi Prius* (London, 1772). The law of *nisi prius* was, to put it overly simply, the archaic law of trial practice, or the law that defined what cases went forward to trial. Not all "complaints" deserve adjudication. The law of *nisi prius* described how a complaint became legally justiciable. It was, through the eighteenth and early nineteenth centuries, a crucial but arcane field of law defined by the rules of pleadings—the old writ system—that largely determined access to the courts. The *"nisi prius* record" was the formal copy of the proceedings leading up to a trial.

16. Stokes v. Lewis, 99 Eng. Rep. 949; 1 T.R. 20 (K.B. 1785); Jenkins v. Tucker, 126 Eng. Rep. 55; 1 H. Bl. 90 (C.P. 1788).

17. Heirs of Potter v. Potter's Widow, 3 N.J.L. 415 (1808).

18. Dunbar v. Williams, 10 Johns. 249 (NY Sup. 1813).

19. Evarts v. Adams, 12 Johns. 352 (NY Sup. 1815); Bartholomew v. Jackson, 20 Johns. 28 (NY Sup. 1822).

20. Force v. Haines, 389–90.

21. Ibid.

22. Searman v. Castell, 1 Esp. N.Pr. 270 (1795); Simmons v. Wilmot, 3 Esp. N.P. 91 (1800).

23. Forsyth v. Ganson (mislabeled as Gansel in Ford's opinion), 5 Wend. 558 (NY Sup. 1830). See Hendrik Hartog, *Someday All This Will Be Yours: A History of Inheritance and Old Age* (Cambridge, MA: Harvard University Press, 2012).

24. His uncle Jonathan Dayton had been an important figure in the early republic, the youngest signer of the U.S. Constitution, the Speaker of the House of Representatives for a time, a land speculator, an entrepreneur, and a partner in steamboat operations first with Aaron Ogden and then with Thomas Gibbons. Others in his family became prominent lawyers both in New Jersey and in New York City.

25. Elmer, *Constitution and Government*, 372–96. See the *New York Times*, February 23, 1860, where Dayton was described as having been "one of the most conspicuous, trusted, sagacious, conservative and moderate, but firm defenders, in the United States Senate, of constitutional principles, and the, until that time, established policy of the Government."

26. The next paragraphs depend on Dayton's opinion in *Force v. Haines*, 393–402.

27. It has for a generation been conventional for historians to regard the law of slavery as a distinctive legal field. See Mark V. Tushnet, *The American Law of Slavery, 1810–1860: Considerations of Humanity and Interest* (Princeton, NJ: Princeton University Press, 1981); Morris, *Southern Slavery and the Law*. That understanding is challenged by the work of Christopher Tomlins. See Christopher Tomlins, *Freedom Bound: Law, Labor, and Civic Identity in Colonizing English America, 1580–1865* (Cambridge: Cambridge University Press, 2010).

28. "An Act Respecting Slaves," March 14, 1798, sections 21–25, A75 (NJDLL).

29. Overseers of Poor of South Brunswick v. Overseers of Poor of East Windsor, 8 N.J.L. 64 (Sup. Ct. 1824). The situation described in this case was one that occurred often throughout the South, as slaveholders abandoned old and "worthless" enslaved peoples when they moved away. Alexandra Lerner, "Aging in Bondage: Slavery, Debility, and the Problem of Dependency in the Old South" (PhD diss., Princeton University, 2016).

30. William Nelson, *Joseph Coerten Hornblower, 1777–1864, Chief Justice of New Jersey, 1832–1846: A Biographical Sketch* (Cambridge, MA: John Wilson and Son, 1894); Paul Finkelman, "State Constitutional Protections of Liberty and the Antebellum New Jersey Supreme Court: Chief Justice Hornblower and the Fugitive Slave Law," *Rutgers Law Journal* 23, no. 4 (1992): 753–87; Daniel R. Ernst, "Legal Positivism, Abolitionist Litigation, and the New Jersey Slave Case of 1845," *Law and History Review* 4, no. 2 (Autumn 1986): 337–65. I have found relatively little on Nevius. He had a

prominent life as a practitioner before a relatively short term on the court. Elmer thought Nevius lacked accurate knowledge of the law; he had a more complex assessment of Hornblower. Elmer, *Constitution and Government*, 347–49, 361–73.

31. The next paragraphs draw from Hornblower's opinion found in *Force v. Haines*, 402–10.

32. On readings of Somerset, see Edlie L. Wong, *Neither Fugitive nor Free: Atlantic Slavery, Freedom Suits, and the Legal Culture of Travel*, America and the Long 19th Century (New York: New York University Press, 2009); Patricia Minter, "'The State of Slavery': *Somerset, The Slave Grace*, and the Rise of Pro-Slavery and Anti-Slavery Constitutionalism in the Nineteenth-Century Atlantic World," *Slavery and Abolition: A Journal of Slave and Post-Slave Studies* 36, no. 4 (June 2015): 603–17; George Van Cleve, "Somerset's Case and Its Antecedents in Imperial Perspective," *Law and History Review* 24, no. 3 (Fall 2006): 601–45.

33. We will return to the relationship between poor relief and gradual emancipation in chapter 2.

34. Force v. Haines, 410–15.

Chapter Two

1. The modern city of Rahway was formed in 1860 by combining Rahway Township with a portion of Woodbridge, in Middlesex County. I suspect that the latter included the area along the Rahway River where Henry Force lived. John P. Snyder, *The Story of New Jersey's Civil Boundaries, 1606–1968* (1969; repr., Trenton: Bureau of Geology and Topography, 2004), 42.

2. Nicholas Murray, *Notes, Historical and Biographical, concerning Elizabeth-Town, Its Eminent Men, Churches and Ministers* (Elizabeth-Town, NJ: E. Sanderson, 1844); Theodore Thayer, *As We Were: The Story of Old Elizabethtown*, Collections of the New Jersey Historical Society, vol. 13 (Elizabeth, NJ: Grassmann, 1964). Between 1820 and 1830, Elizabethtown (borough and township) lost population; by 1840, it had grown modestly to 4,184. Meanwhile, Newark had already grown from 6,507 in 1820 to 17,290 in 1840. (See http://population.us/nj/newark/; http://population.us/nj/elizabeth/.) After 1855, the township and borough of Elizabethtown became the city of Elizabeth, as it is today. It also was separated from Essex County, becoming part of the new Union County.

3. In 1830, there were still 218 slaves in Essex County (http://westjersey.org/ssn.htm). One local historian acknowledged the presence of a slave trade by describing two advertisements placed by his own ancestor, Cornelius Hatfield: one for a "likely Parcel of Negro Boys and Girls from 12 to 20 Years of age, who have all had the Small Pox," dated April 27, 1752, and one from June 4, 1753, for "A parcel of likely healthy Negro Men and Women, from between 14 and 22 Years of Age." He recognized that Elizabethtown, like other slaveholding communities, had been repeatedly subject to "remarkable panics." Such a panic in 1741 led to the burning to death of two African American men from New York City. Enslaved people had fled to Elizabethtown to escape the white violence that had resulted from the infamous "Negro Conspiracy" and fire of that year. White "panic" in New York City ended with the imprisonment

of 154 "negroes," of whom fourteen were burned at the stake, eighteen hanged, and seventy-one transported. Two of those who had fled the city across the Hudson were arrested in Essex County. The historian then reproduced the account book of the "Justices and Freeholders" of the Essex County government, which included both an eleven-shilling allowance granted to Daniel Harrison for carting wood used "for burning" to death those "two Negros," and smaller allowances to three other men who had provided the wood used to carry out that "legal process." Edwin Francis Hatfield, *History of Elizabeth, New Jersey: Including the Early History of Union County* (Elizabeth, NJ: Carlton and Lanahan, 1868), 363–64, 387–88. See also Thayer, *As We Were*. Another historian describes the exploits of some of the heroes of the town during the Revolutionary War. In one incident, the "guard . . . and baggage . . . and horses" of a British Colonel Fox were captured. One of the four men captured was a "colored man," who was taken to Philadelphia, where he could be sold into slavery. Murray, *Notes, Historical and Biographical*, 97.

4. 1830 Federal Census, New Jersey, Middlesex, Woodbridge, 15, 10–18 of 60 (Ancestry.com). On the other hand, at that time there remained 309 enslaved people in the whole of Middlesex County (http://westjersey.org/ssn.htm).

5. See "Persons under the Pension Roles under the Law of the 18th of March, 1818," 479 (Ancestry.com). He called himself a lawyer after having moved to Prince William County, Virginia, during the 1840s. 1850 United States Federal Census, Virginia, Prince William, 84 of 13 (Ancestry.com). On his financial life, see chapter 4, and *Force v. Craig*, 7 N.J.L. 272 (N.J. 1823). New Jersey General Assembly, 1921.001, SAS00001, Tax Ratables (Duplicates), 1768–1846 (Trenton: New Jersey Department of Archives and Records Management) (NJSA). On his first two wives, see cemetery inscriptions for Anna, who died in 1806, and Sarah, who died in 1820. A son died in 1824, at the age of nine (http://www.westfieldnjhistory.com/files/rahwaycem.htm). I suspect his saw mill is the same one that he and the executors of the estate of John C. Marsh advertised in the *New-Jersey Journal*, December 14, 1813 (vol. 30, issue 1572, p. 3). See also Harry B. Weiss and Grace M. Weiss, *The Early Sawmills of New Jersey* (Trenton: NJ, New Jersey Agricultural Society, 1968), 60.

6. Essex County Surrogate, "Will Book A" (1803–14), Benjamin Hains will, GSU Reel #913280 (NJSA); see also New Jersey, Wills and Probate Records, 1739–1991, for Benjamin Hains, Essex Wills, vol. A, 1803–14 (Ancestry.com).

7. Tax Ratables (Duplicates), 1768–1846 (NJSA); *Record of Black Births, Followed by Birth Certificates, and Certificates and Deeds of Manumission, and Slave Receipts* (Essex County, 1804–43), 153–54.

8. The gravestone inscription reads as follows: "His days are number'd, and his spirit fled / He's gone the Husband Father, Friend, is dead; / Nor weeping friend, nor healing art could save / His body from the cold and silent grave" (http://www.find agrave.com/cgi-bin/fg.cgi?page=pv&GRid=7237192&PIpi=41888861). Curiously, there is no mention at all of Elizabeth, and I have failed to find records of their marriage. For Mary Cross's testimony, see Force v. Haines, trial transcript, #12912 (NJSA).

9. For more on Jesse, see chapter 4. Force v. Haines, trial transcript, #12912 (NJSA).

10. *New York Times*, June 14, 1864. New England Historical and Genealogical Register, vol. 19 (1865), 87–89. Letter to Mr. [Ja?] Burt, Joseph C. Hornblower, April 6,

1857, from Newark (printed in a newspaper as well.) Original at the NYHS. Paul Finkelman, "State Constitutional Protections of Liberty and the Antebellum New Jersey Supreme Court: Chief Justice Hornblower and the Fugitive Slave Law," *Rutgers Law Journal* 23, no. 4 (1992): 753–87; James J. Gigantino II, *The Ragged Road to Abolition: Slavery and Freedom in New Jersey, 1775–1865* (Philadelphia: University of Pennsylvania Press, 2014), 220. Gigantino identifies him as a colonizationist who supported gradual emancipation. I think he may understate Hornblower's antislavery commitments. On the multiplicities of what it meant to be an abolitionist, see Padraic X. Scanlan, "The Colonial Rebirth of British Anti-Slavery: The Liberated African Villages of Sierra Leone, 1815–1824," *American Historical Review* 121, no. 4 (October 2016): 1084–1113.

11. Essex County Manumission Book (NJSA), 160–62.

12. New Jersey Wills and Probate Records, 1785–1924. Unrecorded Estate Papers, 852 (Inventory of Estate of Josiah Hornblower); Wills, Vol. A, 1803–1814, Probate May 26, 1808 [this year is incorrect, since Josiah H. lived to 1809], image 373 (Ancestry.com). Essex County Manumission Book (NJSA), 176. On reasons why an enslaved person might not appear in estate distributions, see Stuart Gold, "The 'Gift' of Liberty: Testamentary Manumission in New Jersey, 1791–1805," *Rutgers Race and the Law Review* 15 (2014): 1–72. On Josiah Hornblower, see Richard P. McCormick, "The First Steam Engine in America," *Journal of the Rutgers University Libraries* 11, no. 1 (1947): 21–27; William Nelson, *Josiah Hornblower, and the First Steam-Engine in America: With Some Notices of the Schuyler Copper Mines at Second River, N. J., and a Genealogy of the Hornblower Family* (Newark, NJ, 1883).

13. 1830 United States Federal Census, New Jersey, Essex, Newark, Essex, 117 of 142 (Ancestry.com). Manumission Book (NJSA), 176–78, 37–39, 161. The year after Joseph manumitted his own slave, his brother Josiah Hornblower, who lived in Bergen County, sold his eighteen-year-old slave Samuel Jackson for $225 to the slave trader and plantation owner William Stone, "to have and to hold the said Negro Slave during his natural life . . . forever." Presumably, young Josiah knew that Samuel Jackson would be moved, illegally, to Louisiana sugar plantations. "Subseries 1.2, 1817–1822," Avery Family of Louisiana, 1796–1951 (University of North Carolina, microfilm).

14. Lucius Q. C. Elmer, *The Constitution and Government of the Province and State of New Jersey* (Newark, NJ: M. R. Dennis, 1872), 361–72; William Nelson, *Joseph Coerten Hornblower, 1777–1864, Chief Justice of New Jersey, 1832–1846: A Biographical Sketch* (Cambridge, MA: John Wilson and Son, 1894). The next thirteen paragraphs are drawn from the Hornblower Family Collection, 1760–1900, MG10, Box 8, Folders 1–5, Ann Ogilvie Papers (slavery) (New Jersey Historical Society). MacWhorter's papers are at the Southern Historical Collection of the University of North Carolina, Alexander MacWhorter Papers, 1764–1807 (Collection Number 01235-z).

15. Alexander MacWhorter, *A Series of Sermons, upon the Most Important Principles of Our Holy Religion* (Newark: Pennington and Gould, 1803); Julius Melton, "The Book of Common Worship," *American Presbyterians* 66, no. 4 (Winter 1988): 299–303; Elizabeth Marting, "Alexander MacWhorter's Southern Adversities," *Journal of the Presbyterian Historical Society* 26, no. 1 (March 1948): 1–18.

16. Hoffman, a Federalist, had been attorney general of New York between 1799 and 1805. Andrew Burstein, *The Original Knickerbocker: The Life of Washington Irving* (New York: Basic Books, 2007), 18–28.

17. "An Act Respecting Slaves," March 14, 1798, A75 (NJDLL).

18. Although the gift was from Anne Ogilvie, it is not clear whether she gave Leah or Elsie as her own property or as part of the estate that she was the executor of. Was she fulfilling MacWhorter's last wishes, or was the gift to her niece (and to MacWhorter's granddaughter) a "voluntary" act on her part? MacWhorter's will simply divided his estate between his two surviving children, Anne Ogilvie and a brother. New Jersey, Wills and Probate Records, 1739–1991, Essex Wills, vol. A, 1803–1814 (Ancestry.com). It is, of course, entirely possible that MacWhorter had instructed Ogilvie privately about how he wished Leah or Elsie to be treated. In the records, Beebe is often spelled Bebee. For simplicity, I am using Beebe, which seems to be the family name, in the text.

19. For the contrary argument, see Rebecca J. Scott, "Paper Thin: Freedom and Re-Enslavement in the Diaspora of the Haitian Revolution," *Law and History Review* 29, no. 4 (November 2011): 1061–87.

20. It is possible that Leah or Elsie had come from South Carolina, where MacWhorter had lived until shortly before his death.

21. A similar deposition was taken in August 1822 from Mrs. Eliza H. Robins, who was apparently a stepsister of Mary Beebe.

22. On municipal law, see William Blackstone, *Commentaries on the Laws of England*, ed. William Carey Jones (Baton Rouge: Claitor's, 1976), 44–47. Mansfield's decision in *Somerset v. Stewart* insisted that the right of a master was founded on the "municipal law" of a particular place only and did not continue elsewhere. See Somerset v. Stewart (1772) 98 ER 499. There was, as far as I have found, little effort in New Jersey or New York to justify slavery using biblical law or other forms of natural law. On conflicts of law, see Joseph Story, *Commentaries on the Conflict of Laws, Foreign and Domestic: In Regard to Contracts, Rights, and Remedies, and Especially in Regard to Marriages, Divorces, Wills, Successions, and Judgments* (Boston: Hilliard, Gray, 1834).

23. Why did New York law rather than Pennsylvania law play such an important role in New Jersey? By the early nineteenth century, most New Jersey households that included enslaved people were in the northern and eastern part of the state; as a result, most of the cases occurred in northern counties. Gigantino, *Ragged Road to Abolition*, 66–69. One suspects the influence of Quakers in southern Pennsylvania-bordering counties played a role in the decline of slavery in that region. For justice of the peace manuals, see *The Conductor Generalis, or The Office: Duty and Authority of Justices of the Peace, High-Sheriffs, Under-Sheriffs, Coroners, Constables, Gaolers, Jury-Men, and Overseers of the Poor [...]* (Albany, 1794); James Ewing, *A Treatise on the Office and Duty of a Justice of the Peace, Sheriff, Coroner, Constable, and of Executors, Administrators, and Guardians: In Which is Particularly Laid Down, the Rules for Conducting an Action in the Court for the Trial of Small Causes [...]* (Trenton, NJ, 1805 and later additions in 1832 and 1839); William Griffith, *A Treatise on the Jurisdiction and Proceedings of Justices of the Peace, in Civil Suits in New-Jersey with an Appendix, Containing, Advice to Executors, Administrators, and Guardians, an Epitome of the Law of Landlord and*

Tenant [...] (Burlington, NJ: David Allinson, 1813). For Pennsylvania, see Gary B. Nash and Jean R. Soderland, *Freedom by Degrees: Emancipation in Pennsylvania and Its Aftermath* (New York: Oxford University Press, 1991).

24. Ramage Family Papers, 1766–1856, Mss Collection (NYHS). The two Bobs are confused in the description in the catalog of the New-York Historical Society. It is not clear whether young Bob was included in old Bob's purchase. Dinah might have had three living children, in addition to young Bob who lived apart. It should be noted that Dinah's younger children had probably been born in New Jersey after the passage of New Jersey's 1804 gradual emancipation law. All of those children, including young Bob, had certainly been born after New York had enacted its 1799 gradual emancipation law. Both laws marked the children of enslaved people as not-enslaved. They could still be conveyed, though the period of service would end when they were in their twenties. Was young Bob conveyed to Ephraim Sayre as if he were enslaved or as a young person who was being apprenticed?

25. October 5, 1812, Gibbons Carver Collection, Box 19 (read at Museum of American Finance; now at Hagley Museum). On sojourners, see Anne Twitty, *Before Dred Scott: Slavery and Legal Culture in the American Confluence, 1787–1857* (New York: Cambridge University Press, 2016); Edlie L. Wong, *Neither Fugitive nor Free: Atlantic Slavery, Freedom Suits, and the Legal Culture of Travel*, America and the Long 19th Century (New York: New York University Press, 2009).

26. "An Act Respecting Slaves," March 14, 1798, A75 (NJDLL).

27. In the South, the recognition of slave marriages was regarded as inconsistent with the master–slave relationship. State v. Samuel, 19 N.C. 177 (1836). By contrast, in New Jersey and in New York, the recognition of slave marriages did not necessarily serve as a challenge to the regime. Consider "Miss Dunlap vs. Peggy Thomas, wife of Tom Thomas," reported as "A LAW CASE," in *The New-York Magazine and General Repository of Useful Knowledge (1814–1814)*, July 1, 1814, 1, 162. Dunlap had purchased Peggy in New Jersey more than twenty years before. Dunlap had moved Peggy to New York, where she was hired out, earning her mistress $300. Around 1810, Dunlap had "betrothed" Peggy in marriage to Tom Thomas, a free man, with whom she had one child. In 1812, Dunlap had moved back to New Jersey, and she had applied to a New York court ("a special court of enquiry") to remove Peggy to New Jersey as still enslaved. Peggy's attorney, John Graham, argued on Peggy's and Thomas's behalf, in the face of a New York statute (February 17, 1809) that allowed Dunlap to continue to hold a slave notwithstanding her marriage. (He did so because he described himself as "wedded to *Madam Humanity and* ... no earthly tribunal shall ever *divorce* me from the sweet embraces of her ladyship.") Peggy's marriage, he insisted, amounted to a complete manumission, because the law was "always ready to catch at any thing in favour of liberty." Miss Dunlap had "set her slave on the same footing with herself." Consummation of the marriage constituted the consideration for completing the contract. Had a slave married without a master's consent, the situation might be different. But when a female slave was "given over" to a free man, the master lost all rights of ownership. Or so Graham argued. His argument failed, and the New York court allowed "Miss Dunlap to take the wench to the state of New-Jersey." The court held that marriage did not counter or challenge the continuity of

the master–slave relationship. (Apparently, though, Graham was able to convince Miss Dunlap to free Peggy twenty-one days later.) See Michelle McKinley, *Fractional Freedoms: Slavery, Intimacy, and Legal Mobilization in Colonial Lima, 1600–1700* (New York: Cambridge University Press, 2016), 80, in which marriage is described as co-constitutive with slavery. On the duty to teach enslaved children to read, see section 16 of the 1798 act: "Slaves born since Nov. 26, 1788 to be taught to read." It is hard to find evidence of much awareness on the part of whites of this legal obligation. In nearly all legal documents I have found requiring the "consent" or the signature of an enslaved person, she or he signed with an X. However, in April 19, 1817, when Robert Ogden sold Jupiter Hornbeck, his purchaser, James Fowler, agreed to provide the "Education and Provision as the Law ... requires." Fowler promised "to indemnify and save harmless" Robert Ogden "for all damage which accrues from the Negro Boy's not having such Education and Provision as the Law Requires." Co695 Ogden Family Collection; 1682–1853, Manuscripts Division, Department of Rare Books and Special Collections, Princeton University Library.

28. This is one of those moments when a reading of the New Jersey statute book can only produce raised eyebrows. As we will see, slaves were excluded from benefiting from local poor relief. What possible good did it do them when the legislature directed a fine for slave mistreatment to be paid to the presumptively white local poor? The answer, of course, is that the laws were intended to punish abusive slaveholders, not benefit victimized enslaved peoples.

29. In its relative silence about how discipline was to be maintained over those who served, the New Jersey slave code was little different than the legal structures that defined the relations of ostensibly free servants and their "masters" throughout the northern United States. Labor discipline was labor discipline, left in a private sphere governed (occasionally) by local legal authorities like justices of the peace. For the most part, the work of a household was not a focus of legislative attention, whether the labor was being done by those identified as "free" or those identified as "enslaved." For a portrait of a more or less unified and coercive legal order governing all forms of subordinated labor, see Christopher Tomlins, *Freedom Bound: Law, Labor, and Civic Identity in Colonizing English America, 1580–1865* (Cambridge: Cambridge University Press, 2010). For the larger British imperial context, see Douglas Hay and Paul Craven, eds., *Masters, Servants, and Magistrates in Britain and the Empire, 1562–1955* (Chapel Hill: University of North Carolina Press, 2004). On the politics that lay behind the 1798 code, see Marion Thompson Wright, "Period of Democratic Idealism," *The Journal of Negro History* 28 (1943): 175–76.

30. "An Act for the Gradual Abolition of Slavery," Feb. 15, 1804, A78 (NJDLL). On the New York origins of the law, see Graham Russell Hodges, *Slavery and Freedom in the Rural North: African Americans in Monmouth County, New Jersey, 1665–1865* (Madison, WI: Madison House, 1997), 136; David N. Gellman, *Emancipating New York: The Politics of Slavery and Freedom, 1777–1827* (Baton Rouge: Louisiana State University Press, 2006), 182. The general context for the act is covered in Gigantino, *Ragged Road to Abolition.* The New Jersey Society for Promoting the Abolition of Slavery strongly endorsed the law, and a committee of the society urged members to consider the law as "perfect" as it was practicable to be enacted at that time. The committee

cautioned that no alterations be recommended "until some defect shall have been discovered." Minutes of the Proceedings of the New Jersey Society for Promoting the Abolition of Slavery (Haverford College), http://triptych.haverford.edu/cdm /fullbrowser/collection/HC_QuakSlav/id/12143/rv/compoundobject/cpd/12257, pp. 86–87. According to Moss, many slaveholders banded together to press for repeal. Simeon Moss, "The Persistence of Slavery and Involuntary Servitude in a Free State (1685–1866)," *Journal of Negro History* 35, no. 3 (July 1950): 303–4. The form of the gradual abolition law finds a curious echo in the "free womb" law passed in 1871 as a form of gradual abolition in Brazil. Free Womb Law (The Rio Blanco Law). Enacted September 28, 1871. *British and Foreign State Papers*, vol. 62, 1871–1872 (London: William Ridgway, 1877). (Thanks to Tala Khanmallek for this citation.)

31. David Mitros, ed., *Slave Records of Morris County, New Jersey, 1756–1841* (Morris County, NJ: Morris County Heritage Commission, 1991), 42–79; *The Book of Black Birth in Bergen County, N.J.*, copied by Ackerman Hawkey, with a new introduction and index by Carolyn L. Barkley (Bergen County Historical Society, 1923). Hunterdon County (imaged) Records of Children of Slaves (NJSA). http://www.nj.gov /state/archives/chncl004.html. *Record of Black Births, Followed by Birth Certificates, and Certificates and Deeds of Manumission, and Slave Receipts* (Essex County: NJSA, 1804–43) (NJSA).

32. The law declared that any "negro" enslaved on March 1798 would continue as such for life unless manumitted "in manner prescribed by law." Presumptively, that would also be true of those who were born after March 1798 but before the enforcement date of the gradual emancipation statute of 1804. The "code" was modified by several pieces of legislation over the next twenty-two years and was recodified in 1820. See "An Act for the Gradual Abolition of Slavery, and for Other Purposes Respecting Slaves," Feb. 24, 1820, A87 (NJDLL).

33. Gellman, *Emancipating New York*; Sarah Levine-Gronningsater, "Delivering Freedom: Gradual Emancipation, Black Legal Culture, and the Origins of Sectional Crisis in New York, 1759–1870" (PhD diss., University of Chicago, 2014).

34. Christopher Florio, "The Poor Always with You: Poverty in an Age of Emancipation, 1833–1879" (PhD diss., Princeton University, 2016); Benjamin J. Klebaner, "Poverty and Its Relief in American Thought, 1815–61," *Social Service Review* 38, no. 4 (December 1964): 382–99; Alexandra Lerner, "Aging in Bondage: Slavery, Debility, and the Problem of Dependency in the Old South" (PhD diss., Princeton University, 2016).

35. For a continuous record of prices and valuations, see Mitros, *Slave Records of Morris County.*

36. See Sidney Chalhoub, "The Precariousness of Freedom in a Slave Society (Brazil in the Nineteenth Century)," *International Review of Social History* 56, no. 3 (December 2011): 405–39; Sidney Chalhoub, "The Politics of Ambiguity: Conditional Manumission, Labor Contracts, and Slave Emancipation in Brazil (1850s–1888)," *International Review of Social History* 60, no. 2 (August 2015): 161–91; McKinley, *Fractional Freedoms.*

37. I searched New Jersey newspapers in the American Historical Newspapers database, using the following keywords: "Run Away AND Reward AND Negro." I got

72 hits between 1790 and 1840. There were another 4 hits between 1840 and 1860 (http://infoweb.newsbank.com/iw-search/we/HistArchive?p_action=list&p_top doc=1&PAGE=1&p_queryname=7). The same search using "Ranaway" produced 149 hits, all but 4 of which occurred before 1827. The same search with "Ran Away" produced 35 more hits. See also Shane White, *Somewhat More Independent: The End of Slavery in New York City, 1770–1810* (Athens: University of Georgia Press, 1991), 114–49. On the attractions of New York City, see Shane White, *Stories of Freedom in Black New York* (Cambridge, MA: Harvard University Press, 2002), 30–32; Gellman, *Emancipating New York*, 160; Graham Russell Hodges, *Root & Branch: African Americans in New York & East Jersey, 1613–1863* (Chapel Hill: University of North Carolina Press, 1999), 173–75.

38. McCutchen v. Marshall, 33 U.S. 220 (1834). See Ketletas v. Fleet, 7 Johns. 324 (Sup. Ct. 1811), in which a New York court held a master bound by his agreement, yet at the same time explained that he was bound as the giver of a gift. To the New York court, the gift obligation was stronger than that of a mere contract. An 1830 New Jersey source suggested that a master could be bound by his contract with his slave. William Halsted, *A Digested Index to the Decisions of the Superior Courts of the State of New Jersey* (Trenton, NJ, 1830), 831–32, sec. 26. See also State v. Mount, 1 N.J.L. 292 (1795). On the early modern discourse of gifts and contracts, including a focus on the ways gifts could bind like contracts, see Natalie Z. Davis, *The Gift in Sixteenth-Century France* (Madison: University of Wisconsin Press, 2000).

39. The county manumission books also became a registry for the births of children of slave women. See *Record of Black Births, Essex; Manumission Book of Monmouth County, New Jersey, 1791–1844* (Freehold, NJ: Office of the Monmouth County Clerk, 1992). New Jersey Supreme Court, *[Cases] Adjudged in the Supreme Court of New-Jersey, Relative to the Manumission of Negroes and Others Holden in Bondage* (Burlington, NJ, 1794). How new these practices and that presumption were is unclear. Was it a by-product of Revolutionary republican ideology? On the other hand, the work of Jonathan Sassi suggests that the flurry of post-Revolutionary manumissions continued and developed a set of practices—shaped by early Quaker understandings and strategies—that began well before the Revolution. Jonathan D. Sassi, " 'The Assembly of New Jersey Have a Bill Now under Their Consideration': Anthony Benezet and a Transatlantic-Provincial Abolition Campaign on the Eve of the American Revolution" (unpublished manuscript, 2015). In contrast, Gigantino argues that the American Revolution strengthened pro-slavery forces. Gigantino, *Ragged Road to Abolition*.

40. *Manumission Book of Monmouth County, New Jersey, 1791–1844*, 84–85. The certificate was written in 1790, but it was not recorded until 1807, still before Forman's own death.

41. Nathaniel Bennet conveyed Jink to Henry Baker of Woodbridge for one hundred dollars. Jink was fifteen. But the transaction would terminate when Jink turned twenty-seven, at which time she was to have her freedom. C0234, Winans Collection of New Jersey Documents, Manuscripts Division, Department of Rare Books and Special Collections, Princeton University Library. The 1814 will of Enoch Beach of Morris Township declared that a "black boy" should serve until the age of thirty,

at which point he should pay fifty-three dollars. And Samuel Batson's will in the same year declared that a slave should be free after serving his son for five years after the testator's death. The slave in that instance was more than forty but was valued at $250 in the estate. Amos Grandin's 1817 will conveyed a black woman to serve until age twenty-eight (her value was given as $40), one "boy" to serve until age twenty-five (value $130), and one girl until age twenty-one (value $60). (Obviously, he was borrowing the term limits written into the 1804 law, even though those limits did not apply.) Mitros, *Slave Records of Morris County*, 42–79, 26–28.

42. *Trenton Federalist*, October 4, 1809. Hartshorne papers—Monmouth County Historical Society. Box 6—Folder 9; Richard Hartshorne (1752–1831) Personal Papers, 5 items Blacks, 1794–1812. See Roll #1, I-442 Misc. Book B, Manumission records for Monmouth County—1780–1816 (NJSA), p. 156: James Tapscott to Joseph James, bill of sale of male slave in 1805 (manumission in 1813). Richard Hartshorne was the vice president of the New Jersey Society for Promoting the Abolition of Slavery. See "Minutes of the Proceedings of the New Jersey Society for Promoting the Abolition of Slavery" (Haverford College).

43. See Chalhoub, "Politics of Ambiguity," for a somewhat similar analysis.

44. John Brown Papers, 1761–1835, Mss Collection (NYHS).

45. See Cato's cases and Adam Wyckoff's story, both discussed in chapter 3.

46. See Gigantino, *Ragged Road to Abolition*, for the half-empty view.

47. In New Jersey, as well as in New York, agreements between master and slave were usually understood as enforceable. See Ketletas v. Fleet, 7 Johns. Rep. 324 (NY Sup. 1811), affirming Anthon N.P. Cas. 36 (1808). Of 405 contracts included in the Illinois Emancipation and Servitude Records that specified a term, the average was slightly over thirty years; 9 of the contracts specified a term of ninety-nine years. Twitty, *Before* Dred Scott: *Slavery and Legal Culture in the American Confluence, 1787–1857*, 33–37. For Brazil, see Henrique Espada Lima, "Freedom, Precariousness, and the Law: Freed Persons Contracting Out Their Labour in Nineteenth-Century Brazil," *International Review of Social History* 54, no. 3 (December 2009): 391–416, which explores "the paradigm of contract in a slave society."

48. The growth of private charity was one of the ways that nineteenth-century society confused inherited understandings. We might speculate that the need for voluntary and charitable manumission societies grew in part out of the separation of the enslaved from traditional structures of local care.

49. After the turn of the nineteenth century, township overseers of the poor could in theory place a pauper in a county-run poorhouse. I see no evidence of any use of poorhouses until the 1820s. See "Overseers of the Poor, 1754–1911," Monmouth County Archives, https://co.monmouth.nj.us/page.aspx?ID=4454.

50. Cornelia H. Dayton and Sharon Salinger, *Robert Love's Warnings: Searching for Strangers in Colonial Boston* (Philadelphia: University of Pennsylvania Press, 2014); Kunal M. Parker, *The Constitution, Citizenship, and Immigration in American History, 1790–2000*, New Essays on American Constitutional History Series (Washington, DC: American Historical Association, 2013); Douglas Jones, "The Strolling Poor: Transiency in 18th Century Massachusetts," *Journal of Social History* 8 (1975): 18; Lerner, "Aging in Bondage." On office holding, see Karen Orren, "Officers'

Rights: Toward a Unified Field Theory of American Constitutional Development," *Law and Society Review* 34, no. 4 (2000): 873–910. Problems of settlement law filled the pages of justice-of-the-peace manuals.

51. "An Act Respecting Slaves," March 14, 1798, A75 (NJDLL). Reading the county manumission record books of the early 1790s suggests that similar practices were already becoming routine by then. But in those early years, one also finds less formal manumissions in the records, ones in which the niceties of securing the acknowledgments of local officialdom were not observed. Until 1798, the legal effect of such "private" manumissions was said to be to free enslaved people from their masters without freeing masters from continuing public responsibility for "their" former slaves. See, for example, *Manumission Book of Monmouth County, New Jersey, 1791–1844.*

52. "An Act Respecting Slaves," March 14, 1798, A75 (NJDLL). For a description of parallel provisions in New York, see the critique of *Petry v. Christy* [described as Christie], 19 Johns. 53 (N.Y. Sup. 1821), in *U.S. Law Journal,* 1:174, 178–81 (1822–23).

53. State v. Emmons, 2 N.J.L. 10 (1806); State v. Isaac Emmons, Hunterdon, Habeas Corpus, New Jersey Supreme Court Case File #35074 (NJSA). It is not clear how the case came into being. Since the case was much attended to in the minutes of the New Jersey Society for Promoting the Abolition of Slavery, it could be that Ewing was bringing the case on the society's behalf. See Proceedings of the New Jersey Society for Promoting the Abolition of Slavery, 1793–1809, 96, 105, 112, 111 (Haverford College Quaker and Special Collections).

54. "An Act for Regulating of Slaves," March 11, 1713/14, A13 (NJDLL), and "An Act for Laying a Duty on the Purchasers of Slaves Imported into This Colony," Nov. 16, 1769, A24 (NJDLL).

55. State v. Emmons, 2 N.J.L. 10 (1806); State v. Isaac Emmons, Hunterdon, Habeas Corpus, New Jersey Supreme Court Case File #35074 (NJSA). A committee of the society was formed to seek a reversal before the court of errors of the state. A year later, the committee had done nothing. At one of the last meetings of the society, which was going out of business, John Newbold noted that he would take responsibility to hire an attorney to bring a new case. But nothing ever happened. Minutes of the Proceedings of the New Jersey Society for Promoting the Abolition of Slavery, 1793–1809, 105–12 (Haverford College Quaker and Special Collections).

56. "An Act to Repeal the Third Section of an Act Entitled, 'An Act for the Gradual Abolition of Slavery,'" March 6, 1806, A80 (NJDLL). For the later history of the payments, see "An Additional Supplement to the Act Entitled 'An Act for the Gradual Abolition of Slavery,'" Nov. 27, 1809, A82 (NJDLL) and "An Act concerning the Abolition of Slavery," Feb. 22, 1811, A83 (NJDLL).

57. "An Act for the Gradual Abolition of Slavery," Feb. 15, 1804, A78 (NJDLL), "An Act to Repeal the Third Section of an Act Entitled, 'An Act for the Gradual Abolition of Slavery,'" March 6, 1806, A80 (NJDLL), "An Additional Supplement to the Act Entitled, 'An Act for the Gradual Abolition of Slavery," Nov. 26, 1808, A81 (NJDLL).

58. See *New Jersey Journal,* April 8, 1799; *Centinel* [sometimes *Sentinel*] *of Freedom* (Newark), listed April 22, 1806 (actually April 17, 1807); *True American* (Trenton), April 24, 1809; *Centinel of Freedom,* May 2, 1809 (advertisements for both

New Barbadoes and for Bergen); *Trenton Federalist*, May 8, 1809; *Sentinel of Freedom*, April 17, 1810; *Centinel of Freedom*, April 16, 1811. In 1809, the legislature passed a supplementary law framed by the suspicion that some who possessed the services of abandoned children were making illegitimate claims on the state bounty. "An Additional Supplement to the Act Entitled 'An Act for the Gradual Abolition of Slavery,'" Nov. 27, 1809, A82 (NJDLL). For an example of the routine form of advertisement offering to bind out (usually white) apprentices, see "That the Overseers of the poor of the borough of Elizabeth will meet at Stephen Crane's innkeeper ... on Saturday the 13th ... for the purpose of putting out the poor for the ensuing year—Those persons that would wish to take all or a part of them, will please to attend." *New-Jersey Journal*, April 8, 1799. For Newark, see *Centinel of Freedom*, April 17, 1807 (listed in Evans as April 22, 1806).

59. "An Act Respecting Slaves," March 14, 1798, A75 (NJDLL). Overseers of Poor of South Brunswick v. Overseers of Poor of East Windsor, 8 N.J.L. 64 (Sup. Ct. 1824). On creditors' rights to enslaved property in most jurisdictions in early America, see Claire Priest, "Creating an American Property Law: Alienability and Its Limits in American History," *Harvard Law Review* 120, no. 2 (December 2006): 385–459.

60. Overseers of Poor of South Brunswick v. Overseers of Poor of East Windsor, 8 N.J.L. 64 (Sup. Ct. 1824). Lerner, "Aging in Bondage."

61. "A Supplement to an Act Entitled 'An Act for the Settlement and Relief of the Poor,'" June 10, 1820, A89 (NJDLL).

62. In Graham Russell Hodges's study of Monmouth County, Tallman is described as an owner of several slaves. Hodges, *Slavery and Freedom in the Rural North: African Americans in Monmouth County, New Jersey, 1665–1865*, 152.

63. Tallman v. Washington, 2 N.J.L. 242 (Sup Ct. 1807); Brooks v. Farmer, 3 N.J.L. 475 [640] (Sup. Ct. 1810).

64. A Westlaw search using the keywords "entice" and "slave" nationally comes up with approximately 70 cases. Nearly all occurred under state statutes that forbade the enticement of slaves, though a few occurred under common law understandings applicable to servants generally. The vast majority of cases, something more than 50, occurred after 1830. The legal practices in early Dutch New Netherlands had not distinguished clearly between the governance of enslaved Africans and that of mostly white indentured servants. See Patricia U. Bonomi, "'Swarms of Negroes Comeing about My Door': Black Christianity in Early Dutch and English North America," *Journal of American History* 103, no. 1 (June 2016): 34–58.

65. "An Act Respecting Slaves," March 14, 1798, A75 (NJDLL).

66. "A Supplement to the Act Entitled, 'An Act for the Punishment of Crimes,' Passed March 18,1796," March 7, 1801, A77 (NJDLL).

67. "An Act Respecting Slaves," March 14, 1798, A75 NJDLL).

68. Fish v. Fisher, 2 Johns. Cas. 89 (NY Sup. Ct. 1800).

69. Link v. Beuner, 3 Cai. R. 325 (NY Sup. Ct. 1805). See also Dubois v. Allen, Ant. N.P. Cas. 94 (NY Sup. Ct. 1809).

70. State v. Quick, 2 N.J.L. 413e (NJ Sup. Ct. 1807). A case file for a habeas case, *State v. Quick* (1806–8) concerns the freedom suit of "Negro Frank," not Dick. I have no idea if William Quick was sued twice, or if Negro Frank was a renamed Dick.

State v. Quick, Bergen, Habeus Corpus/Slavery, New Jersey Supreme Court Case File #37625 (NJSA).

71. "An Act Supplemental to the Act Entitled 'An Act Respecting Slaves,'" Feb. 1, 1812, A84 (NJDLL). It may be significant that the New Jersey Society for Promoting the Abolition of Slavery had effectively gone out of business by 1807 or 1808. There are no recorded meetings after 1808, though it was not formally dissolved for another decade. See Haverford College Quaker and Special Collections, MC.975.09.018.

72. See, generally, Lacy K. Ford, *Deliver Us from Evil: The Slavery Question in the Old South* (New York: Oxford University Press, 2009), 81–111.

73. Jacob Van Wickle had become a judge of the Middlesex Court of Common Pleas in 1803, apparently replacing his father, Evert. *New-Jersey Journal*, November 8, 1803, 3. Advertisements in newspapers across the North during the 1790s and early 1800s indicate that Evert Van Wickle was an active dealer in real estate, who moved to western New York. In 1808 and 1812, Jacob Van Wickle was the chair of the Middlesex County Republican Party. *Sentinel of Freedom*, September 6, 1808, 3. In 1812, he married Idia Morgan, the daughter of Major General Morgan, whose son, Charles Morgan, owned a plantation in Point Coupée, Louisiana. *New-York Weekly Museum*, May 9, 1812, 3. Other traders who were active in New Jersey included John C. Marsh and his partner, William Stone, who had settled on Petite Anse Island in Louisiana by 1818, and who would develop the Avery Plantation there (Marsh would be identified in many of the documents as being from New York City, at least when he was dealing in New York enslaved peoples). Another trader was Lewis Compton. For a broader view of the trade, see "Subseries 1.2, 1817–1822," Avery Family of Louisiana, 1796–1951 (University of North Carolina, microfilm). In July 1818, Josiah Hornblower, Joseph's brother, sold Samuel Jackson to William Stone for $225. See Ann Patton Malone, *Sweet Chariot: Slave Family and House Old Structure in Nineteenth-Century Louisiana*, Fred W. Morrison Series in Southern Studies (Chapel Hill: University of North Carolina Press, 1992), 92–103.

74. All the releases cited here are located in the NJSA, in the Middlesex County Manumission Book (NJSA). Earlier works that deal with this story include James J. Gigantino II, "Trading in Jersey Souls: New Jersey and the Interstate Slave Trade," *Pennsylvania History* 77, no. 3 (Summer 2010): 281–302; Frances D. Pingeon, "An Abominable Business: The New Jersey Slave Trade, 1818," *New Jersey History* 109, no. 3–4 (1991): 14–35; Jarrett M. Drake, "Off the Record: The Production of Evidence in 19th Century New Jersey," *NJS: An Interdisciplinary Journal* 1, no. 1 (Summer 2015): 104–25.

75. Scott, "Paper Thin."

76. Middlesex County Records, microfilm #241 (NJSA).

77. For an example of a free person "kidnapped" to Louisiana, see the Petition of Phillis Gray, 30 August 1815 (Race and Slavery Petitions Project Series 2, County Court Petitions, The University of North Carolina at Greensboro, PAR #20881514; Proquest, History Vault); and the Petition of Phillis Gray and son, 31 March 1817 to 6 March 1819 (ibid., PAR #2088175). The Avery Plantation records include a variety of similar deeds and records, a few of which carry Van Wickle's name. A certificate declares that Jase, a black boy, was born a slave and that he was "regularly" transferred to William Stone

when a small child, and he had continued "the property" of Stone "ever since." A May 20, 1817, deed between Aaron Ball of Essex County and Martha Phillips conveyed Ball's "Mulatto boy George" to Phillips for $150. George was sixteen years old, and he was identified as a "limited slave" by Ball. According to the deed, Phillips would be able to "have and to hold" George until he reached the age of twenty-eight, at which point he would be "set at liberty." In July 1818, however, Martha Phillips sold "Mulatto boy George" to John C. Marsh for $200. According to this second deed, what Marsh received was limited by the "term of time" mentioned in the earlier deed between Ball and Phillips, which was attached. But, of course, we are free to imagine that once George got to Avery Plantation, he would have become just another enslaved person. "Subseries 1.2, 1817–1822," Avery Family of Louisiana, 1796–1951 (University of North Carolina, microfilm).

78. Representative articles about the scandal include *New-York Evening Post*, June 20, 1818, 2; *Trenton Federalist*, June 29, 1818, 3; *New-York Daily Advertiser*, July 29, 1818, 2; *Trenton Federalist*, August 3, 1818, 2; *New-York Daily Advertiser*, August 6, 1818, 2; *Intelligencer and Weekly Advertiser*, August 15, 1818, 1. The articles identified the 1804 law as the source of the requirement of consent, which was, of course, a mistake.

At the moment, I have no idea what happened to the black people taken off the boat and impounded and held. The newspapers quickly lost interest. On the other hand, the captain of the boat was libeled in admiralty, a case that would eventually end up being heard by the U.S. Supreme Court. The Mary Ann. 21 U.S. (8 Wheat.) 380 (1823). That case, along with clues from New Orleans and perhaps from Point Coupée, leaves a paper trail that may allow us ultimately to trace what happened to those New Jerseyans, apparently enslaved and apparently free, who were conveyed to New Orleans by Charles Morgan and the younger Van Wickle. Much thanks to the ongoing brilliant sleuthing and guidance of Rebecca Scott and Priya Khangura, with the aid of Gautham Rao.

79. "An Act to Prohibit the Exportation of Slaves or Servants of Colour out of This State," Nov. 5,1818, A85 (NJDLL) and "A Supplement to the Act, Entitled 'An Act to Prohibit the Exportation of Slaves or Servants of Colour out of This State,'" A86 (NJDLL).

80. In the matter of Jane Wilson, a black woman, on habeas corpus, New-York City-Hall Records, vols. 3–4 (1819), 42–52; Gigantino, *Ragged Road to Abolition*. See also State v. Raborg, 5 N.J.L. 545 (1819), which indicates that Raburgh or Raborg had been declared in contempt of court for not abiding by the habeas corpus writ.

81. I did not find this "release" among the Middlesex County releases at the NJSA. However, there is a release dated September 28, 1818, for Hannah, the property of Abraham Van Vlast (sp?) of the township of Reading in Hunterdon County. She came before the judges of Somerset County, where she was, so the release claimed, given a "private examination" to test her consent "to be sold to William Raburg and remove with him . . . to the territory of Alabama." The release notes that her "condition" was "healthy" and that there was "no other reason of her removal than her own desire to go." "Subseries 1.2, 1817–1822," Avery Family of Louisiana, 1796–1951 (University of North Carolina, microfilm).

82. Commentary on Jane Wilson's case put it in the context of the Marshall Court's recent decision, in *Dartmouth College v. Woodward*, 17 U.S. 518 (1819), that had mobilized the U.S. Constitution's "contracts clause" to prohibit states from passing laws impairing the obligation of contracts. But the commentary agreed with Colden that there was no violation of the contracts clause in Jane Wilson's case: "The law that impairs the obligation of contracts must operate *on the contract.* The only contract here is the contract of sale between the original master and Raburgh the purchaser. It is no part of the contract that Raburgh should have the right to transport the slave." "Thursday; June; Supreme Court; United States; Constitution; Mayor," *New-York Daily Advertiser,* June 3, 1819, 2.

83. It is not at all clear that Mayor Colden was even interpreting contemporary New York law correctly. See Glen v. Hodges, 9 Johns. 67 (NY Sup. Ct. 1812). By 1833, Justice Baldwin of the U.S. Supreme Court, while riding circuit in Pennsylvania, gave a jury charge in a case involving the recapture of a slave owned by a man from Princeton, New Jersey. In that case, Baldwin forcefully rejected the constitutionality of personal liberty laws. He denied the very notion that state law could make free, by operation of law, anyone who was legally enslaved in another state. And he rooted his charge in a constitutional history that presaged the argument later made by Chief Justice Taney in *Dred Scott.* Johnson v. Tompkins, Baldw. 571, 13 F. Cas. 840 (1833). During the *Gibbons v. Ogden* litigation, New York's laws forbidding the importation of slaves were characterized as commercial regulations. In his argument to the Supreme Court in 1824, in support of Gibbons and against the New York "monopoly," Daniel Webster was uncertain whether those laws were "constitutional and valid." He left the question of determining the matter for a later day. Gibbons v. Ogden, 22 U.S. 1, 9–10 (1824). See H. Robert Baker, "The Fugitive Slave Clause and the Antebellum Constitution," *Law and History Review* 30, no. 4 (November 2012): 1133–74.

84. For the free labor analogues, see Robert J. Steinfeld, *The Invention of Free Labor: The Employment Relation in English and American Law and Culture* (Chapel Hill: University of North Carolina Press, 1991); Christopher L. Tomlins, *Law, Labor, and Ideology in the Early American Republic* (New York: Cambridge University Press, 1993).

85. For the use of prisons, see Hay and Craven, *Masters, Servants, and Magistrates in Britain and the Empire, 1562–1955.* Laura Edwards gives such discretionary actions a kinder and gentler quality than I do. Laura F. Edwards, *The People and Their Peace: Legal Culture and the Transformation of Inequality in the Post-Revolutionary South* (Chapel Hill: University of North Carolina Press, 2009).

86. Martha Hodes, *White Women, Black Men: Illicit Sex in the Nineteenth-Century South* (New Haven, CT: Yale University Press, 1997); Geneva Smith, "Subversive Revenge: An Analysis of White Women, Black Men, and Their Children, in Maryland and Virginia from 1681 to 1800," (undergraduate thesis, Columbia University, 2014).

Chapter Three

1. Daniel Rogers, ed., *Report of the Trial of John Quay, vs. the Eagle Fire Company of New York; Before the Honourable William W. Van Ness, One of the Justices of the Supreme Court of Judicature of the State of New-York, at the City-Hall of the City of New-York;*

Commencing on Friday the Sixth, and Ending on Tuesday the Tenth Days of December, 1816 (New York, 1817), 1–5. For an example of the many advertisements for the hotel, see *Relfs Philadelphia Gazette*, June 21, 1811, 1; *Federal Republican*, July 13, 1811, 2. For a visual image of the sea near there, see George Harvey, *Thunder Storm: Shore at Long Branch, New Jersey, High Tide* (1830s–40s). Collection (NYHS).

2. In part, her "melancholy" early on was caused by the naval war that was going on before her eyes. She felt "constantly exposed to . . . misery," which she could not "relieve." There were two English frigates "always in sight" whenever she went out walking. CA 51 Dupont, Letters, 1814, Collections of the Monmouth County Historical Society. See also Betty-Bright P. Low, Margaret Manigault, and Josephine du Pon, "The Youth of 1812: More Excerpts from the Letters of Josephine du Pont and Margaret Manigault," *Winterthur Portfolio* 11 (1976): 173–212. Writers' Program of New Jersey, *Entertaining a Nation; the Career of Long Branch*, American Guide Series (Bayonne: Jersey Printing, 1940), 22.

3. *Relfs Philadelphia Gazette*, March 27, 1815, 4; *New-York Gazette & General Advertiser*, April 22, 1815, 4.

4. Rogers, *Report of the Trial of John Quay*, 3–4; "John Quay vs. the Eagle Fire-Company of New-York," trial transcript, *New-York City-Hall Recorder* 2, no. 1 (January 1817): 1–22. Citations are to the pamphlet version.

5. New Jersey, Wills and Probate Records, 1739–1991, Letters of Administration, Vol. A-B, 1804–1858, images 47 and 66 (Ancestry.com). For advertisements, see *Trenton Federalist*, April 1, 1811, 3, in which Bennet announces a public auction of the property of Henry Green, deceased; and *Mercantile Advertiser*, October 3, 1814, 4, in which Bennet announces a second public auction, after his purchase of the property at the earlier auction. The neighboring property had been purchased from Jacob and Rachel Corlies and Thomas Chandler. Much information is found in the sheriff's deed, identified as "Joshua Bennett to John Quay," found in Book Y, p. 105, of the Monmouth County Records (NJSA). (One imagines that Quay and Bennet had worked together to gain control of the property.) The Federal Writers' Project History of Long Branch suggests that Bennet bought the property in 1806. Writers' Program, *Entertaining a Nation*, 22.

6. According to Judge Van Ness, what Quay bought "at sheriff's sale" was "the equity of redemption, . . . with some other property, for the summ of one thousand and five dollars." According to Catherine Bennet, the sale occurred because Quay was in control of Bennet's affairs. Early on, Quay had offered to let them stay if they gave security for rent payment. And, according to her, "a respectable man" had volunteered to become security. But Quay had refused to accept him. Rogers, *Report of the Trial of John Quay*, 19, 4–5, 9, 17–18. The sheriff's deed, identified as "Joshua Bennett to John Quay," may be found in Book Y, p. 105, of the Monmouth County Records.

7. For a selection of political correspondence and advertisements, see *Trenton Federalist*, October 12, 1807; December 28, 1807; September 25, 1809; October 30, 1809; November 27, 1809; and *True American* (Trenton), October 2, 1809; November 9, 1809; November 13, 1809.

8. *New-Jersey Journal*, September 30, 1806, 3; *American Citizen* (New York), October 6, 1806, 1. *Manumission Book of Monmouth County, New Jersey, 1791–1844* (Freehold, NJ: Office of the Monmouth County Clerk, 1992) [Originally "Monmouth County Miscellaneous Book B"], 16, 120, 121, 133, 134, 143–44, 147, 151, 159, 160, 163, 164. On June 12, 1809, he freed slave Charles. Ibid., 110. See also *True American* (Trenton), November 25, 1816, 2, in which two notices of the Monmouth Orphan's Court include him present as one of the judges.

9. For more on one of the first fire insurance companies in the United States, see Samuel Latham Mitchell, *The Picture of New-York, or The Traveller's Guide, Through the Commercial Metropolis of the United States* (New York, 1807), 47–49; Louis N. Geldert, *The Eagle Fire Company of New York: A History of Its First Century with Portraits and Illustrations / Compiled from Official and Various Other Sources at the Request of the Directors* (New York, 1906). A copy of an 1816 insurance policy for a house in Jersey City owned by Richard Varick can be found in volume 4 (miscataloged as volume 5) of the Richard Varick Mss Collection (NYHS). I have drawn the language in the text from Varick's policy, since I have not found Quay's. I expect that the policy is indistinguishable from the one that John Quay signed. It is worth noting that the policy does not require an inspection. See also Insurance Policy #17,523, to Gerald Rutgers of Bloomfield, NJ, in the Misc. Mss. Eagle Fire Insurance (NYHS).

10. Rogers, *Report of the Trial of John Quay*, 18–20. Quay sued Barnes Smock for $5,000 in damages; Smock defended himself by insisting that the accusation was true. According to him, in 1798 Quay had gotten possession of "a certain running horse" called Harmless that belonged to Isaac Staatger. Quay took the horse out of state and sold it. Unfortunately, Smock's witnesses lived in Kentucky and did not make themselves available. And in April 1816, a jury held Smock guilty, but assessed damages of only $50, plus six cents in costs. John Quay v. Barnes Smock, Case no. 31355 (1816), New Jersey Supreme Court Case Files (NJSA).

11. Rogers, *Report of the Trial of John Quay*, 18; "John Quay vs. the Eagle Fire-Company of New-York," 15.

12. *True American* (Trenton), September 4, 1815, 3.

13. Van Ness had been a prominent attorney in New York City. He had clerked in the office of James Kent and served with Alexander Hamilton in the famous Croswell criminal libel trial. He was appointed to the New York Supreme Court in 1807. Van Ness would later be charged with corruption. The legislative commission that inquired into the matter exonerated him, but he resigned from the court. "William W. Van Ness," http://www.nycourts.gov/history/legal-history-new-york/legal-history-eras-02/history-era-02-van-ness.html.

14. Wells and Emmet were friends but rivals, each of whom could claim to being the best trial lawyer of his generation. They also came from opposite sides politically. Wells was a Federalist, while Emmet, who had been an Irish revolutionary, was a Jeffersonian Republican. On Emmet, see G. Edward White, ed., *The Marshall Court and Cultural Change, 1815–1835*, vol. 3–4 of *Oliver Wendell Holmes Devise History of the Supreme Court of the United States* (New York: Macmillan, 1988), 204–14. There is less available on John Wells. He was the founder of the predecessor of Cadwalader,

Wickersham, and Taft law firm. He originally partnered with George Washington Strong. See *Memorial of the Life and Character of John Wells, with Reminiscences of the Judiciary and the Members of the New York Bar* (New York, 1874).

15. "John Quay vs. the Eagle Fire-Company of New-York," 23–25; Rogers, *Report of the Trial of John Quay*, 23–26.

16. There are too many Wyckoff's in this story. Jacob Wyckoff was John Quay's partner. William Wyckoff was the former master of Adam Wyckoff, John Quay's quondam slave. And Henry I. Wyckoff was the first president of the Eagle Fire Insurance Company in New York City. Geldert, *Eagle Fire Company of New York*, 20. Spellings are haphazard. I will use first names where necessary for clarity.

17. On the competence of a slave's testimony, see Jacob D. Wheeler, *A Practical Treatise on the Law of Slavery. Being a Compilation of All the Decisions Made on That Subject, in the Several Courts of the United States, and State Courts. With Copious Notes and References to the Statutes and Other Authorities, Systematically Arranged* (New York: Allan Pollock, Jr.; New Orleans: Benjamin Levy, 1837), 193–97. For New York law on slave testimony, see "Diana Sellick's Case," transcript in *The New-York City-Hall Recorder* (New York, 1816), 185–91, and Rogers v. Berry, 10 Johns. 132 (1813).

18. Rogers, *Report of the Trial of John Quay*, 27.

19. See chapter 2. Colden was also deeply involved in the affairs of the insurance company, having sold the company the house in which it conducted business. Geldert, *Eagle Fire Company of New York*, 30.

20. See discussion in chapter 2.

21. Rogers, *Report of the Trial of John Quay*, 27–28. It is worth noting that Colden and Ogden had made directly contradictory arguments in several earlier cases. See Aza v. Eitlinger, Ant. N.P. Cas. 73 (Sup. Ct. 1808); Dubois v. Allen, Ant. N.P. Cas. 94 (Sup. Ct. 1809).

22. Rogers, *Report of the Trial of John Quay*, 28–30.

23. On Diana Sellick's legal status: Philip Hone testified that "legally, I suppose the prisoner is my slave. I purchased her in 1807, and told her that in 1819 I would free her. While she continued in my family, though she was an excellent servant at times, and particularly fond of children, yet she was restless and unsteady: she was, at times, flighty, which became a subject of serious conversation in the family. I liberated and discharged her; and when she went away, the understanding was, that she was to work in other families, and pay for her time; but I never calculated that she would pay any thing and had never any idea of claiming her service. After she had left the family some time she returned, but we refused to receive her. . . . I have long since relinquished all claim, and am willing to execute a formal manumission." In the midst of the trial, a paper "for that purpose" was "then immediately drawn and executed by Hone." "Diana Sellick's Case," transcript in *The New-York City-Hall Recorder* (New York, 1816), 185–91.

24. "Diana Sellick's Case," transcript in *The New-York City-Hall Recorder* (New York, 1816), 185–91. On the marriage of Elizabeth Alexander and John Jaques, see Hendrik Hartog, "Wives as Favorites," in *Law as Culture and Culture as Law: Essays in Honor of John Phillip Reid*, ed. Hendrik Hartog and William E. Nelson (Madison, WI: Madison House, 2000), 292–321.

25. See discussion of conditional or term-limited manumissions in chapter 2.

26. Rogers, *Report of the Trial of John Quay*, 29–30.

27. Ibid., 30–31. In 1808 and 1811, Van Ness had been the judge in the important case of *Kettletas v. Van Fleet*, Anthon C.P. Cas 36 (1808) and 7 Johns. 324 (1811), involving an effort to sell an enslaved person, Tom, for life after having covenanted to free him. In Van Ness's opinion, the covenant was understood as binding the seller not on principles of a contract "depending on a consideration" but as "an act of benevolence, sanctioned by the statute, and made obligatory, if in writing." In his argument for the defendant Van Fleet, Thomas Addis Emmet insisted on the validity of contracts between masters and slaves in New York (in order to void the contract between seller and purchaser): "It is," he claimed, "the universal understanding in the community, that such contracts are binding. Such certificates are given every day." He implicitly acknowledged that there might not be any ruling precedent to that effect, but the community norms were clear. 7 Johns. 324. See also the case of Tom, a negro man, in 5 John. 365 (Sup. Ct. 1810). In the early New Jersey case of *State v. Mount*, 1 N.J.L. 292 (1795), by way of comparison, the court held that a covenant to free Grace after ten years of further service if she did not have children did not void the sale of Grace to a purchaser "for life," because she had had a child in the interim. The fact that such a condition would be void if applied to a free white woman (as violating policies in support of marriage and childbirth) was held to be of no relevance.

28. Rogers, *Report of the Trial of John Quay*, 31.

29. This testimony had already been heard over two days in July 1816 during a preliminary hearing before the New York City recorder. Rogers, *Report of the Trial of John Quay*, 31–40.

30. For one of many possible references, see James Oakes, "The Political Significance of Slave Resistance," *History Workshop Journal* 22, no. 1 (Autumn 1986): 89–107. See also Wendy Warren, *New England Bound: Slavery and Colonization in Early America* (New York: Liveright, 2016), 193–99.

31. He was probably referring to John Stillwell, a prominent Federalist in Monmouth County, a regular candidate for the assembly. As a Federalist, he would have been Quay's political opponent. See *Trenton Federalist*, September 10, 1809.

32. Who the Philadelphians were remains a mystery.

33. One should note that this commonsensical reading of the meaning of slavery was countered by the actual liability of enslaved people for crimes in all jurisdictions in the United States where slavery was practiced.

34. After Adam's testimony, Jonathan Morris testified that Brewer had told him that he was actually asleep in the wagon when the man passed him. Morris and Haight disagreed about the landscape of the place where Adam supposedly met the wagon. Haight claimed that he and another man had examined the place. Adam had testified that there was a hickory tree there; Haight agreed that there was a tree, but he thought it was a black walnut. Morris thought there was no tree at all and that the spot was too narrow for a man on horseback to pass between a wagon and the fence. These disputes created new litigations (see below).

35. Rogers, *Report of the Trial of John Quay*, 42–44. Trotter did say that Adam had a fight in the jail with a Mr. M'Dowell. Another witness, David Craig Jr., who lived in

New York, also reported that he had a conversation with Adam around that time. Adam told him he had come "up" to New York to give testimony against his master. Adam admitted that he had set the fire. But, according to Craig, Adam answered in the negative when asked if he had done so on his master's orders. Craig had once lived in Monmouth County, and he remembered that Adam had been tried there for some offence, and he was pretty sure he had been whipped. But David Craig Jr.'s father, the sheriff of Monmouth County, later testified that his son was "subject to intoxication."

36. Rogers, *Report of the Trial of John Quay*, 46–51.

37. See "Quays Trial Just Arrived," *Trenton Federalist*, March 10, 1817, 1; *Relfs Philadelphia Gazette*, December 18, 1816, 3; *Messenger*, December 19, 1816, 2.

38. Pennington v. Quay, Monmouth, Debt, New Jersey Supreme Court Case Files, #30540. See also Pennington v. Bennett, Monmouth, Debt, #29154; Britton v. Bennett, Monmouth, Trespass on Case, #2081 (NJSA).

39. The only later mention of the Long Branch property is in 1818, when John G. Wachsmuth, a Philadelphia merchant, put the property up for resale. The advertisement emphasized how much of the structure remained and how little expense it would be to put it back in repair. There was still a billiard room, kitchens, and stables sufficient for two hundred horses. *Trenton Federalist*, March 23, 1818, 1. I have no idea how the property ended up under Wachsmuth's control.

40. *Manumission Book of Monmouth County*, 16. See also *True American*, November 25, 1816, 2, in which there are two notices of the Monmouth Orphan's Court, which include him present as one of the judges. Quay obviously still had friends in Monmouth County. One might wonder if the risk of criminal prosecution might have kept him from traveling to New York.

41. Quay v. McNinch, 2 Mill Const. 78, 1818. The absconding slave might have been Tone, for whom Quay had advertised a twenty-dollar reward in October 1806. See *American Citizen*, October 6, 1806; *New-Jersey Journal*, September 30, 1806.

42. New Jersey, Wills and Probate Records, 1739–1991, Monmouth Wills, Vol. C-D, 1826–1844, image 27 (Ancestry.com).

43. Haight v. Morris, 7 N.J.L. 289 (1824).

44. 1830 United States Federal Census, New Jersey, Monmouth, Freehold, 334 (Adam Wikoff) (Ancestry.com). I am grateful to Rebecca Scott for leading me to Adam Wikoff.

45. Coleman had been a Federalist, closely associated with Alexander Hamilton. "From Alexander Hamilton to the Editor of the *Evening Post*, 10 August 1802," http://founders.archives.gov/documents/Hamilton/01-26-02-0001-0029. He was often attacked and sued for libel. See *Connecticut Herald*, April 21, 1818.

46. Advertisements for his boats, *Freedom*, *Friendship*, *Liberty*, and *Industry*, appeared regularly in the New Jersey papers. See, for example, *New Jersey Journal*, April 14, 1807, and February 2, 1811. Apparently he inherited his ferry business from Morris Hetfield. See advertisement, *New Jersey Journal*, May 23, 1803. John Hatfield was originally from Hartford, Connecticut. He married Mary Cutter of Woodbridge, New Jersey, in June 1801, and then moved to New York. From there he came to New Jersey, apparently to take over the family business. He died in

May 1819. See Connecticut Town Marriage Records, pre-1870 (Barbour Collection) (Ancestry.com).

47. *Evening Post*, November 4, 1816, 2. The article was widely reprinted in newspapers throughout the northeast. "William Coleman's Case," *New-York City-Hall Recorder*, vol. 2, April 1817, 49–53.

48. *Evening Post*, April 9, 1817, 2.

49. See Correspondence of Thomas Gibbons, 1818, GFP, Drew University.

50. For a similar contract for service that constituted what we might see as voluntary slavery, see *Manumission Book of Monmouth County*, 122–23. Wicoff Conover manumitted Robert Conover on May 2, 1810. Then Robert Conover bound himself to serve Wicoff Conover "of his own free will and accord" to serve for a term of seven years—"keep secrets, not contract matrimony, follow all commands, etc." Soon thereafter, Robert sold Wicoff for $300 to a third Conover, who lived in Bristol, Pennsylvania. On the question of the plausibility or possible legality of re-enslavement, see Rebecca J. Scott, "Paper Thin: Freedom and Re-Enslavement in the Diaspora of the Haitian Revolution," *Law & History Review* 29, no. 4 (November 2011): 1061–87. What is clear, as the material on "kidnapping" in chapter 2 suggests, is that re-enslavement occurred often. For examples in the Midwest, see Anne Twitty, *Before* Dred Scott: *Slavery and Legal Culture in the American Confluence, 1787–1857* (New York: Cambridge University Press, 2016), 65. For Brazilian practices, see Keila Grinberg, "Re-enslavement, Rights and Justice in nineteenth Century in Brazil" (unpublished manuscript, 2013).

51. In the March 4, 1817, issue of the *New Jersey Journal*, it was noted that the house of General Jonathan Dayton, one of the prominent people in the town and at the time a close associate of Thomas Gibbons, had been "forcibly entered by a Negro belonging to John Hatfield." A "quantity of goods" had been taken. But "providentially" he had been discovered and apprehended and now awaited trial. I assume this was not Cato Richards.

52. He had earlier owned at least two other boats. I'm not sure what happened to them, but it seems clear that he left the business around then.

53. In Thomas Gibbons's correspondence, 1818, a copy of the sale is dated January 21, 1818. GFP, Drew University.

54. Thomas Gibbons, Correspondence, 1817, 5; 1818, 13–15; 1819, 86; 1821, 22 Dec. 1821. GFP, Drew University.

55. Maurice G. Baxter, *The Steamboat Monopoly: Gibbons v. Ogden, 1824*, Borzoi Series in United States Constitutional History (New York: Knopf, 1972); Richard Primus, "The *Gibbons* Fallacy," *University of Pennsylvania Journal of Constitutional Law* 19, no. 3 (2017): 567–620.

56. Gibbons v. Morse, 7 N.J.L. 25 (NJ Sup. Ct. 1821); Gibbons v. Morse, Essex, Debt, Case Files #25408 (NJSA). At first I thought that the *Nonpareil* and the *Industry* were the same boat, renamed after Gibbons's purchase. See Box 34, gtt 503 #477—Documents relating to Gibbons ferryboats 1817–1826, from the Gibbons Carver Collection, then at the Museum of American Finance (NYC), now at the Hagley Museum (Delaware), where repair bills for each are mixed together in the folder. But the *Nonpareil* was purchased from John Bodine. I am reasonably certain that Cato

Williams was once Cato Richards, since the number of free black men who captained ferry boats to New York was surely small. To add to the mystery, in 1815–16, a Cato Johnson sued Daniel Hendrickson in Monmouth County in habeas corpus for the freedom of his sons, Joseph and Richard Williams, who were being held as slaves in Hendrickson's household. (He would lose.) Ancestry.com offers nothing on a Cato with any of those three last names. But it is at least suggestive that Cato Johnson's children had the same last name as Cato Williams. State v. Hendrickson, Monmouth, Habeas Corpus in Manumission, Cases #35939 and 35939* (NJSA).

57. According to a history of the local medical society, Dr. Morse was well known in early nineteenth-century Elizabethtown as a relentless practical joker. "Stories of his management of hypochondriacs, his practical jokes, his witty sayings, and his facetious acts, full of humor, always kind in intent if apparently harsh, could be multiplied to any extent." According to the history, the case that would become *Gibbons v. Morse* revolved around a "useless slave" named "Pete," who went off in one of "William Gibbons' steamers." (William Gibbons was Thomas Gibbons's son, and he would eventually inherit Gibbons's holdings, which he would sell to Cornelius Vanderbilt.) According to this text, Dr. Morse sued Gibbons for the loss of Pete and recovered $800. He told Gibbons afterward "that if he brought him back he would sue him for $300 more. Said Mr. Gibbons, "Did you not want him?" "No, I offered him twenty to run away and never come back." J. Henry Clark, *The Medical Men of New Jersey, in Essex District, from 1666 to 1866* (Newark, 1867), 18–23.

58. According to Cato, Zadock Tooker was also wrong in his claim that they had first landed in Staten Island before going on to Manhattan. Gibbons v. Morse, 7 N.J.L. 253, 255–56, 259–60 (1821).

59. "An Act Respecting Slaves," March 14, 1798, A75 (NJDLL). Gibbons v. Morse, 7 N.J.L. 253 (Sup. Ct. 1821).

60. "Memorandum," Court Documents: Thomas Gibbons vs. Isaac Morse (Decided: 1821) 1818–1819, File 20:18. GFP, Drew University.

61. Gibbons v. Morse, 7 N.J.L. 253, 267.

62. Gibbons, Memorandum. Strikethrough in original.

63. Gibbons v. Morse, 7 N.J.L. 253, 257–58.

64. Ibid., 259–60.

65. In his brief on the appeal, William Halstead, Gibbons's attorney, also gestured toward the notion that the court might properly regard Cato Williams as responsible. "But the law is, if a man command a servant to do what is lawful, and he misbehave himself, or do more, the master shall not answer for the servant, but the servant for himself, for it was his own act; otherwise it would be in the power of every servant to subject his master to what actions and penalties he pleases. Ibid., 268.

66. Ibid., 263–64. On Kirkpatrick, see Lucius Q. C. Elmer, *The Constitution and Government of the Province and State of New Jersey* (Newark: M. R. Dennis, 1872), 308–10; James Grant Wilson, *Memorials of Andrew Kirkpatrick, and His Wife Jane Bayard* (New York, 1870).

67. Gibbons v. Morse, 7 N.J.L. 253, 260–62. In 1820, Zadock Tooker had manumitted a slave named Keziah. I have no idea whether Keziah was kin who had been pur-

chased. See *Record of Black Births, Followed by Birth Certificates, and Certificates and Deeds of Manumission, and Slave Receipts* (Essex County: 1804–43), 85–87 (NJSA).

68. We have met Stone and Marsh before, in chapter 2, as slave traders involved in the "kidnapping" controversy. Remember that in November 1818, a new law went into effect that presumptively put an end to the trade in moving enslaved people out of state. Marsh had married Morse's daughter Elizabeth. Ann Patton Malone, *Sweet Chariot: Slave Family and House Old Structure in Nineteenth-Century Louisiana*, Fred W. Morrison Series in Southern Studies (Chapel Hill: University of North Carolina Press, 1992), 92–103.

69. See Gibbons, Memorandum; this witness's words do not appear in the case report.

70. Ibid.

71. Gibbons v. Morse, 7 N.J.L. 253, 264.

72. Nineteenth-century evidence treatises distinguished presumptions of law from presumptions of fact. Kirkpatrick's presumption was both, since it presumed the need for legal proof of freedom (we will see in the next section how that played out) while providing an evidentiary inference that all African Americans in New Jersey were enslaved. The classic form of a presumption of fact was the presumption that when a man and a woman lived together they were married (unless, of course, they were of different races, because of anti-miscegenation rules). See John D. Lawson, *The Law of Presumptive Evidence, Including Presumptions Both of Law and of Fact, and the Burden of Proof Both in Civil and Criminal Cases, Reduced to Rules* (Littleton, CO: Fred B. Rothman, 1982). Chalhoub notes that in nineteenth-century Brazil, the police chief of Rio de Janeiro imposed a presumption of slavery. Sidney Chalhoub, "The Precariousness of Freedom in a Slave Society (Brazil in the Nineteenth Century)," *International Review of Social History* 56, no. 3 (December 2011): 431. See also R. H. Helmholz and W. David H. Sellar, eds., *The Law of Presumptions: Essays in Comparative Legal History*, Comparative Studies in Continental and Anglo-American Legal History, vol. 27 (Berlin: Duncker & Humblot, 2009).

73. See Wheeler, *A Practical Treatise*, 406. The note explained: "It is a general rule in all the states where slavery exists, that every negro is to be presumed a slave." Ibid. It should be added that Kirkpatrick's jury instructions also directly challenged the implicit acceptance of the conventional nineteenth-century reading of *Somerset*: that slavery was inconsistent with the common law and that sustaining it required direct legislative action. Halstead, in his brief to New Jersey's Court of Errors, tried to reintroduce what might be called the Somerset principle: "If slavery did not exist at common law, the principles of that system [of the common law]" were "not applicable to a case of this description." Gibbons v. Morse, 7 N.J. L. 253, 269. See Joseph Story, *Commentaries on the Conflict of Laws, Foreign and Domestic: In Regard to Contracts, Rights, and Remedies, and Especially in Regard to Marriages, Divorces, Wills, Successions, and Judgments* (Boston: Hilliard, Gray, 1834), 92–93. The "presumption" became emblematic of chattel race-based slavery and of the North–South divide in the 1850s and was made constitutional in the *Dred Scott* decision. Thomas R. R. Cobb, *An Inquiry Into the Law of Negro Slavery in the United States of America. To*

Which is Prefixed, an Historical Sketch of Slavery (Philadelphia: T. & J. W. Johnson; Savannah: W. T. Williams, 1858), vol. 1, sections 66–69.

74. Gibbons v. Morse, 7 N.J.L. 253, 270.

75. Cutter v. Moore, 8 N.J.L. 219 (Sup. Ct. 1825).

76. Thomas Gibbons, Correspondence, 1824, Folder 3:9. GFP, Drew University.

77. For details of the demurrer, see George Boice v. Thos. Gibbons, Essex, Debt, Supreme Ct. Case File #3121 (NJSA). Boice v. Gibbons, 8 N.J.L. 324–33 (Sup. Ct. 1826). By then, Gibbons was dead.

78. Fox v. Lambson, 8 N.J.L. 275 (Sup. Ct. May term 1826), and 8 N.J.L. 366 (Sup. Ct. Sept. term 1826). The 1813 case was Potts v. Harper, 3 N.J.L. 1030 (Sup. Ct. 1813). Several readers have suggested that gender might have played a role, distinguishing a possible male witness from a possible female witness.

79. The next seven paragraphs rely on Ogden v. Price, Essex, Appeal/Trespass on Case, NJ Supreme Ct. Case File #28776 (NJSA). See Ogden v. Price, 9 N.J.L. 167 (Sup. Ct. 1827).

80. Edwin Francis Hatfield, *History of Elizabeth, New Jersey: Including the Early History of Union County* (Elizabeth: Carlton and Lanahan, 1868), 622–26. In his journals, Morrell notes, without criticism, the slavery he saw during a trip through the South in the 1790s. The journals end long before the time that he acquired Prime, Jude, and Betty. Michael J. McKay, ed., *The Journals of the Rev. Thomas Morrell: The Maverick Strain: Dissent and Reform in the United Methodist Tradition* (Madison, NJ: Historical Society, Northern New Jersey Conference, 1984). Earlier, in 1805, he had apparently advertised for a black couple who were promised their freedom at the end of a term of service. See Theodore Thayer, *As We Were: The Story of Old Elizabethtown*, Collections of the New Jersey Historical Society, vol. 13 (Elizabeth: Grassmann, 1964), 169. The length of time that Prime and Jude would have to serve before they would be freed is rendered inconsistently in the trial record.

81. The price might also have incorporated the risk that Price assumed he might have to pay for the future care of aging and not-yet-emancipated enslaved people.

82. As of 1830, Oliver Ogden, Elihu Price, and Thomas Morrell were near neighbors (they all appear on the same sheet of the census return). Robert Price and Joseph D. Price lived near as well (one census page on either side). At that time, none of the five white heads of household had reported that he had slaves in his household, although Thomas Morrell, alone of the five, still had three persons of color living with him. See 1830 United States Federal Census for New Jersey, Essex, Elizabeth, 51–52, 49–50, 53–54 of 62 (Ancestry.com). (It is altogether possible that Prime and Jude were also in Oliver Ogden's household or nearby.)

83. Ogden v. Price, 9 N.J.L. 167 (Sup. Ct. 1827).

84. The attorney's questions for Stoutenborough's witnesses included the following: Whether the waggon was to be exchanged by Heavilan with Stoutenborough for a negro boy? Whether the said boy was not a free black boy? Bound out by the Trustees of the County house? Whether Mr. Stoutenborough had not at the time in his possession the original Indenture from the Trustees of the County house for the boy? Whether at the time the contract or exchange was agreed upon Mr. Stoutenborough informed Mr. Heavilan that said boy was a free boy bound out as aforesaid or whether

any intimation of the kind was given at the time? . . . Whether a bill of sale of said boy was to be delivered or assigned to Mr. Heavilan? and when? Whether this was offered or done? and when? Whether it was accepted by Mr. Heavilan? Whether the waggon was not by the terms of the contract or exchange to be delivered at the time the negro boy and the note was to be delivered & the bill of sale to be made or assigned whether the indenture annexed to the appeal papers, is not the original indenture under which Mr. Stoutenborough held said boy?

All those questions were objected to and were overruled by the Monmouth County court as improper. Heavilan's attorney then tried to prove that the assignment from Stoutenborough to Heavilan, written on the back of the indenture, had been produced after the taking of the wagon, after Heavilan had seen and read the front of the document—the indenture from the poorhouse. But, again, the court refused to allow such evidence to be introduced. And it affirmed the one hundred dollar award.

85. Stoutenborough v. Haviland, 15 N.J.L. 266–69 (Sup. Ct. 1836). Stoutenborough v. Heaviland, NJ Supreme Ct. Case File #35864 and Heavilan v. Stoutenborough, NJ Supreme Ct. Case File #17744. (NJSA).

86. For mention of the Thistle, see Edward J. Renehan, *Commodore: The Life of Cornelius Vanderbilt* (New York: Basic Books, 2007), 102, 106–7. For mention of Jenkins, see *National Advocate*, May 24, 1827, 2; *Emporium and True American* (Trenton), June 23, 1827, 3; *Poulson's American Daily Advertiser*, July 04, 1827, 2 (his rescue of a rude man); *New-York Spectator*, September 14, 1835, 2 (he exceeds all others in his speed on the Delaware); *New Brunswick Fredonian*, December 1, 1824, 4.

87. Stille v. Jenkins, 15 N.J.L. 302 (Sup. Ct. 1836); Stille v. Jenkins, Middlesex, Trespass on Case, NJ Supreme Ct. Case File #36311 (NJSA).

88. Stille v. Jenkins, 15 N.J.L. 302 (Sup. Ct. 1836).

89. For the Burlington slave case, see *Philadelphia Enquirer*, August 16, 1836, reprinted in *Baltimore Gazette and Daily Advertizer*, August 17, 1836; *New-Bedford Mercury*, August 19, 1836; and also *Connecticut Courant*, August 22, 1836, 2. There are other steamboat captains with the last name Jenkins. In 1830, Stille or Stelle held two female slaves, and there were two free black young men in his household, according to the census. 1830 United States Federal Census, New Jersey Middlesex Piscataway, 13–14 of 36. In the 1840 census (Stelle), 1840 United States Federal Census, New Jersey, Middlesex, Piscataway, 35 of 40, there were two adult women of color in his household (Ancestry.com).

90. In the census, he is listed as William Ienkius. 1830 United States Federal Census, New Jersey Middlesex North Brunswick, 61–62 of 66 (Ancestry.com).

91. See *Emancipator* [Pennsylvania Freeman], under the heading "Freedom in New Jersey!" May 10, 1838 (vol. 3, no. 2, p. 6. [NewsBank]). On Baldwin's mental condition, see White, *Marshall Court and Cultural Change*, 298–302. Verus, "Slavery in New Jersey," *Friend: A Religious and Literary Journal*, January 18, 1840, 13, 16.

Chapter Four

1. Note that a book begun by the Essex County clerk to record "slave receipts"— transactions for the conveyance or alienation of slaves—was almost never used. Only

three transactions were ever recorded. Unlike land transactions, slave sales and leases remained in a private sphere. See *Record of Black Births, Followed by Birth Certificates, and Certificates and Deeds of Manumission, and Slave Receipts* (Essex County: NJSA, 1804–43) (NJSA). Neither the New Jersey legislature nor the courts created or imposed rules requiring the recordation of slave transactions.

2. 1830 United States Federal Census, New Jersey, Essex, Elizabeth, 3–4 of 62 (Ancestry.com). For the birth of Minna's child, Jesse, see *Record of Black Births, Essex* (NJSA).

3. For an example of someone doing it right, see *Manumission Book of Monmouth County, New Jersey, 1791–1844.* (Freehold, NJ: Office of the Monmouth County Clerk, 1992), 155.

4. On Pennington, see William Henry Smith, *Speakers of the House of the United States with Personal Sketches of the Speakers with Portraits* (1928), 1:149–53. On Rogers, see W. Woodford Clayton, *History of Union and Middlesex Counties, New Jersey, with Biographical Sketches of Many of Their Pioneers and Prominent Men* (Philadelphia: Everts & Peck, 1882), 117.

5. The next paragraphs are drawn from the trial transcript, *Force v. Haines*, Middlesex, Trespass on Case, New Jersey Supreme Court Case File #12912 (NJSA).

6. For Morse, see 1830 United States Federal Census, New Jersey, Essex, Rahway, 21–22 of 26 (Ancestry.com).

7. 1830 United States Federal Census, New Jersey, Essex, Elizabeth, 3–4 of 62 (Ancestry.com).

8. 1830 United States Federal Census, New Jersey, Essex, Rahway, 21–22 of 26 (Ancestry.com).

9. Amzi Armstrong, the son of a prominent minister with the same name, was a member of the New Jersey Council of the state legislature and an active attorney. He died in 1845, at the age of thirty-eight. On Williamson, see Edward Quinton Keasbey, *The Courts and Lawyers of New Jersey, 1661–1912* (New York: Lewis Historical, 1912), 2:731–36.

10. The levy is listed both in the case materials for *Clark v. Force* and for *Southwick v. Force*. Since the levy is almost identical in each case—in Southwick, the sawmill is not mentioned—I'm assuming that there was one single levy in favor of both sets of plaintiffs. See Clark v. Force, Middlesex, Trespass on Case, New Jersey Supreme Ct. Case File #6981* and Southwick v. Force, Middlesex, Trespass on Case, New Jersey Supreme Ct. Case File #35334* (NJSA).

11. Wing v. Force, Middlesex, Trespass on Case, NJ Supreme Ct. Case File #44802 (NJSA).

12. In December 1840, Sheriff James M. Brewster levied on him once again. There was still property to take: "one clock, bureau, two tables, twenty four chairs, looking glass, lots of carpeting, candle and works stand, two desks, three beds bedding and bedsteads, closet and contents, consisting of crockery, earthenware, knives and forks etc. Cooking stove and fixtures, meals chests, lot of potatoes, beers, three casks and contents, lots of empty boxes and barrels, work bench, lot of old lumber, lot of stone, and forty acres of land more or less, again situated in the Township of Woodbridge, . . . bounded by the road leading from mills formerly belonging to the said Henry Force

to the Essex and Middlesex turnpike, and the lands of Robert L. Jaques and William Stone." Finch v. Force, Middlesex, Debt, New Jersey Supreme Court Case File #12862* (NJSA). It is hard to decipher from the case records what had produced Force's bankruptcy. It is easy to say that he had been unable to pay his debts. But beyond that, the case files reveal little.

13. See discussion in chapters 1 and 2.

14. 1840 United States Federal Census, New Jersey, Middlesex, Woodbridge, 17 of 58 (Ancestry.com). According to Nicholas Murray, *Notes, Historical and Biographical, concerning Elizabeth-Town, Its Eminent Men, Churches and Ministers* (Elizabeth-Town, NJ: E. Sanderson, 1844), 166, the 1840 census revealed only one enslaved female person in Elizabethtown (and no enslaved men). There were at the same time 277 free colored persons in the town (along with 3,906 white people). Is it possible that Minna was that one enslaved person?

15. In the 1850 census, an elderly Elizabeth Haines was living on a farm in Hamilton in Mercer County headed by Benjamin, aged fifty-four, and Abraham, aged forty-five. 1850 United States Federal Census, New Jersey, Mercer, Hamilton, 28 of 67 (Ancestry.com). This Benjamin was undoubtedly the oldest son of husband Benjamin Haines, as mentioned in his will. But who was Abraham Haines? In the will, Benjamin Haines's other son was named Richard. Richard had died sometime around 1830 (see evidence in *Force v. Haines*). Abraham could have been a child of Elizabeth's from an earlier marriage, who had been adopted by Benjamin. Or he could have been a cousin. For Henry Force, see 1850 United States Federal Census, Virginia, Prince William, 84 of 135; 1850 U.S. Federal Census—Slave Schedules, Virginia Prince William, 20 of 30 (Ancestry.com).

16. 1850 United States Federal Census, Pennsylvania, Philadelphia, Philadelphia Spruce Ward, 45 of 164 (Ancestry.com).

17. "An Act to Abolish Slavery," revision approved April 18, 1846, Revision of 1846, A98 (NJDLL). Overseers of Morris v. Overseers of Warren, 26 N.J.L. 312 (Sup. Ct. 1857). Janet Halley, "What Is Family Law? A Genealogy, Part One," *Yale Journal of Law and the Humanities* 23, no. 1 (2011): 1–109.

Index

McNinch, John, 104

Meadow Ridge, 49

mere voluntary courtesy, 2, 4–5, 12–38, 69, 144

Middlesex County, 76, 80, 119–20, 131, 140, 145, 164n1, 175nn73–74, 176n81, 187n89, 189n12–14

Middlesex County Court of Common Pleas, 74, 140, 175n73

Middlesex County District Court, 3

Minna (slave), 1–41, 52, 67, 69, 135–49, 157n1, 189n14. *See also Force v. Haines*

Monmouth County, 56–57, 88–89, 126–29, 174n62, 181n31, 182n40, 184n56, 187n84

Moore, Henry, 119

Moore, Phineas, 122–23

morality, 2–12, 17–26, 96, 138–44, 158n5, 159n11, 162n12

Morgan, Charles, 74, 76–77, 175n73, 176n78

Morrell, Thomas, 122, 186n80, 186n82

Morris, Jonathan, 104, 181n34

Morse, Anthony, 142, 147, 184n57

Morse, Bill, 112

Morse, Harry, 112, 117

Morse, Isaac, 111–18

municipal law, 31, 47, 167n22

Nevius, James Schureman, 30, 37, 130, 144, 163n30

Newark, 38, 66, 164n2

New Jersey. *See* care; gradual emancipation; law; legal regime; manumissions; slaves and slavery

New Jersey Court for the Correction of Errors, 105, 119, 185n73

New Jersey Courts of Common Pleas, 74, 92, 128, 140, 175n73

New Jersey Society for Promoting the Abolition of Slavery, 63, 172n42, 173n53, 175n71

New Jersey Supreme Court, 2–3, 24, 40, 43, 62, 66–68, 122, 128–30, 143, 147. *See also specific cases*

New Orleans, 74–75, 77, 176n78

New Providence, 57

New York: case law, 20–24, 36; emancipation in, 44–46, 78–79, 105, 168n24; law, 48–49, 52, 69, 82, 98, 102, 109, 167n23, 171n38, 177n83; transfer of slaves and, 70–77, 81

New York City, 2, 54, 71, 79–82, 100, 109, 130, 164n3, 175n73, 179n13, 180n16

New York City Court of Common Pleas, 92

New-York City-Hall Recorder, 78

New York Evening Post, 106

New York Manumission Society, 78, 96, 107

New York Supreme Court, 92, 179n13

nisi prius, 19, 162n15

Nonpareil (boat), 111–12

North Brunswick, 132

North Carolina, 16, 27

Northwest Territory, 59

officious intermeddlers, 4, 18, 31, 147. *See also* good Samaritan; mere voluntary courtesy; volunteerism

Ogden, Aaron, 111, 113, 115, 163n24, 180n21

Ogden, David, 94

Ogden, Oliver W., 122, 124, 186n82

Ogden, Robert, 169n27

Ogden, William, 113

Ogden v. Price, 122–26, 143

Ogilvie, Anne, 43–45, 47, 167n18

Olive Branch (ship), 119

Outcalt, John, 74–77

Overseers of Poor of South Brunswick v. Overseers of Poor of East Windsor, 28–29, 163n29, 174n59

overseers of the poor, 19–37, 45–46, 51–53, 60–67, 126, 136, 172n49. *See also* manumissions; poor relief; settlements

The Path of the Law (Holmes), 4

paupers, 19, 23, 29, 60, 66–67, 148

Pennington, William, 63, 73, 135, 138, 143
Pennsylvania, 48, 78, 80, 167n23, 177n83
Periam, Joseph, 114
personal liberty law, 30, 177n83
Perth Amboy, 57, 75, 102
Philadelphia, 2, 54, 123, 182n39
Philadelphia Inquirer, 132
plantations, 58, 74, 116–17, 166n13
Point Coupée, 74, 176n78
poor relief, 7, 19, 27, 33–36, 53, 59–63, 95, 98, 149, 169n28. *See also* manumissions; overseers of the poor; settlements
population decline, 2, 37–39, 69, 82, 85, 134, 158n4
Potter v. Potter, 20–21, 34, 36
presumption of slavery, 72, 86, 95, 118–19, 126–33, 146, 185n72–73
Price, Elihu, 122–24, 186n81–82
Price, Joseph D., 123, 186n82
Price, Robert, 123
Price, William, 114–15, 122
Princeton University, 24, 38, 162n12
promises, 31, 36. *See also* contracts
property, 10, 15–30, 55, 61, 70, 79, 81–84, 178n5. *See also* slaves and slavery

Quakers, 40, 50, 70, 133, 171n39
Quay, Agnes, 104
Quay, Henry, 88
Quay, John, 87–106, 178n5–6, 179n9–10, 180n16, 181n31, 182n40
Quick, William, 73, 174n70

Raburgh, Thomas, 78–81, 84
racism, 59, 85, 109. *See also* slaves and slavery
Radcliff, Jacob, 71–72
Rahway, 66, 138, 164n1
Rahway River, 38–39
Ramage, Dinah, 49
Republican Party, 3, 24–25, 138, 171n39, 175n73

Revolutionary War, 89, 95, 104, 165n3
Rhea, Mary, 57
Rhea, Robert, 57
Richards, Cato, 106–12, 183n51, 184n56. *See also* Williams, Cato
Rogers, Edward Y., 138, 140, 178n6
Roman law, 4, 21
Rossell, William (Justice), 63, 68
Ruffin, Thomas, 16–17, 27
Ryerson, Thomas C. (Justice), 128–31, 133

Salem County Quakers, 133
Sayre, Ephraim, 49, 168n24
Scott, Rebecca, 75
Scudder, Smith, 122, 125, 143
Sellick, Diana, 96, 180n23
settlements, 22–23, 28–29, 35, 53, 60–61, 65–67, 148–49, 173n50
slave code, 50–51, 61–64, 69–70, 117, 120, 169n29. *See also* law
slaves and slavery: care of, 12–38, 61, 66, 135–49, 163n29, 172n48; children of, 36, 51, 64–65, 122–30, 168n24, 169n27; contracts, 13, 110, 172n47, 175n77, 177n82, 181n27, 186n84; enticement of, 67–69, 130–34, 174n64; gradual emancipation and, 5–6, 38–55, 60–66, 79–84; harboring of, 111–17, 120–25; kidnapping and, 73–78; legal regime of, 1–12, 47–52, 161n4, 163n27, 185n73; liability and, 99–105, 120, 181n33–34; manumissions and, 52, 56–59, 67; map of, 156; marriage and, 160n20, 168n27; morality and, 138–44, 167n22; presumption of, 67, 72, 85–86, 95, 118–19, 126–29, 146, 185n72–73; regime of, 1–12; sales of, 49, 70–72, 110; testimony and, 90–106, 180n17; transfer of, 44–54, 69–75, 78–79, 81, 167n18, 168n27, 176n78, 176n81, 185n68, 187n1. *See also* apprenticeships; freedom; labor
slave trade, 1, 11, 54, 70–78, 185n68. *See also* kidnapping